Observations on the Real Rights of Women
and Other Writings

Legacies of Nineteenth-Century American Women Writers

HANNAH MATHER CROCKER

Observations on the Real Rights of Women
and Other Writings

Edited and with an introduction by
CONSTANCE J. POST

University of Nebraska Press   Lincoln & London

A small portion of the introduction was
previously published in *The Dictionary of
Literary Biography: American Women Prose
Writers to 1820*, ed. Carla Mulford, Angela
Vietto, and Amy E. Winans (Detroit:
Bruccoli-Clark-Layman, 1998). © 1998
by Gale, a part of Cengage Learning, Inc.
Reproduced by permission. www.cengage
.com/permissions.

Publication of this volume was assisted by
The Virginia Faulkner Fund, established
in memory of Virginia Faulkner, editor in
chief of the University of Nebraska Press.

Library of Congress Cataloging-in-
Publication Data

Crocker, Hannah Mather, 1752–1829.
Observations on the real rights of women
and other writings / Hannah Mather
Crocker; edited and with an introduction by
Constance J. Post.
p. cm.— (Legacies of nineteenth-
century American women writers)
Includes bibliographical references
and index.
ISBN 978-0-8032-1615-0 (pbk.: alk. paper)
1. Women's rights. I. Title.
HQ1423.C9 2011
814.7—dc22
2010042425

Set in Adobe Caslon.

To My Family

Contents

Preface

In doing research for *Signs of the Times in Cotton Mather's Paterna: A Study of Puritan Autobiography* (2000), I traveled to Boston to consult "Biblia Americana," Mather's vast commentary on the Bible, at the Massachusetts Historical Society. While there I also worked at the American Antiquarian Society in Worcester, where I came upon a reference to Cotton Mather's granddaughter, Hannah Mather Crocker, in the Mather Family Papers. That bit of serendipity led me to the collection of her many unpublished texts at AAS and her unpublished "Reminiscences and Traditions of Boston" at the New England Historic Genealogical Society, in addition to her published texts, *A Series of Letters on Free Masonry* (1815), *The School of Reform, or Seaman's Safe Pilot to the Cape of Good Hope* (1816), and *Observations on the Real Rights of Women* (1818).

Although I found a few scattered references to Hannah Mather Crocker in the secondary literature, the dearth of material about her made it clear that the project of reclaiming neglected women authors is not yet complete. To give Crocker the attention she deserves I first wrote entries about her for *The Oxford Companion to Women's Writing in the United States*, edited by Cathy N. Davidson and Linda Wagner-Martin (New York: Oxford University Press, 1995), 222–23, and *The Dictionary of Literary Biography: American Women Writers to 1820*, edited by Carla Mulford et al. A more recent piece appears in *An Encyclopedia of American Women's History*, edited by Hasia Diner (New York: Facts on File, forthcoming). I have also given papers on Crocker at meetings of the Society of Early

Americanists, the American Literature Association, and the Transatlantic Studies Association and contributed to the scholarly conversation about her in print. See, for example, my essay about Crocker's participation in the transatlantic culture of creating catalogs of illustrious men and women in "Making the A-List: Reformation and Revolution in Crocker's *Observations on the Real Rights of Women*," *Resources for American Literary Study* 29 (2003–4): 67–88.

An important step in my project to recover the writings of Hannah Mather Crocker is to make her work widely available in a modern, annotated edition. Of the three texts published during her lifetime, only *Observations on the Real Rights of Women* has been reprinted in its entirety but without the benefit of an introduction or notes. Most of Crocker's texts, however, have never appeared in print. I am grateful that Sharon Harris and Cindy Weinstein, general editors of the Legacies of Nineteenth-Century American Women Writers series at the University of Nebraska Press, believed in the importance of the project, which gives readers unparalleled access to the broad range of Crocker's writings for the first time.

Editing the writings of Hannah Mather Crocker is a project that has taken me many years to complete, in large part because of the challenges presented by her unpublished manuscripts. My debts to others are many, especially to staff at the American Antiquarian Society, the Massachusetts Historical Society, and the New England Historic Genealogical Society, as well as the Hollis Library at Harvard and the Beinecke Library at Yale. The generosity of Iowa State University, including grants from the Center for Excellence in the Arts and Humanities, the College of Liberal Arts and Sciences, and the Department of English, made it possible for me to travel to collections and to have time to write. For their encouragement and helpful suggestions about my work on Crocker I especially want to thank Kathleen Diffley, Mary Kelley, Carla Mulford, and Priscilla Wald, as well as Sacvan Bercovitch and the late Emory Elliot. I owe a special debt to my colleague Matthew Wynn Sivils for his knowledge of the intricacies of textual editing and to my copy editor, Judith Hoover, and project editor, Sara Springsteen, for their careful attention to detail. The insights of my husband, Danny, into the politics of the period as well as other matters have greatly enriched this volume, and I am grateful to him for this and so much more.

Introduction

On August 14, 1765, the office of Andrew Oliver, stamp master for Massachusetts, was destroyed and his home ransacked by the Loyalist Nine, later known as the Sons of Liberty; an effigy of Oliver was later found hanging in a tree. The Nine also surrounded the home of Thomas Hutchinson, lieutenant governor and chief justice of the Province of Massachusetts Bay, but they moved on when persuaded by a speaker who rose to Hutchinson's defense. On the night of August 26 a mob paid a visit to the homes of Charles Paxton and William Story. Paxton's was spared by the offer of free drink, but Story's was completely destroyed. A second mob trashed Capt. Benjamin Hallowell's home before the two parts joined to reach their third target that evening. The lieutenant governor was not so lucky this time. Enthusiasm was running high to seize the man suspected of supporting the Stamp Act and known to support the writs of assistance that gave the British government the right to conduct a search without needing to provide a reason to do so.[1] Finding no one at home, the crowd burst into the house and began smashing furniture and hauling out stacks of manuscripts and books that Hutchinson had amassed over many years for his projected history of the Massachusetts Bay Colony. In "Reminiscences and Traditions of Boston" his niece, Hannah Mather Crocker, notes that the manuscripts, some of which belonged to her father, Samuel Mather, were dumped in North Square.[2] The mob, however, did not consider its work finished until it had also gutted the interior walls of the stately home, cut off the cupola, and removed most of the slate roof. Dismantling the roof took several hours.[3]

On hearing that Hutchinson had fled to the home of his brother-in-law, Samuel Mather, some of the men rushed over there. Mather, however, refused to let them in and soon determined that it was unsafe for Hutchinson to remain with them a moment longer. According to Crocker, she "was sent to shew and escort him the pass, a back way through an alley to the house of Mr. Thomas Edes, father of the late Edward Edes, baker and grandfather of the present Senior Minister in Providence. Mr. Hutchinson continued there till 6 o'clock the next morn. The present writer," notes Crocker, "continued his companion through the night without sleep, then escorted him in safety to his sister's house the same way he retreated. He was calm through the whole scene and partook of Breakfast with the family. After breakfast he went to court in his common dress as his bagwig and robes were destroyed."[4] The sister's house was none other than the home of Hannah Crocker's parents, Hannah Hutchinson and Samuel Mather, from which the girl had escorted Thomas Hutchinson the previous evening. The incident, which occurred when Crocker was thirteen, appears in her miscellany, "Reminiscences of Boston," in which she recalls the details about her modest role in a major incident leading up to the Revolutionary War. Crocker's part in the episode encapsulates several themes in her writing: the conviction that women have a part to play in public affairs, the devotion to things antiquarian, and the determination to reconcile opposing viewpoints in an effort to achieve harmonious relations.

The daughter of Samuel and Hannah Hutchinson Mather, Hannah Crocker was born in Boston on June 27, 1752, and died in nearby Roxbury on July 11, 1829, at the age of seventy-seven. She is buried in the Mather tomb at Copp's Hill in Boston. A direct descendant from what she called "the four-fold line of Mathers," ministers all, Crocker was the great-great-granddaughter of Richard Mather, who emigrated to the Massachusetts Bay Colony in 1635; the great-granddaughter of Increase Mather, president of Harvard University (then Harvard College) from 1685 to 1692; the granddaughter of Cotton Mather, the most prolific writer in the colonies; and the daughter of Samuel, Cotton Mather's sole surviving son. On her mother's side she was the descendant of Anne Hutchinson, banished from Boston in 1638.[5] In 1779 Hannah married Joseph Crocker, the son of Josiah Crocker, a minister of Taunton, Massachusetts. A graduate of Harvard, Joseph Crocker served as a captain in the revolutionary army. The Crockers had ten children, but Hannah waited until her "olive branches," as she refers to them, were grown before she fulfilled her aspiration to become a writer.[6]

Crocker believed that the ideal time for a mother to take up writing is after her children "have spread forth to form new circles in society," leaving an empty nest that enables her to enter "a fully ripe season to read, write, meditate and compose, if the body and mind are not enfeebled by infirmities."[7] Although she believed the chief end of such activities is to be mindful of the needs of the next generation, the personal satisfaction to be gained from activities that cheer the "furrows of age" did not escape her notice. In an 1821 poem, "A Petition," she pleads with an old friend who told Crocker's granddaughter to hide Crocker's pen and ink in order to speed her recovery from lung fever. "Thinking," writes Crocker, "keeps your friend alive. / I live to think; I think to live" (182). In the juxtaposition of living and thinking the chiasmus includes nothing about writing, an activity that Crocker regarded as inseparable from thinking and pursued as twin activities well into the last year of her life, when she finished her reminiscences in 1829 at the age of seventy-seven.

That text and others remain unpublished until now. Even before the 1815 publication of her first essay under the pseudonym "A Lady of Boston," Crocker tried her hand at writing a fast sermon, dated August 20, 1812, under the pseudonym "Increase Mather Jun. of the inner Temple" for that sermon and for a Thanksgiving sermon dated November 18, 1813. She also completed the manuscript of a short play, *The Midnight Beau*, in 1819. Several undated manuscripts make it difficult to fix the date of her first sustained attempt: "The United Trinity or consistant [*sic*] Catholic Christian" by "Candidus Maximus Originalis"; "Jephthah Vow, explained," for which no author is given; and "An Humble Address to the reason, and Wisdom of the American Nation," a third essay written under the pseudonym "Increase Mather Jun. of the inner Temple." There are also three versions of an essay on "Antiquarian researches, Pleasant and easy, By an original Antiquarian." A fragment of her writing is dated as early as 1772. Considered in their entirety Crocker's published and unpublished texts provide ample evidence of a sustained effort to develop her skill at writing in several genres, chiefly the essay but also poetry, drama, and the commonplace book.[8] The essay, however, remained a favorite vehicle for the expression of her ideas about a wide range of contemporary issues and thus a means by which to enter into public life.

Crocker did so as a "sublime amateur," the phrase applied by Susan Phinney Conrad to women writers of the period who wanted to avoid the negative associations of professionalism with femininity.[9] As Conrad notes, women with intellectual aspirations in the period 1830–60 usually had a father who was a professional. Crocker fits this pattern. Although she wrote in the period before 1830, men on her father's side of the family had been professionals for many generations. Little is known, however, about her education. Unlike the women writers examined by Mary Kelley in *Learning to Stand and Speak: Women, Education, and Public Life in America's Republic*, there is no record that Crocker attended a female academy or seminary.[10] Though largely self-taught, Crocker at least had the advantage of her father's library with its hundreds of books that included many volumes written by her male forebears. Other women writers of the early republic, such as Phillis Wheatley, Judith Sargent Murray, Mercy Otis Warren, and Hannah Adams, also lacked a formal education. Given their scant resources the achievements of women writers in Crocker's generation seem all the more extraordinary when compared to women writers of the next generation, who had the benefit of the formal education available at female academies and seminaries.

The lack of formal education, however, did not produce a uniform career path among women writers in the early republic. Phillis Wheatley (1753?–84), a child prodigy, was writing poetry long before the 1773 publication of *Poems on Various Subjects, Religious and Moral*, when she was about twenty; the first major work of Hannah Adams (1755–1831), *An Alphabetical Compendium of the Various Sects*, appeared in print in 1784, before she was thirty; "On the Equality of the Sexes," the landmark essay in the March–April issue of *Massachusetts Magazine* by Judith Sargent Murray (1751–1820), was published in 1790, before her fortieth year; Mercy Otis Warren (1728–1814) saw nothing in print with her name on it until 1790, although her play *The Adulateur* was published anonymously in 1772, when she was forty-four. Similarly the name Hannah Mather Crocker (1752–1829) did not appear on the title page of her first major publication, *A Series of Letters on Free Masonry*. Published in 1815, when she was sixty-three, the author is identified only as "A Lady of Boston."

Crocker did not let her delay in entering public life as a writer prevent her from taking on a wide variety of issues, whether a spirited defense of women's rights, Freemasonry, American exceptionalism, the need for reform, or the promotion of antiquarian research. These matters, treated singly or in combination in her writings, place her squarely within the political and cultural developments of the period of the early republic in the United States as well as the transatlantic context of Great Britain and the Continent. The advancement of Enlightenment values, those undergirding the American Revolution in particular, permeate her work, as do those of Scottish Enlightenment writers in the matter of common sense and rights.[11] Crocker is also representative of the period's renewed interest in literary genres such as the epistolary essay to articulate her support of Freemasonry; drama, in particular farce, to instruct foolish young men by entertaining rather than sermonizing; and satiric verse to excoriate physicians who cared more about their fees than the well-being of their patients. The sermon and the commonplace book also figure prominently in her writings; she relied heavily on the former in her jeremiads and on the latter in her two longest texts, *Observations on the Real Rights of Women* (1818) and "Reminiscences of Boston" (1829).

This book includes both published and unpublished writings by Hannah Mather Crocker. Of her published writings it provides the complete texts of *A Series of Letters on Free Masonry* (1815), *The School of Reform, or Seaman's Safe Pilot to the Cape of Good Hope* (1816), and *Observations on the Real Rights of Women* (1818). Many of her unpublished writings are also included: the complete texts of "Fast Sermon" (1812), "Thanksgiving Sermon" (1813), and the farce *The Midnight Beau* (1819), as well as one of the three versions of the essay "Antiquarian researches, Pleasant and easy, By an original Antiquarian" (n.d.) and "An Humble Address to the reason, and Wisdom of the American Nation" (n.d.). Selections from Crocker's 1829 miscellany, "Reminiscences of Boston," convey the breadth of her interests, ranging from anecdotes about the early founders to a description of a spinning contest on Boston Common, a story about Benjamin Franklin learning to stoop and one about a ten-foot-long rattlesnake placed in her lap by Sir John Dalton, reflections on the origins of the Liberty Tree, and a no-fail recipe for clam chowder.

To understand Crocker's development as a writer, a useful place to start is with her earliest extant pieces, considered here under "Beginnings: 1772–1811." These are followed by selections arranged chronologically in three major groupings: "Finding a Voice, 1812–1814," "Becoming an Advocate, 1815–1819," and "Taking Stock, 1820–1829." These groups, it should be noted, are not mutually exclusive. For example, Crocker uses a pseudonym in both the first and second groups, but the pseudonyms vary. Likewise although she supported a variety of causes, the last essay in "Finding a Voice" is the first of her writings in which she describes herself as "a warm advocate," in this instance, "for the forming of associations for literary and scientific improvement" (34). The assumption of a public role for her advocacy, however, becomes much more apparent in the second group, which includes three published texts and an unpublished play. "Taking Stock," a lifelong interest of Crocker's that surfaces in many of her writings, reaches its fullest expression in "Reminiscences and Traditions of Boston."

Beginnings, 1772–1811

Miscellaneous papers of Hannah Mather Crocker dated 1772, 1778, and 1786 shed light on her beginnings as a writer. The earliest of these highlights the importance she attached to respecting those with whom you differ, an idea found throughout her writings and usually combined with an emphasis on the need for mutual respect. The account notes with approval the high praise of Governor Thomas Hutchinson for the integrity and intelligence of clergymen in New England even though their views were far from his on the subject of politics. Hutchinson presumably extended this respect to his brother-in-law, Samuel Mather, the father of Hannah Mather Crocker, but whether the respect was reciprocated by the clergymen in their assessment of Hutchinson is absent from the unsigned document, dated September 21, 1772, and identified only as "recorded by a friend to all good men, tho' they differ, in their political, civil, or religious opinions."[12] The importance of the anecdote for Crocker is twofold: not only does it express the idea of mutuality that informs most of her writing, but it also serves as an example of her habit of collecting material from a wide variety of sources.

The conscious effort to produce a commonplace book surfaces in one of her miscellaneous papers, titled "A new collection of fragments taken from the public papers for rustick amusement in a winter evening by a friend of rural contentment." It is followed by a poem about the entertainment value these may have for the entire family.[13] Among the fragments gathered in her miscellaneous papers at the American Antiquarian Society is her poem "A Short Address, By the Mistress of St. Ann's Lodge," first printed in the public paper the *Boston 1778 Centinel*, according to Crocker. (The poem appears with the same date in *A Series of Letters on Free Masonry*, although the actual date of publication was February 24, 1798, in the *Columbian Centinel*.[14]) Crocker's miscellaneous papers, however, are not limited to her own attempts at versifying. A poem attributed to Tabitha Frost about Shay's Rebellion, which Crocker dated December 13, 1786, may have sparked a poem of her own on the taking of Daniel Shays that she prefaces with a note to the editor: "The following lines must give pleasure to your readers[,] please insert them in your Centinel," the same paper in which Frost's poem was published.

Crocker's beginnings as a writer show a marked preference for poetry as well as for the commonplace book as a repository of material that might be useful for subsequent projects. Among the poems in her miscellaneous papers that appear in "Reminiscences" are "Washington's Birthday, Calm Thoughts the Day of Celebrating for Peace, by a Washingtonian" and "To a Young Lady Who Was a Little Prudish." As a harbinger of Crocker's ideas about women's rights, the Hutchinson anecdote about the need to respect difference is revealing. Most important of all, however, is "North Square Creed, 30 Years ago," a manifesto she elsewhere dated 1787, more than three decades before the publication of *Observations on the Real Rights of Women*. The ringing declaration in the opening line, "I believe woman is the ostensible source of man's happiness," is reinforced by assertions, one rooted in the Bible and the other in Enlightenment values, that Crocker will greatly amplify in her pamphlet on women's rights: "I believe it was not good for man to be alone, and that God in infinite mercy provided for him an help meet. I believe a prudent wife is the greatest blessing man can attain [in] this world."[15]

Finding a Voice, 1812–1814

Essays about the War of 1812

Most of Crocker's unpublished writings in this period focus on the War of 1812. Included in this section are the complete texts of three sermons, the first dated August 20, 1812, the second dated November 18, 1813, and the third, which is undated. There is also an essay on antiquarian research. All three of the essays about the war were written under the pseudonym "Increase Mather Jun. of the inner Temple," a nom de plume that likely recalls her great-grandfather. (Other Mathers with the same first name were Increase Mather's son, Crocker's uncle, who was lost at sea before 1728, and her brother, who was killed in Havana in 1765.) Crocker's appropriation of Increase Mather in these early attempts at sermonizing made it possible for her to imagine coming into public life by adopting the male persona of a public figure, one who not only served as a minister but also played a prominent role in renewing the charter of the Massachusetts Bay Colony.[16] A trope for her inward meditations, the pseudonym "Increase Mather Jun. of the inner Temple" refers to the holy of holies in Solomon's Temple, a key element of Freemasonry that appears in many of her writings.[17]

The first of these sermons, "Fast Sermon, Preached Mr. Madison's fast day, By Increase Mather Jun. of the inner Temple, August 20, 1812," responds to the Proclamation of Public Humiliation and Prayer issued by President James Madison on July 9, shortly after the start of the War of 1812 on June 18. The proclamation, which specified the third Thursday of August, the date of Crocker's sermon, was followed by similar proc-lamations issued by Madison on July 23, 1813, and November 16, 1814.[18] Invoking a tradition practiced by earlier generations in Massachusetts Bay, including Crocker's forebears, the fast day sermon recalled the community's special relationship with God and warned of dire consequences if it failed to live up to its obligations.[19] Such sermons enjoyed a resurgence during the Revolutionary War period and in the years of the early republic, from 1800 to 1820. During the War of 1812 ministers not only in New England but well beyond its borders used the fast day sermon to inveigh against "Madison's War," which they opposed on the grounds that an alliance with France would benefit the United States neither politically nor religiously. In Crocker's hands the jeremiad is first used to sound an alarm against precipitate action in going to war, which she believes is justified only for reasons of defense. Given that the war has already commenced, she quickly moves from the concern about a just war to the staples of the jeremiad: first, by mentioning a litany of sins such as materialism, extortion, and oppression to illustrate how the people of God's "American Israel" have gone astray; and second, by holding out the promise of great blessing if the people submit to God, who is using the war as a means of chastising them.

Crocker's "Thanksgiving Sermon, Preached Novemb^r 24, 1813," the second of her three sermons about the war, owes more to established custom than to a specific proclamation from President Madison, who did not issue a proclamation declaring a Day of Thanksgiving for the end of the war until March 4, 1815. (Although the Treaty of Ghent was signed on December 24, 1814, the Battle of New Orleans, the final battle in the war, did not take place until January 8, 1815.) Citing Philippians 4:6 as her text, "Be careful for nothing; but in everything by prayer and supplication with thanksgiving let your request be made known unto God," Crocker expounds on its meaning for the United States as the beneficiary of divine favor. Her gratitude extends from the simple mess of clams enjoyed by those who attended the first Thanksgiving in Plymouth to the wise providence that produced a Washington and other leaders during the Revolutionary War, but stops far short of blessing members of the current administration, whom she castigates for their part in waging "a cruel, and imprudent, unjust war against the innocent inhabitants of Canada."[20] Praying for peace for "our American Israel," Crocker contrasts the United States with the chaotic political scene in Europe as she contemplates the likelihood that the United States is "the last rising empire" on the world stage.

A third piece, undated, delineates Crocker's opposition to the War of 1812 in even greater detail. In "An Humble Address to the reason, and Wisdom of the American Nation, By Increase Mather Jun. of the inner Temple," she inveighs against the Madison administration for not building a strong navy to prevent the impressment of American seamen by the British. Blame is assigned to southerners and northerners alike for the threat they pose to the body politic. Hailing Washington as the true Federalist, Crocker expresses disbelief that southerners would vote against their interests, a reference to their continued support of economic sanctions that began with the Embargo Act of 1807, initiated by President Thomas Jefferson. At the same time she is sharply critical of the foes of Federalism in the North, the Federalist stronghold, for their stubborn refusal to be mindful of their own need for commerce. Although she refrains from airing the controversy that led to cries in favor of secession in the New England states, she does warn of anarchy, for which she finds Hydra, the many-headed monster, a fitting symbol. Her willingness to acknowledge that political viewpoints in the nation may be as diverse as climatic conditions, however, does not deter her from invoking the theme of mutuality that is repeated here and elsewhere in her writings. On the contrary, in this address Crocker lets it serves as a reminder that "we are formed in one federal band," a political triumph that she identifies with George Washington and cites as the reason why the nation once enjoyed wide respect in Europe.[21]

"Antiquarian researches"

The final selection in Crocker's early unpublished writings from 1812 to 1814 is "Antiquarian researches, Pleasant and easy, By an original Antiquarian." Although undated the essay is included in this period because of the likelihood that it was written around the time that Isaiah Thomas established the American Antiquarian Society, on March 13, 1812, and his subsequent acquisition of the Mather Family Library from Crocker in 1814. The three versions, filed in Folders 4, 5, and 6 in Box 12 of the Mather Family Papers at the American Antiquarian Society, have considerably more similarities than differences. Each acknowledges the importance of conducting antiquarian research and cites ancient Masonic principles based on biblical texts in support of such activities. All three include the passage "the prudence of even a matron [may be the means of saving a nation]."[22] Although the immediate context refers to records that could settle boundary disputes, restore ancient landmarks, and recover the rights of original owners, Crocker's larger concern is the preservation and dissemination of ancient knowledge that may usher in the millennium.

Despite the similarities, differences among the three versions are striking. The version in Folder 4, "By H. M. Crocker," is the shortest of the three. The version in Folder 6, signed "H. Mather Crocker," contains lengthy passages about the religions of Egypt, Persia, and India that celebrate a trinity in unity, which Crocker also believes can be found in the Jewish tradition. All nations of the world have a belief of this sort, asserts Crocker, who primarily relies on Claudius Buchanan and other scholars to support her claim that the ubiquity of the tradition prepared the way for the Christian doctrine of the Trinity.[23] "The United Trinity or consistant [*sic*] Catholic Christian," an undated essay not included in this book, provides further insight into her beliefs about the Christian doctrine of the Trinity in considerable detail. Of special interest to Crocker is the continuity of this belief as represented by the Masons.

The unsigned version of the essay in Folder 5 differs from the other two by ending with Crocker's imitation of Timothy Dwight's poem "Columbia," in which she celebrates the splendors of America that have been brought to light by the learning and knowledge of those who pursue antiquarian researches. Their work will never be done, she suggests, because the growth of the empire from east to west will bring in its wake a concomitant expansion of learning and knowledge about it. The praise of Columbus and his namesake, Columbia, highlights a process whereby the rise of America will culminate in the millennium, a period Crocker continued to believe was fast approaching. Of the three versions of her essay promoting antiquarian research, this is the only one with an inscription on the back of the last page that links it directly to the founder of the American Antiquarian Society: "Isaiah Thomas Esqr. Worcester. Belonging to the Antiquarian Soc[ie]ty."

Becoming an Advocate, 1815–1819

Although Crocker maintained her interest in things antiquarian long after the war ended in 1815, other matters engaged her attention, especially women's education, social reform, and women's rights. Becoming an advocate for each of these issues broadened her range considerably, and it is during the period 1815–19 that she came into her own as a published author. For each of these concerns she wrote a book; however, not until her second, *The School of Reform*, did she use the name "H. M. Crocker," and not until her third did she use the name "H. Mather Crocker." This highly productive period in Crocker's life ended with a foray into a very different genre, the writing of *The Midnight Beau*, her only play.

A Series of Letters on Free Masonry

Crocker's first major publication, *A Series of Letters on Free Masonry* (1815), contains three letters from "A. P. Americana" of Boston and a brief reply after each from "Enquirer." The letters are dated September 7, September 30, and October 20, 1810, and the replies from the Enquirer of Montpelier, Vermont, are dated September 21, October 9, and October 31, respectively. Following the letters are two poems attributed to the "Mistress of St. Ann's Lodge" and a poem "By a lady, who sat in the east gallery of the Old South meeting" at a Grand Lodge Masonic ceremony to commemorate George Washington, the most well-known Freemason in the United States, where Masonry was first introduced in 1730. Written when Freemasonry was enjoying great popularity in the country, Crocker's 1815 essay was particularly well-timed: eleven years later the attempts to silence William Morgan for his exposé of Masonic secrets in 1826 unleashed a firestorm of criticism from which the Masons never recovered.[24] The criticism that Crocker seeks to deflect is of a very different sort, and in the first letter it is eclipsed by her more immediate concern about the deplorable state of women's education.

Acknowledging that many will think it "a bold attempt for a female to even dare enter on the subject at all," the first letter in Crocker's series asserts that "a truly independent mind will rise above the fear of man."[25] That many women were already possessed of such an independent mind is evident in her observation about the new role women envisioned for themselves that extended beyond basic literacy. "If women could even read and badly write their names it was thought enough for *them*, who by some were esteemed as only 'mere domestick animals,'" writes Crocker, who identifies a growing awareness among women that "they were given by the wise author of nature, as not only helps-meet, but associates and friends, not slaves to man." The call for companionate marriage is coupled with conventional warnings about wasting time "in frivolous calls" or "with some foolish novel" and ends on the theme of the importance of cultivating virtue, which is best done by acquainting young people with the history of virtuous persons in their own country.[26]

For Crocker the link between female education and Freemasonry began with an attempt to allay the fears of her female friends who were worried about their husband joining a disreputable group, an inquiry that eventually led to her becoming the mistress of a similar institution, St. Ann's Lodge. According to Crocker, there is "reason to think this institution gave the first rise to female education in this town, and our sex a relish for improving the mind" because of the desire on the part of several women to study languages.[27] The twin aims of the group, friendship and improvement of the mind, bear a resemblance to those of the Junto, a male club for mutual improvement formed in 1727 by Benjamin Franklin, who drew up rules and qualifications that guided his group and its offshoots for more than forty years.[28] Although members of the Junto helped Franklin form an academy that later became the University of Pennsylvania, they did not take great pride, as Crocker's group did, in studying a variety of subjects while "performing every domestick duty with ease and harmony" (45). The assurance that the smooth running of the household would not be affected by membership in the group suggests that Crocker was aware of such criticism and sought to deflect it. In 1815 the lodge was no longer active, but Crocker harbored the hope that the institution would be revived. A possible model would be the female benevolent societies for the education of the poor that she knew were already in existence.

The next two letters address the charges leveled against the Masons directly but also serve as a vehicle for Crocker's ideas about the value of institutions. In the letter dated September 30, 1810, Crocker argues that leaving the Society of Masons because of the behavior of some of its members could serve equally well as a reason to leave any institution, including a literary society to which she once belonged. The learning available to its members was not embraced by everyone to the same degree, notes Crocker, who attributes the failure to reap the benefits provided by the association to the individuals rather than the institution. She holds institutions of all sorts in high esteem, as long as they are based on reason, because of their "tendency to promote the general utility and happiness of our fellow creatures" (49). The value of benevolent institutions in spreading goodwill receives added emphasis in the final letter, in which Crocker extols the link between Freemasonry and the Christian dispensation, and in turn the links between these and the earlier Jewish dispensation that she believes they supersede.

An alternative title for *A Series of Letters on Free Masonry* put forward by Crocker in one of her miscellaneous papers titled "Thinks I to myself" demonstrates a sense of humor as well as the recognition that a book needs to be marketed. In an unacknowledged reference to *Thinks-I-to-Myself: A Serio-Ludicro, Tragico-Comico Tale*, written by Thinks-I-to-Myself, Who? (1814), Crocker uses the phrase to speculate on the fact that "an odd, or singular title will give zest to a work" that otherwise would go unread.[29] Citing as an example the title of one of the many books written by Hannah Adams, *The History of the Jews*, Crocker wonders how much wider Adams's readership might be had she modernized the title by calling it "The Jews, an Historical Novel called *The Clincher*." In this instance Crocker focuses attention on the popularity of the novel as a genre and not just the matter of a snappy title. Repeating the phrase "Thinks I to myself," Crocker notes that she has "been reading some letters written by a Lady to a young friend on masonry" and wants to have them published with an attention-grabbing title such as "The Clincher of Clinchers, Or a Series of letters on Masonry by a Lady." She ends the humorous piece by acknowledging her desire to attract young people as her readers, recognizing that "a song may catch him whom a sermon flies."[30]

The School of Reform, or Seaman's
Safe Pilot to the Cape of Good Hope

A Series of Letters on Free Masonry was followed by a homily
for sailors, *The School of Reform, or Seaman's Safe Pilot to the
Cape of Good Hope,* by the Seaman's Friend, H. M. Crocker
(1816). In both pamphlets Crocker uses the same pseudonym
and variations of the same signature, P. Americana and
A. P. Americana in the former and Prudencia Americana
in the latter. Although the adoption of a Roman name was
widely shared by writers in the early federal period (e.g., Judith
Sargent Murray's use of "Constantia" and Sarah Wentworth
Morton's use of "Philenia"), Crocker's joining of "Prudencia"
to "Americana" recalls the distinctively American consciousness of her grandfather, Cotton Mather, in assigning such
names to his biographical subjects as Nehemias Americanus
for John Winthrop. Crocker's two essays also share a similar
purpose, specifically the use of disruptive male behavior as a
springboard to register womanly concerns about matters of
consequence for the common good. A significant difference is
that *A Series of Letters* relies on Masonic imagery, whereas *The
School of Reform* depends on sailing for its major tropes; the
symbols of Masonry, however, are not entirely absent in this text
or, for that matter, in almost any text by Crocker. Addressing
her "messmates" she announces that she has "taken passage for
the Cape of Good Hope, in the fast sailing ship Time; owner,
Columbus; commanders, Fortitude, Perseverance; Wisdom
and Reason helmsmen; the hard arms all manned with skill
and prudence, sound hearts and clear heads" (62).

A poem directed to "Brave seamen" bookends the essay
that serves as ballast for the solemn vow of temperance that
Crocker enjoins them to take in the first twenty-four lines of

the poem at the beginning of the essay and the final eighteen lines at the end. In exhorting sailors to be guided by reason she inveighs against the habit of intemperance but carefully refrains from counseling total abstinence. Instead her admonition to the sailor to let reason, not drink, steer the course of his life is tempered by the advice not to drink too hard or too deep. Never, though, does she advise him not to drink at all. Crocker's moderate views on the subject are closely aligned with those of her contemporary Benjamin Franklin, whom she quotes at length on the debilitating effects of excessive drinking. They also recall the balanced stance of her forebears on the subject, a stark contrast with the hard line taken against drinking by the Society for the Suppression of Intemperance, a group to which Crocker refers and with which she was in sympathy, but only to a degree.[31]

To help the intemperate Crocker advises that they embrace religious faith and a rational mode of living, the latter of which she views as a necessary adjunct of being Christianized. To keep the problem from spreading she promotes education as the primary means of prevention, especially the education of poor children. In her view males and females alike should attend schools of industry, a vocational education program in the nineteenth century that did not focus on classroom study exclusively but also included wage work. While industriousness as an antidote for idleness receives warm praise from Crocker, she judges the importance of cultivating the mind to be as important as cultivating the land. Mindful of the attention given to education by the settlers of Massachusetts Bay, she suggests that the movement to send missionaries abroad should be paralleled by a movement to send them "from north to south, and from east to west" in the United States, a clear indication of the centrality of the Northeast as an exemplary model for Crocker.

Throughout the essay Crocker tacks back and forth between the literal and metaphorical treatment of the trope of the journey, dispensing much of the same advice to those on the voyage of life as she gives to sailors on a ship. The effect deepens both the figurative and the literal use of the trope; what goes largely unremarked, however, is the metaphor of the Ship of State, although the idea conveyed by it is given some attention. Having invoked Columbus as the owner of the ship on which she and her messmates have embarked Crocker argues throughout about the interconnections between the good habits of individuals and the good order of society, with special reference to the home, which serves for her as an important middle ground between private and public well-being. The enjoinder "Steady! Boys, Steady!" at the end of the essay as well as in the closing lines of the poem serves as a reminder of the Masonic emphasis on steadfastness, a trait rooted in classical, biblical, and Enlightenment ideals.

Observations on the Real Rights of Women

Crocker's concern for private and public well-being finds its fullest expression in *Observations on the Real Rights of Women, with Their Appropriate Duties, Agreeable to Scripture, Reason and Common Sense* (1818), one of the first books on women's rights written by an American to be published in America.[32] By listing the author as H. Mather Crocker on the cover, the book highlights her connection to the Mathers but obscures her female identity. Readers, though, were unlikely to miss the reference in the dedication to another Hannah, the English writer "Miss H. More."[33]

Crocker begins *Observations* with an introduction, followed by eight chapters and an appendix. The first two chapters concentrate on the religious roots of women's rights: the story of the Creation and the Fall as it pertains to women's status in chapter 1 and women's restoration through the plan of redemption in chapter 2. After a catalog of outstanding religious and secular women in chapter 3, she asserts in chapter 4 that contemporary women's writing is equal to that in any previous period and provides numerous examples.[34] The next three chapters constitute the heart of *Observations on the Real Rights of Women, with Their Appropriate Duties* by focusing on the second half of the title: *Agreeable to Scripture, Reason and Common Sense.* The argument chiefly rests on a series of correspondences whereby women's rights are linked in three ways: with their rights as Christians, based on scripture (chapter 5); with their rights as heirs of the Enlightenment, grounded in reason (chapter 6); and with their rights as citizens in a democracy, depending, as it does, on common sense (chapter 7). The first four chapters, together with the last, chapter 8, and the appendix, reinforce the central idea of the book: the bond of mutuality as the primary means of assuring unity, whether that of husband and wife, members in an association, or citizens of a country.

A distinctive feature of the treatise is its heavy reliance on the writings of others, so much so that it raises the question of exactly whose observations these are. More than half of the material is not Crocker's own but is taken from a wide variety of texts by her contemporaries, including *A Vindication of the Rights of Woman* by Mary Wollstonecraft and *Strictures on Women* by Hannah More; essays from *The Rambler* by Samuel Johnson, as well as his abridged biography of Rochester in *Some Passages in the Life and Death of John, Earl of Rochester* by

Gilbert Burnet. Other texts used by Crocker include *History of the Rise, Progress and Termination of the American Revolution* by Mercy Otis Warren; *A Commentary on the Bible* by the Methodist minister Thomas Coke; the poetry of Lucy Aikin and Isaac Watts; and compendia for young people such as *Beauties of History; Or, Pictures of Virtue and Vice, Drawn from Real Life* by L. M. Stretch and *Elements of General Knowledge, Introductory to Useful Books in the Principal Branches of Literature and Science* by Henry Kett. The preponderance of her borrowings, however, come from studies such as *The History of Women* by William Alexander; *Sacred Biography, Or, The History of the Patriarchs, To Which Is Added, The History of Deborah, Ruth, and Hannah* by Henry Hunter; *Essay on the Character, Manners, and Genius of Women in Different Ages* by Antoine Leonard Thomas and enlarged by Mr. Russell; and *The Friend of Women* by Boudier de Villemert, translated by Alexander Morrice.[35]

Most of Crocker's borrowings are direct, but not all. The commentary on the temptation of Adam and Eve attributed to Jacques Saurin, for example, is not taken directly from his writings but from a note on Genesis 3:6 in Thomas Coke's extensive commentary on the Bible. Likewise Mary Wortley Montagu's reflections on whether Islam considers women to have souls are not borrowed from Montagu's correspondence but indirectly by way of William Alexander's *History of Women*, as is the anecdote about the Tahitian queen. In discussing the physical strength of women Crocker notes Captain Wallis's recollection that the queen effortlessly carried him over the marsh; the source for the passage, however, is Alexander's *History* and not Wallis himself in John Hawkesworth's *An Account of the Voyages*. Although some of Crocker's borrowings are acknowledged, many are not. The material directly borrowed, moreover, often does not have quotation marks placed around it, which makes it difficult for the reader to determine where the quotation begins and ends. Minor changes to the quoted material are made without comment: the substitution of a word or phrase for another, alterations in spelling, changes in punctuation, and so on. The same holds true for major changes, such as the deletion of a sentence or an entire paragraph or a line or section of a poem without signaling the omission to the reader by the use of ellipses.

While these lapses in documentation may be considered egregious by modern scholars, many of them fall within the range of standard practice by nineteenth-century writers. The habit of quoting extensively without benefit of quotation marks, however, problematizes the text by raising the issue of whether Crocker's *Observations* might best be described as a commonplace book.[36] In many instances large blocks of material drawn from a variety of sources are organized under major headings in such a way that the text appears to be a collection of quilted squares banded by Crocker's occasional comments. The recent claim put forth by Eileen Hunt Botting and Sarah L. Houser that Crocker is the most important theorist on women's rights in the eighteenth century in the United States is therefore open to debate.[37] Instead of dismissing *Observations* out of hand as a commonplace book or lavishly praising it as cutting-edge political theory of the period, a third possibility is to consider it chiefly as a rich repository of ideas that were circulating about the *querelle des femmes* during the period of the early republic on both sides of the Atlantic. As a participant in the long-standing debate about the nature and status of women Crocker contributed by raising the issue of whether some countries were more congenial than others in extending the progress of those rights.

In particular the value of *Observations* lies in its articulation of the ideals of freedom and equality for women that are linked to the American struggle against Great Britain during the Revolutionary War. Many of the assumptions underlying Crocker's text, however, were widely shared on both sides of the Atlantic by the time her book appeared in 1818. The belief that men possessed greater physical strength, for example, appears in most of the writings by advocates of women's rights regardless of political affiliation. Nor does Crocker depart from the view that the mental powers of women are equal to those of men, with any differences attributable to education. On these and many other matters those committed to the rights of women were in agreement, especially their ability to do more than sew and spin. A different sort of spinning occupies Crocker's attention: the swift rotation caused by political revolution in America that not only transformed opinion about women's rights in the late eighteenth century but also changed the discussion about those rights in the United States.

Much of the debate after the Revolutionary War centered on the need for both men and women to cultivate virtues essential for the survival of the republic, although their cultivation is cast more as a duty than a right. According to Rosemarie Zagarri, duties and rights began to acquire a gendered distinction during this period, when Americans "applied the more open-ended concept of rights, associated with Locke, to men and the more duty-bound theory, associated with the Scots, to women."[38] Raising well-regulated individuals was deemed an important duty for women, but the indirect influence they could thereby exert on the course of public affairs is extolled by Crocker as an important right. Allied with the need for well-ordered lives was the fear of luxury and dissipation, a fear frequently invoked by Crocker's forebears but one that took on a more pronounced political cast after the war. Crocker praises the period when women had time to study history and pursue other intellectual interests rather than waste time sitting in front of the mirror or reading worthless novels. Although the emphasis on virtue was deeply rooted in the Puritan assumption that human nature is fallen but capable of regeneration, it also had roots in the ideas of Whig liberty, especially those of Montesquieu. As a newspaper article of the period put it, "No virtue, no Commonwealth."[39] The idea of public virtue as rooted in private virtue, argues Gordon S. Wood in *The Radicalism of the American Revolution*, is what gave the Revolution its "socially radical character—an expected alteration in the very behavior of the people."[40]

By the time Crocker's book was published in 1818 two additional events had influenced the progress of women's rights beyond the first tentative steps to challenge the boundaries imposed on women that confined them to making pudding and plying their needles. In the eyes of the American public the two were inextricably intertwined: first, the scandal surrounding Mary Wollstonecraft, and second, the French Revolution. Noting that little attention had been devoted to women's rights, Crocker speculates, "Perhaps it has not been necessary in a land where the rights of women have never appeared a bone of much contention." Independent people, she argues, are likely to have ideas that "will be more liberal and expanded respecting the sexual rights." What did become a bone of considerable contention was William Godwin's 1798 *Memoirs of the Author of A Vindication of the Rights of Woman*.[41] Although Godwin, Wollstonecraft's husband, sought to defend his wife's reputation in *Memoirs*, it had the opposite effect when readers learned from its pages about Wollstonecraft's many affairs and attempts to commit suicide. The effect on her reputation was disastrous, and those who defended her were open to charges of loose morals.[42] Crocker, however, praised *A Vindication*, although she differed with Wollstonecraft on several points.[43] Her praise, coming in 1818, suggests that the passage of time had softened the criticism against Wollstonecraft; it also signaled a major shift in attitudes about women's rights whereby the radical and conservative forces no longer seemed to be diametrically opposed to each other.

For Crocker the treatment of women's rights through a series of correspondences begins with the family circle and widens to include the entire nation. Noting that women in early America had always enjoyed the right to choose whom they would marry, she does not explicitly repudiate an older system of correspondences whereby women were seen as inferior to men. She nevertheless challenges its assumptions by establishing a series of correspondences based on equality and mutuality, beginning, as most arguments about women's rights at this time did, with Adam and Eve. Echoing Milton, Crocker informs us in chapter 5 that the two "walk side by side, as mutual supports in all times of trial" (84), thereby serving as models for a number of couples throughout history whom she praises for the mutuality of their marriage. From Henry Hunter's *Sacred Biography* she cites the marriage of Hannah and Elkanah as based upon "one common interest" (97). Her description of an ideal pair reflects what Lawrence Stone has identified as a movement toward "affective individualism" in marriage at the end of the eighteenth century.[44] Crocker lauds men who wrote about companionate marriage, especially Sir Thomas More, who described an ideal wife as serene, well-educated, and a constant friend. She likewise quotes Boudier de Villemert and Samuel Johnson approvingly. The example par excellence is Aurelius and Prudencia, an ideal couple likely based on the lives of her parents.

The final chapter of *Observations* ends on a note of joyful anticipation of heaven, where the spiritual distinction of the sexes does not exist, for all are equally redeemed. The advantage of forming "sacred love and friendship here," argues Crocker, is "that it shall be the foretaste of our future bliss" (130). Recalling the biblical assertion that God is no respecter of persons or sexes, she invites the reader to draw the conclusion that neither are we to be on earth. After all, she says, quoting Hannah More, who in turn quoted a prelate, "Women make up one half of the human race, equally redeemed by the blood of Christ" (91). Crocker did not believe that the equal redemption of women meant they were relegated to the home as their sole area of influence, even though she accepts it as their dominant sphere. From the earliest days of the nation's history, she says, women availed themselves of the opportunity to be educated and were often consulted on matters of public concern. She points with obvious pride to Sarah Kemble Knight, an instructor of writing in Boston in the early eighteenth century whom she credits with wielding considerable influence.[45] She lauds other women for "their writings and advice" during the American struggle for independence, a time when the "cult of true womanhood," to borrow Barbara Welter's phrase, was not yet deeply entrenched.[46]

An important way the redemptive or regenerative force of women was not confined to the individual household can be seen in the numerous female associations, chiefly maternal and religious, the second in Crocker's series of correspondences. The insistence that "women have an equal right, with the other sex, to form societies for promoting religious, charitable and benevolent purposes" (86–87) is a reminder of Crocker's active role in forming a female society of Masons and her strong advocacy for the establishment of an antiquarian society. According to Crocker, such mutuality would benefit the community and by extension the entire country.

The correspondences between mutual partners in a marriage and mutual members of an association are reinforced in *Observations* by the third in her series of correspondences, the mutuality of citizens. Here she parts company with Hannah More, Mary Wollstonecraft, and a host of other contemporaries, some of whom considered the role in women in raising good citizens, but few of whom argued that a specific form of government was more congenial to women's rights. In contrast Crocker argues in chapter 7 that to maintain peace in "our American Israel," a phrase that resonates in the literature of the early republic, "a free, federal, republican government . . . requires more sense and judgment to preserve it from disorder and disunion; therefore the union and right understanding of the sexes will have a tendency to strengthen, confirm and support such a government, and common sense must allow women the right of mutual judgment, and joining with the other sex in every prudent measure for their mutual defence and safety" (126).

Crocker mentions few examples of women's contributions to the Revolutionary War effort, although she singles out Mrs. Ackland for praise, from Mercy Otis Warren's *History of the Rise, Progress and Termination the American Revolution.*[47] Mrs. Washington and Mrs. Jackson are also hailed as examples of American women who were willing to leave the comforts of home to endure the privations of life at the front. In so doing they illustrate "the mutual virtue, energy, and fortitude [by which] the freedom and independence of the United States were attained and secured" (110).[48] Of special concern to Crocker is that the egalitarian rhetoric of the Revolution may disappear and with it the right of a woman to participate directly in matters outside the home.[49] That some women were already doing so in the postrevolutionary period is a source of obvious pride to Crocker, whose survey of the mutual accomplishments of the citizens of the new republic enlarges Jefferson's argument in query 6 of his *Notes on the State of Virginia*. Like Jefferson, Crocker asserts, "America, though as yet but young in the arts and sciences, will not long remain in the background" (108). Unlike Jefferson, who concentrates on the achievements of men, Crocker states that the country "can now claim the birth-right of many respectable female writers, both in prose and verse." Among those whom she praises are the poet Sarah Wentworth Morton and the historians Mercy Otis Warren and Hannah Adams. Crocker not only contributes to the dialogue about American genius highlighted by Jefferson but also expands it by offering evidence that women who lived during the Revolution were already extending its egalitarian ideals to a group not originally envisioned as a part of "We, the People."

Concerned lest she be guilty of partiality in her *Observations*, Crocker ends with a roll call of illustrious men as a counterweight to the list of outstanding women enumerated in chapters 3 and 4. For example, Old Testament figures such as Deborah, Ruth and Naomi, and Hannah in chapter 3 are offset in the appendix by Moses, Job, Solomon, and Isaiah, and from ancient Rome Pliny and Cicero balance Zenobia and Cornelia. Likewise her citing of Marie Le Jars de Gournay, Mary Schurman, Catherine Macaulay, and Mary Wollstonecraft as female writers is matched by her listing in the appendix of male counterparts Dryden, Pope, Addison, and Johnson, although perhaps unevenly. The historians Mercy Otis Warren and Hannah Adams cited in chapter 4 are balanced in the appendix by the historians Jeremy Belknap and George Minot. As Crocker enumerates illustrious men throughout the course of history, she gives high praise to more than thirty from her native land. In fact, she writes, were she to include "the catalogue of old Harvard, and the other Universities, it would swell our work to the frightful size of a huge folio" (139). The narrative of Aurelius and Prudencia at the end of the appendix offers the reader a model of mutuality on all three levels. The two also recall Crocker's pseudonym for herself as A. P. Americana in *A Series of Letters*: Aurelius and Prudencia as the model of mutuality in an independent country where women as well as men are accorded rights.

The Midnight Beau

The Midnight Beau: A Farce in 2 Acts is Crocker's sole surviving attempt at drama. Completed in 1819, the unpublished play apparently was never staged, even though it provides a further demonstration of Crocker's versatility in performing advocacy. It also contributes to our understanding of the early republic by signaling the dramatic change in attitudes toward the theater between late seventeenth- and early nineteenth-century Boston. Unlike her great-grandfather Increase Mather, who inveighed against the theater as a "danger to the souls of Men," Crocker praised it as an alternative to the pulpit for those who may find a play more congenial than a sermon.[50] Finding many genres congenial, Crocker had already tried her hand at several, including memoir, sermon, essay, and poetry.

Not only did she seek to reinvigorate the sermon, the genre most closely identified with the long line of ministers on her father's side of the family, but she also embraced the genre of drama, an unprecedented Matherian move beyond theatrical metaphor to theater itself, albeit a move she made fairly late.[51] Crocker's play thus illustrates the expanding number of genres practiced by women writers for which Mercy Otis Warren may have served as Crocker's primary model. An example of a subgenre of drama long favored in Great Britain and on the Continent, Crocker's farce is also important as a measure of its growing popularity among American playwrights.

Situating her work in the context of a current event is typical of Crocker's attempt through writing to enter into public life. *The Midnight Beau* is no exception. Steeped in the Panic of 1819 the play juxtaposes the sinking fortunes of credulous investors with the fallen reputations of credulous women who place their confidence in men, allowing them to "first gain their affections, then ruin and destroy their reputation."[52] Although confidence men pose a threat to both groups, Crocker maintains the farce by satirizing Captain Spoilation's boast that he will discount their notes at 50 percent to demonstrate "how it is done by the way of modern friendship," but drops it when she presents Angelica Bloomly's grave concern about the jeopardy in which a woman is placed when she finds her currency devalued. In a rare appearance by a mother in an American play during this period, Amilia Prudencia, mother of Stripling, affirms her solidarity with Angelica by casting moral consciousness as a republican virtue available to all, rather than the exclusive preserve of a particular class or gender. Concern about the rising generation takes center stage in *The Midnight Beau*, a play that not only interrogates speculation by examining its economic and sexual variants, and the links between them, but also reflects on their ramifications for the well-being of the nation.

Taking Stock, 1820–1829

"Reminiscences and Traditions of Boston"

The longest of Crocker's unpublished manuscripts is her miscellany, "Reminiscences and Traditions of Boston," which defies easy categorization despite the suggestion in the title that it is a memoir and a history. Divided into three major sections, the first of these is subdivided into several parts, with entries on a wide variety of topics, including people and their houses, fires, lawyers, churches, laws, doctors, and epitaphs. An appendix at the end of the section contains poems, anecdotes, letters, and elegies before Crocker brings it to a final close with material "of modern date, to shew the recent feelings of patriotism in the heart of a real Washingtonian." For the second and third sections of this sprawling work, Crocker used the title "Interesting Memoirs and original anecdotes." Shorter versions of narratives in the first section appear in the second, together with material of the sort found in the first section: epitaphs, anecdotes, an essay, and more poems. Section 3, which has lengthy extracts from an old law book, contains fewer narratives and many more poems than section 2. Most of the poems are occasional, covering public events such as the launching of the frigate *Independence*, the choice of a new governor in Massachusetts, and the opening of a school, as well as private matters, including thanks for a gift of bread, gratitude for the kindness of an official in arranging for her care, and a plea to a misguided friend who thinks Crocker's failing health will improve if only she will give up her writing. Some of these, however, combine the personal and the political, for example, a blistering criticism of doctors who refuse to treat patients unless the fee for their services is assured. Although some of the poems are clustered together, many are interspersed with anecdotes and letters. Crocker likewise made no attempt to separate material of her own composition from that by others in her sprawling miscellany, which also functions as a commonplace book. Letters and documents are pasted onto the final pages of the collection, including a note from A. Holmes dated September 5, 1822, thanking her for the account of the Mather family high chair that Crocker donated to the American Antiquarian Society.

The collection exhibits the broad range of Crocker's interests in the city's history, which coincides at many points with the history of both sides of her extended family, given the prominent role played by Mathers and Hutchinsons in the Massachusetts Bay Colony. As a result the miscellany gives her wide berth in fulfilling her lifelong passion for antiquarian research, which she believed to be of great benefit for the rising generation. Sometimes an anecdote draws in sharp relief the change from the past to the present, as the story of the father of Sarah Kemble Knight suggests. Returning home from a long voyage he greeted his wife by kissing her in public upon his arrival, which happened to be the Sabbath, and for that infraction he was punished. Other anecdotes reveal Crocker's recognition that memorable occasions in her own day would be deemed antiquarian a few decades hence. One such event was an exhibition in 1762 on Boston Common that began with the performance of Highland reels, followed by a contest to determine the best spinner among the women operating nearly fifteen hundred spinning wheels. According to Crocker, who relies on the reminiscence of her friend Madame Turell, one of the participants, the event pitted the "spinning school scholars" from North Boston against "the West Boston factory girls" (187). The miscellany also serves as a record of Crocker's personal experiences, for example, her recollection of meeting Phillis Wheatley and several lines of a poem by Wheatley that she inscribed to Crocker. "Reminiscences" also serves as an important repository of material such as "North Square Creed" and an essay on antiquarian research that appear in other texts by Crocker. Although the first section is dated 1827, Crocker worked on the manuscript as late as 1829, the year of her death.

Hannah Mather Crocker's growth as a writer from 1772 to 1829 offers a striking parallel to the development of the United States during the period of the Revolution and the early republic. As a result the material included here broadens our understanding of the achievement of women writers in the early republic who sought to expand the idea of who constituted "We, the People." Despite scholarly efforts to recuperate lost or neglected texts by early women writers, Crocker nevertheless remains an author who has yet to receive her due. Had she written nothing else but *Observations on the Real Rights of Women* that alone would be sufficient reason to place her at the forefront of the project to recuperate the work of women writers in the United States. Until very recently, however, Crocker has been entirely omitted from most histories of American feminism, even though *Observations* has been cited by one historian as the first "feministic" book in America.[53] This glaring omission is rectified by the publication of a modern edition of the complete text of Crocker's *Observations on the Real Rights of Women, A Series of Letters on Free Masonry,*

The School of Reform, The Midnight Beau, several sermons and essays, as well as selections from "Reminiscences of Boston" and other material.[54]

As part of the continuing effort to reclaim neglected women writers of the early republic, this edition traces the development of Crocker as a writer gradually coming into public life. In doing so it refigures the period 1800–1830, which is often slighted by scholars in their haste to leapfrog from the Revolution of the 1770s to the purported American Renaissance of the 1850s. At the same time this edition decenters the nation-state by situating Crocker's writings transatlantically, thereby challenging prevailing views of early American women in its exploration of the ways that Crocker illuminates the debates on both sides of the Atlantic about women's rights and other issues. The work of the Continental writers Anna Maria van Schurman and Madame de Staël and the English writers Mary Wollstonecraft and Hannah More, for example, are as important for an understanding of Hannah Mather Crocker as are the work of the American writers Phillis Wheatley, Mercy Otis Warren, Hannah Adams, and Judith Sargent Murray.

This edition also focuses on the broad swath of American history that includes Crocker's formidable forebears, many of whom were ministers, statesmen, and writers — some of whom were all three — although Crocker was the first woman in the Mather family to take up the pen. In her efforts to cross generational boundaries she reveals elisions and evasions shared by many writers in the early republic who wanted to celebrate the past but could not take it all in their embrace. The high chair she donated to the American Antiquarian Society was occupied successively by the numerous offspring of several generations of Mathers, including the children of Richard, the first Mather to emigrate from England, and the children of Hannah, his great-great-granddaughter. Many who sat in it scarcely lived long enough to outgrow the need for it; others went on to write volumes. A modern edition of Hannah Mather Crocker's writings serves as a helpful reminder that not every Mather who sat in the chair and later became a writer was male. For insights into the efforts of women writers of the early republic to enter into public life, her writings offer the reader an unprecedented opportunity to trace the development of a writer who sought to champion women's rights, promote education, support reform, encourage the formation of an antiquarian society, and grapple with the pressing political issues of her day.

A Note on the Text

Previously published texts by Hannah Mather Crocker appear in this edition with minor alterations. These include the complete texts of *A Series of Letters on Free Masonry*, *The School of Reform*, and *Observations on the Real Rights of Women*, which have not been altered except for changes in formatting and a few changes in punctuation and capitalization in cases where there is an apparent printer's error. Changes that do not fit the categories below appear in brackets within the text.

Crocker's unpublished manuscripts present a different challenge. Spelling, punctuation, grammar, and other matters have been changed to conform with the editing practices evident in her texts in the aggregate, both published and unpublished. To start a new sentence, Crocker often does not use a capital letter. To start a new paragraph, she rarely indents. Sometimes she leaves the preceding line partially unfilled and thus appears to start a new paragraph by beginning a new line in the far left margin of the paper; however, this is often the same way she continues a sentence, so it is unreliable as a paragraph marker. For *The Midnight Beau*, which has spelling and punctuation issues not found elsewhere in her unpublished material, a note has been added to the text of the play itself.

The spelling of proper names for all of Crocker's texts has been standardized, with variants placed in endnotes. Lines of poetry are numbered at line 5, 10, 15, 20, and so on.

Changes Made to Crocker's Texts

Changes in Grammar

1. Forming verbs: e.g., "bet" has been changed to "bit," "begain" to "begun," "eat" to "ate," "meet" to "met," "set" to "sit"; and verbals: e.g., "advance" to "advanced," "setting" to "sitting," "threaten" to "threatened," "wrote" to "written."

2. Making the subject and verb agree in number; e.g., the use of a plural verb with a collective noun has been changed to a singular verb: e.g., "have" to "has," "are" to "is."

3. Making a relative clause agree in number with the noun that it modifies: e.g., "loadstone that attract" to "loadstone that attracts."

Changes in Spelling

1. Separating into two words phrases formed by adding "a" to a single word: e.g., "ahappy," "amost," "anavy," "apeople," "asociety," "awar," "avery," "awise."

2. Joining the following words spelled as two: "news papers," "to night," "stock broker." When the second of the two words appears in uppercase, the words have been joined together and capitalized: "grand Father" to "Grandfather."

3. Using a single initial, medial, or final consonant rather than a double: e.g., initial — "inniquity"; medial — "cappitulate," "carreer," "collour," "depossit" or "depossited," "feellings," "promissed," "reelling," "rulling," "satturday," "seatting," "tranquillity," "triffling"; and final — "beautifull," "dispell," "excell," "gratefull," and "wonderfull."

4. Doubling a single consonant preceded by a vowel: e.g., "alowance," "biten," "mery," "milions," "recolect," "tyrany."

5. Doubling a final consonant preceded by a vowel to which

"-ed" has been added: e.g., "beged," "cloged," "commited," "compeled," "permited," "possesed," "stoped," "suped," "worshiped."

6. Doubling a final consonant when added to "-ing": e.g., "beging," "earings," "stagering," "trapings."

7. Doubling a final consonant preceded by a vowel to which "-ly" has been added: e.g., "continualy," "especialy," "habitualy," "literaly," "providentialy," "realy."

8. Adding an "e" to the following words: "determin," "hast," "imped," "tast."

9. Dropping the "e" in the following words: "animale," "eate," "controles," "customes," "guarde," "lightening" for "lightning," "longe," "shope," "speake," "truely," "weake."

10. Dropping the "e" in a word preceded by a consonant to which "-ing" has been added: e.g., "haveing," "improveing," "liveing," "placeing," "riseing," "sendeing," "takeing," "undertakeing."

11. Replacing a letter or letters omitted in a word: e.g., "exort" and "exortation," "govenor," "govment," "govement," "safty," "ploushares," "sout" for "sought."

12. Using appropriate homonyms: "an" for "and" and "and" for "an," "Quincy" for "Quinsy," "sculptor" for "sculpture," "where" for "were" and "were" for "where," "there" for "their" but not the reverse, "than" for "then" and "then" for "than," "the" for "thee," "it's" for "its" but not the reverse. Homonyms are sometimes used both correctly and incorrectly in the same text, occasionally on the same page, and even in the same sentence. "Then" is used correctly more often than any other homonym.

13. Forming the plural of a word ending in "y" preceded by a consonant by changing "y" to "i" and adding "-es" instead of adding "-s" to "y": "seminarys" to "seminaries," "Sentrys"

to "Sentries"; also forming the plural of a word ending in "y" preceded by a vowel by adding "s" instead of changing "y" to "i" and adding "-es": "chimnies" to "chimneys."

14. Forming a verb from a word ending in "y" preceded by a consonant by changing "y" to "i" and adding "-ed": e.g., "applyed" to "applied," "tyed" to "tied."

15. Reversing letters of words that have been transposed: "angle," "beleive," "beleiving," "Britian," "buckel," "Gaurd-ian," "Gosple," "Isarel," "Isarelites," "itslef," "peices," "reigons," "teir," "thier," "thurst," "viens," "veiw." Some transpositions, such as "knigs" for "kings" and "snigs" for "sings," appear infrequently.

16. Changes in the spelling of vowels and consonants:

Table 1. Vowels

"a" to "e"	"franzy," "inconsistant," "shepard" (to which "h" has also been added)
"a" to "o"	"accessary," "aften"
"e" to "a"	"continuel," "descendent," "secred," "segacious" (but "sagaciously"), "Yeomenry"
"e" to "ea"	"relms"
"e" to "ae"	"Cesar"
"e" to "i"	"embibed," "mellennium"
"e" to "o"	"contributers"
"i" to "e"	"dispised"; "dispond"; "distroy," "distroyed," and "distroying"; "distruction"; "enimies"; "ingage"; "intirely"; "intreat"; "privail"
"i" to "y"	"mistery," "paroxism," "Poliphemus," "stiled"
"o" to "e"	"phylactory"
"o" to "i"	"Bason," "frivoloties"
"o" to "u"	"Fon"
"oo" to "o"	"rood"
"u" to "eu"	"grandur" to "grandeur"
"ui" to "u"	"Bruit" to "Brute" (with final "e" added)
"y" to "ee"	"Jubily"

Table 2. Consonants

"c" to "s"	"cherry" (for "sherry"), "distructing" (for "distrusting"), "immence." (An exception is *Centinel*, the name of a newspaper, which has not been changed.)
"c" to "t"	"ingraciate"; "negociate," "negociated," "negociating"
"ck" to "k"	"strick" for "strike" and "stricking" for "striking"; "strock" for "stroke"
"k" to "ck"	"shakles" and "shakled"
"s" to "c"	"ansestors," "predesessors"
"s" to "t"	"repass"
"w" to "r"	"horrow" to "horror"

17. Other spelling changes: "artical" to "article," "Bretheren" to "Brethren," "Elijah mantles" to "Elijah's mantle," "mear" to "mere," "Methodis" to "Methodist," "perswaid" to "persuade," "priviledge" to "privilege," "potatoes popes" to "potato popes," "shew" to "shewed" for the past tense, "some olds womans hen roost" to "some old woman's hen roost," "stimulous" to "stimulus," "tabanacle" to "tabernacle," and "vians" to "viands."

18. Correcting what appear to be obvious errors: "age to ages" to "age to age," "ara avis" to "rara avis," "bagig" to "bagwig," "bleive" to "believe," "disgust" to "discuss," "dispostion" to "disposition," "evenig" to "evening," "finialy" to "finally," "goodess" to "goodness," "plitical" to "political," "poety" to "poetry," "secred" to "secret" and "sacred," "thirly" to "thirdly," "whent" to "went."

19. Silently deleting obvious repetitions: "lead lead," "our our," "she returned she returned," "the the."

Changes in Punctuation

1. Using an apostrophe to form a contraction. Crocker rarely uses an apostrophe for a verb form contracted with "not": e.g.,

"cant," "dont." Nor does she use an apostrophe with other contracted forms: e.g., "heres," "thats." An exception is the use of an apostrophe for the contraction of a pronoun and a verb: e.g., "We'll" and "I'm." Crocker omits it, however, in "Lets."

2. Using an apostrophe to show possession. Although Crocker occasionally uses an apostrophe for this purpose, most of the time she omits it: e.g., "Balaams," "Copps hill," "Gods," "Madisons," "Natures," "Washingtons."

3. Using an apostrophe and "-s" to show possession: e.g., "almighty" for "almighty's."

4. Deleting the apostrophe in "her's," "their's," and "your's."

5. Using a period for the following abbreviations: "am" to "a.m.," "capt" to "capt.," "Coll" to "Col.," and "Mr" to "Mr."

6. Using a question mark to signify the end of a direct question.

Changes in Capitalization

Crocker sometimes makes little distinction between upper- and lowercase letters in her unpublished texts, so her published texts are a useful guide. Changes in capitalization have been made for the following:

1. Using a capital for the first letter of the first word of a sentence. Crocker rarely does this, although she typically uses a capital for the first letter of the first word at the start of a major section of a published text and often capitalizes each letter in that word.

2. Using a capital for proper nouns: "christian," "english," "latin," "mahometan," and "puritan"; including days of the week: e.g., "monday" and "satturday"; and names of towns: e.g., "roxbury."

3. Using a capital letter for each word in a salutation: "August hearers," "Respected friends," and "My respected hearers."

4. Making all words uppercase in the following phrases: "Little red riding hood," "revolutionary War."

5. Making both words lowercase in the following phrases: "august Body," "howling Wilderness."

6. Regularizing the use of a capital for words in a series: "Cats, rats"; "Theology, Law, physic, astronomy, geography, and . . . chymistry."

Other Matters

1. Titles of newspapers have been italicized: e.g., *Courant*.

2. A hyphen has been added only to such words as "re-echo."

Changes That Have Not Been Made in Crocker's Texts

Spelling That Has Not Been Changed

1. The use of "an" before "h" whether silent or not: "an handful," "an heated," "an helpmeet," "an heroine," "an highly favoured people," "an historical," "an honourable," "an honest," "an host," "an hour," "an house," "an howling wilderness," "an humble."

2. The ending of words spelled with "ck": "electrick," "energetick," "fabrick," "panegyricks," "physick," "publick," "relick," "traffick," "tunick"; cf. "scientific" and "sceptic." The few instances in which Crocker uses "-c" instead of "-ck" to spell a word have been retained.

3. Words spelled with "ou" rather than "o": e.g., "ardour," "errour," "humoured," "horrour," "honour," "labouring," "Saviour," "vapours," "venoum," "vigour." Although Crocker uses both "honorable" and "honourable" on the very same page and in one instance spells "governor" as "governour," more often than not she employs "ou" rather than "o" in such words.

All such spellings have been regularized as "ou" except for "governor."

4. Contractions such as "tho'" for "though" and "thro'" for "through."

5. Formation of the past participle as a contraction: "clos'd," "powder'd," "prov'd," "restor'd," "rev'd" for "revered," "smoak'd." "Pitty'd" and "take'd," however, have been changed to "Pity'd" and "taken'd."

6. Words such as "chymistry," "compleat," "chastize," "contributers," "Enquirer," "Enterprize," "merchandize," "oeconomized," "practise."

7. Compounds formed with "well" or "ill" (e.g., "well regulated," "ill judged") have been left unchanged.

Punctuation That Has Not Been Changed

1. The omission of a period for abbreviations formed with the use of a superscript: e.g., "D^r" and "M^{rs}."

Capitalization That Has Not Been Changed

1. The use of capitalization to show emphasis: "Audience," "Children," "Nation," "Navy."

2. The use of a lowercase word before a proper noun that is capitalized: "almighty God," "apostle Paul," "fort William," "inner Temple," "king Lemiel [Lemuel]," "king Solomon," "late governor Sam Adams," "mother Nature," "mount Ephraim," "queen of Sheba," "saviour Jesus Christ."

3. Capitalization of a proper noun preceding a common noun: "Copp's hill," "Lord's day."

4. Retaining the mix of lower- and uppercase in the following phrases: "brave Boy" and "brave Boys," "high Bucks."

Observations on the Real Rights of Women
and Other Writings

I

Finding a Voice, 1812–1814

Fast Sermon

Preached Mr. Madison's fast day, August 20, 1812

By Increase Mather Jun. of the inner Temple

My Respected Hearers,

We have this day assembled in the house of the Lord in compliance with and direction of the head government of this Nation.[1] As specified by proclamation thro' the medium of the public newspapers, it may be expected by them that we join in fervent prayer for the divine blessing to attend the present war.

But every judicious person must be sensible it is the duty of a wise Nation to seek direction of heaven before they engage in a war. If they do not, but rush into one without seeking direction from him who is the wise ruler and disposer of all events of Mankind, we can have no reason to expect a blessing will attend the undertaking till we have sought out heaven to direct our path. I feel very confident no war can be justifiable in the eye of the God of peace except a defensive one. And when his people are labouring under the yoke of tyranny, and oppression, it is the duty of such a people to call on the Lord and be of good courage, and commit their cause to him if a just one. We may expect a blessing will attend us, if we fervently pray [to] him to appear on our behalf, that he would protect us and break to pieces the power of every cruel and proud oppressor, for wherefore go we forth except the Lord go with us.

Now if any Nation do go forth in a rash manner, not first seeking direction of heaven as to the justness of the cause, it may indeed be called a war of passion, or the rage of men in power. God forbid this nation, as a people, should engage in such a war, for which reason I have chosen for our present meditation these words,

Numbers, the 22 chap[ter], 12 verse
And God said unto Balaam thou shalt not go with them, thou shalt not curse the people for they are blessed.

I would recommend to you, my hearers, to read the whole of this chap[ter], when you return to your own houses, that you may take into view the wonderful interposition of divine providence on behalf of his ancient people Israel. Now at that time they, the Children of Israel, were many, and Moab was sore afraid of them, and Balak the son of Zippor was king of the Moabites at the time. And Moab was greatly intimidated and sore afraid, on account of the vast number of the Children of Israel, whom it seems had pitched their tents on the plains of Moab, on this side [of] Jordan, by Jericho. Now Balak, tho' he was irritated to a degree of desperation, yet he had not the hardiness or imprudence to wage war against the Israelites till he had secured Balaam in his interest, as he supposed him to be a prophet, or one versed in divination.

In the first place I shall take notice of the unhappy situation of the Moabites and their poor king Balak, that they could not call on the God of Israel as the God of their Fathers, and they dare not for their cause was a bad one. For it doth not appear that the Israelites made any war upon them but were quiet in

4

their own tents. But such was the pride of Moab and Balak, they could not bear to let them go on quietly to the land of Canaan, read Canada,[2] and they must have them routed to gratify their own pride and ambition. And how can it be done, they must needs have recourse to a false prophet, for a righteous one they would not listen to. So they repeatedly sent to Balaam, with the offer of large bribes, to come and curse the people of the most high God. Now we see in the words of our text, God said, go not with them, curse them not, for they are blessed. We, my hearers, have reason to hope we are the people of God. Tho' in many instances we have sinned and come short of his Mercy, yet we have experienced the divine favour towards us in as striking a manner as his peculiar people of old did. Did he not take a most gracious care of our venerable ancestors when they, for the sake of a free enjoyment of civil and religious liberty, forsook their native Land and came into this then howling wilderness?[3] Their cause was a good one, for they sought a place of refuge where they might worship God in truth and uprightness and obtain peace, liberty, and independence for their Children. And heaven never suffered any Balak to prevail against them. Tho' they were but an handful in number at that time, he scattered the heathen before them. When we have been oppressed with internal Tyrants, or foreign enemies, this people have always sought refuge in the Lord of hosts and the God of their Fathers; and he has never said to their seed, Seek ye me in vain. When we have sought him with our whole heart,[4] he has always heard our prayers and sent a gracious answer of peace to our country.

Secondly, I shall consider the folly of Balak, and Balaam, in attempting to curse the people whom the Lord pleases to own and bless. Now, my hearers, how wonderfully was the power of the almighty displayed in rebuking the madness of the prophet, and turning his curse so soon to a blessing. The prophet evidently appears to refuse the first offers, or bribes, but finally God permitted him to go on in his career till rebuked by the very Beast that he rode. He could go no further, but his eyes were opened, and he beheld the Angel of the Lord. And at the 25 verse we read, and when the Ass saw the Angel of the Lord, she thrust herself against the wall. And yet, he smote her again, and continued his rage till the Lord was pleased to open his eyes and he was convinced of his folly; and he fell on his face fully ashamed of his guilt in attempting to curse those whom the Lord pleases to own and bless as his people.

Thirdly I shall consider what a happy people they must be whom the Lord delights to own and bless as his; they may be encouraged to trust in him at all times. Tho' clouds and thick darkness may hang over them, yet he will point out some way for their escape. Tho' any Balak, or Balaam, attempt to curse us by an ill judged and imprudent war, if we humble ourselves under his mighty hand, he can and will turn their machinations from the curse of war to peace. War is always a sore judgment to a Nation and never ought to be resorted to, till no other refuge is left to preserve our lives, and Liberty. Then it is our duty to stand fast in the Liberty wherewith God has made us free,[5] and trust in him to deliver us from all our enemies. We, my hearers of these United States, have ever been the peculiar care of a most kind and gracious God. Has he not upheld us, from our first settlement to the present day? When we have had reason to think our vessel had nearly foundered, did not he that raised up a Joshua of old, has he not raised up a Washington in our own remembrance? He can yet save our American Israel.

For if the God of peace bless us, we need not fear the wrath of Man. We have reason to hope much from the wisdom, and prudence, of the head rulers of this State. We have reason to think heaven directed our choice in a ruler for peace. We have reason to bless God we have yet peace so far, that we are preserved from intestine war among ourselves in this part of our land. We have reason to bless God for the faithfulness of our Clergy for they are heard to say, almost to a man, peace be within your walls,[6] prosperity in all your dwellings. From these things we may be encouraged and hope the wrath, indignation, and horror of war will soon pass over if we will take the advice of Isaiah, to God's own people. When there was great tribulation coming on the land, he saith in Isaiah 26 chap[ter], 20 verse, Come my people, enter thou into thy Chamber, shut thy door about thee. Hide thyself as it were for a little moment until the indignation be over past. What a tenderness is here shewed to the people of God, that tho' there was great evil coming on the city, yet he would protect and save his own. Let me entreat of you, my Christian friends, every one of you, to retire and examine himself, and see, how far we fall short of our duty to God and our fellow creatures. Let us not give way to our angry passions, but let us all consider what we can do for the good of our country and the honour of God's holy name. Every individual can do something. Much may be done by prayer, for we read the prayer of the righteous availeth much.[7] We, my friends, must be prudent, quiet, and discreet; let not contentions be heard among us. Don't let party spirit shut your eyes to the truth.

I must be plain and explicit here, for I wish the meanest capacity to comprehend our present situation. For some years past we have been the happiest people on the Globe; we have been blessed with every favour heaven could bestow on a favoured people, but we have done evil in the sight of the Lord. We have gone astray from the living God. We have forsaken the path of our ancestors, we have gone astray from the living God and have worshipped the Idols of silver and gold. We have made haste to be rich. Our land groans under the Yoke of extortion and oppression, and tis for our follies and sinfulness we are now involved in a war, which is indeed a gloomy scene. And as it appears a war of party and the rage of men in power, nothing can save us from intestine animosity but the good sense of the people attended with a divine blessing. For God almighty's sake, don't let party spirit prevail among us and destroy all our happiness. Let us bear in mind [that] if we differ in opinion, we also differ in our looks; and we can no more make men think alike than we can make them look alike. Our frames, our whole organization, are so different, tis impossible we should think just alike. But we can all be so far orthodox as to do good to our fellow creatures. We can love and shew mercy and walk humbly before God.[8] If we differ in some points respecting religion or politics, we can all bear in mind that our country was settled on the firm basis of liberty, freedom, and independence for the free enjoyment of civil, and religious privileges but not licentiousness.

Let us then, my hearers, continue firm in the real interest of our beloved Country. Let us unite in one body for the joint interest of all its members. For we are indeed a very great and numerous people, and the Lord Jehovah will not as yet give us up if we do not provoke him by our sins and follies, which are indeed very great. It behooves us then, my friends, to forsake every evil way. Let me beg of you to begin by paying more regard to family government. If we do not, tis greatly to be feared our Children will not be found walking in the path of our venerable ancestors. We of these New England

States have been blessed in a most particular manner in having wise, and good Men to rule over us. We now call on all Magistrates to perform their duty, to restrain all profaneness, and debauchery in the land. It is now indeed a crying sin in our land and calls loudly for reformation. Tis reformation alone can save the city. If every one will consider and do his part, we may yet be that happy people whose God is Jehovah.[9] Be yet encouraged, my friends, for I doubt not we can find ten righteous ones amongst us.[10]

Let us all then join heart and hand and do justly, love and shew mercy[11] and put our trust in the God of our Fathers for he is ever Merciful. I have been Young, tho' I am now old.[12] And I can say I have never seen the righteous Man forsaken, or his seed. Tho' reduced to begging bread, the God of Jacob has been their support. Fear not then, my people, tho' an host should encamp against thee, and Balak and Balaam go forth to curse us with an ill judged war, yet the Lord will take a gracious care of his own people and will meet their enemies in the way. He can turn the curse of war into the blessing of peace. It is our duty to be firm, trusting in the Lord, commit all our affairs to him who ruleth among the Nations and can turn the hearts of Men from the curse of war to peace. When he sees us fully humbled under his correcting hand, he can, and will, put a stop to Balaam's career and turn his curse into a blessing and cause him to say in such language as this: tho' Balak would give me his house full of silver and gold, I cannot go beyond the commandment of the Lord. —

Don't let us rail so much at second causes but look to the great first cause who has permitted the great evil of war in our country. He has been pleased to permit it for our chastisement, for we have indeed been very ungrateful for the mercies we have enjoyed. Turn then, my people, return unto the path of your ancestors. Seek the Lord whilest he may be found, fervently commit the cause of your country and your wholeselves to his guidance and protection in and thro' his beloved son Jesus Christ, who is able to keep what we commit unto him, and to his name be adoration and praise.

Amen.

Thanksgiving Sermon

Preached Novemb[r] 24, 1813

By Increase Mather Jun. of the inner Temple

Respected Friends,

It has long been an established custom to celebrate an anniversary thanksgiving even from the first settlement of our country.[1] Our pious and venerable ancestors, deeply impressed with a sense of the divine goodness for preserving mercy and protecting them, even in an howling wilderness,[2] they then with fervent gratitude of soul gave thanks to almighty God. When their repast was no more than a simple mess of Clams, they even then appointed a day for thanksgiving prayer and praise in firm expectation of further help. They sought refuge in the Lord Jehovah by prayer and supplication with thanksgiving. From that time to the present day, there has been a day of anniversary thanksgiving kept by our government. Our respected governor, with the council, has now called on us as a people by proclamation to celebrate the goodness of the Lord, as specified in that he has been doing us good, and giving us rain from heaven and fruitful seasons, and art filling our hearts with good and gladness. Therefore tis our duty to praise the Lord with supplication and prayer. Having meditated on several passages of sacred scripture, I remained undetermined what would be most suitable for the present day till I was providentially directed to these words:

Philippians, 4 chap[ter], 6 verse.
Be careful for nothing; but in every thing by prayer
and supplication with thanksgiving let your request
be made known unto God.

I shall first consider it the duty of every Christian to be careful for nothing with an anxious solicitude, as it is distrusting the goodness of God. Secondly, I shall consider it the duty of Christians in every age to make known their wants to their heavenly parent by prayer and supplication; and thirdly, I shall shew, we should make our request known with thanksgiving and gratitude of heart for every favour and blessing we enjoy. The text we have read is in the general exhortation of Paul to the Philippians. Paul was a man of a very strong mind and the only scholar among the first called apostles, and he was very energetick in every undertaking. When he persecuted the Christians before his conversion, he pursued them with great rigour.[3] After he became a convert to the Christian system, he was more zealous to have others partake of the like joy in believing that he had experienced in himself. He writes to the Philippians with energy and affection. He had resided with them some time and found them willing to embrace his doctrine. And he with his fellow laborer Timotheus was filled with gratitude for the kindness and attention they had received from the Philippians.

Paul writes to them, and with Timotheus prays for them with the warmth and affection of a Christian parent. With what energy and feeling he writes to them: I thank my God upon every remembrance of you; always in every prayer of mine, for you all, making request with joy after praying. And commending them to the keeping of God, he goes on to exhort them to rejoice in the Lord always, and again I say rejoice.[4] As in the text, be careful for nothing, that is, be not too anxious respecting the things of this world, but be faithful in doing your duty and leave the event to providence. A man of Paul's energy and industry could not mean they should be inattentive to their particular calling. No. Neither did he mean they should neglect any of the moral virtues for he is careful to remind them thus: Finally, Brethren, whatsoever things are true, honest, just, pure, lovely or [of] good report, if there be any praise, think on these things.[5] He says again, those things which ye have both learned, and received, and heard, and seen in me do; and the God of peace shall be with you.[6] Now, my hearers, if in the very heat of the Christian persecution, the apostle Paul could exhort his friends and followers to be careful for nothing with doubtful anxiety, we, my Christian friends in this present day, must not despond nor hang down our heads like a bulrush. Tho' a very heavy cloud hangs over our country, we must not give way to anxious care.

Secondly, I shall consider it our duty to draw near to God at all times, more especially in a time of war and adversity, for surely the peace of God passeth all understanding.[7] We, my friends, have seen [a] very great display of the divine favour. From the first settlement of this country to the present day, we have had reason to sing of the mercy and lovingkindness of the Lord Jehovah, for he scattered the heathen to make room for our pious predecessors. Has he not appeared for and upheld us from one Generation to another, and shall not one Generation praise him and tell of his great goodness and mercy to the rising Generation, and Children's Children shall tell their Children of his wonderful works that he has done for our Fathers of old times? Many now on the stage of action

at this very day can recollect with gratitude the memorable
era of the Revolutionary War when but Children in arms and
knew not the sound of war. Did not heaven then appear on
our behalf and raise up for us a Washington and other brave
spirits to defend the cause of liberty and justice, and under
Washington's wise and prudent administration this country
enjoyed every blessing and comfort heaven could bestow on a
favoured people? No Nation ever enjoyed so wise an administration since the reign of Solomon, and his administration
was attended by the wisdom of God for he sought direction
from Jehovah himself. And the consequence was he negotiated
peace with all nations as the first prelude to the happiness of
his subjects, well knowing war a bane to all morality, virtue,
and religion.

Then surely it must be a duty incumbent on every sincere
Christian and true friend of his country to make known his
request to God by prayer and supplication, that peace may be
restored to our now suffering country and that the very God of
peace may bless us with his presence and be with us as he was
with our fathers. Let us then by prayer and supplication make
known our request unto God, that he would open the eyes of
our infatuated rulers of this nation, for the leaders of the people
have caused them to err in declaring a cruel, and imprudent,
unjust war against the innocent inhabitants of Canada, and that
only under this false colour of protecting the seamen's right. Let
us then unite in praying: Oh that they were wise, and would
understand their duty, and turn their attention to protecting
the lives, liberty, and right of the Citizens at home. We have
great reason to pray, supplicate, and deplore[8] the present state
of the country. I shall further consider, that it is the duty of
every Christian, not only by prayer and supplication, but with
thanksgiving to bless and praise God that the government of

this state has not been accessory in promoting this unhappy war. But as the innocent must suffer with the guilty, we feel the sad effect, in some degree. Yet what reason have we for thankfulness that while our friends on the frontiers are now suffering all the hardship and fatigue of war, we in this part of the land can sit quietly under our own vine and have none to make us afraid? We have reason to be thankful for a wise and prudent administration in our own state.

We have reason to be thankful for the union and faithfulness of our Clergy that they cry aloud and spare not, that they pray unitedly for the peace and prosperity of our American Israel. When we take a retrospect of the convulsive state of the powers in Europe and consider, I may say, the millions that are sacrificed to swell the proud triumphs of our lawless Tyrant, it almost makes the Blood chill in our veins and we shrink with horrour from the gloomy scene. But I will not harrow up your feelings on this anniversary day of thanksgiving. I wish only to remind you to be careful for nothing with anxiety of mind or distrusting the care of a gracious providence, but by prayer and supplication with thanksgiving at all times make your request known unto God and commit the cause of your country and yourselves to his care and keeping. For he governs among the nations and can turn the hearts of men as the waters are turned, and in his own time will bring about that happy period foretold of by the prophet Micah, fourth chap[ter], 3 verse: he shall judge among many nations afar off, and they shall beat their swords into ploughshares and their spears into pruning hooks: nation shall not lift up sword against nation, neither shall they learn war any more. Then will commence that happy period called the millennium; from this convulsive state of the world in general, there is great reason to expect one universal peace will take place before long. Let us be encouraged, my American friends, and hope the Lord will visit us soon with his mercy and in some particular manner, as we have reason to be thankful that we are the only nation under whose government his own peculiar people, the Jews, have never been persecuted. —

Let us bless the Lord Jehovah that in the midst of the judgments that are abroad in the earth that he is still visiting us in mercy, and has preserved us from intestine broils and animosities. And tho' we feel the evil of war in restricting our commerce and trade, yet bless the Lord oh our Souls, for he has indeed been doing us good and giving us rain from heaven, and blessed our agriculture and the labor of the husbandman, and has crowned the year with multiplied mercy and goodness. We have been an highly favoured people from our first settlement to the present day. This Western part of the world in all probability will be the last rising empire and the knowledge of the gospel will spread even to the going down of the setting sun.[9] Our pious ancestors began the good work, by early establishing churches, schools, and seminaries of learning; and I think it is a happy presage of future prosperity that so many institutions for benevolent purposes are now established among us. They all have a happy tendency in making man mild and sociable to man.[10] All the societies for promoting Christian knowledge and learning must have a good effect in promoting the cause of God, and his people. The historical and antiquarian researches must have a good effect in bringing to light many hidden treasures that without the aid of the antiquarian must have been lost in oblivion.

And by bringing out of the hidden treasury, all things in time shall become new. And the fruit of industry and labor shall be rewarded with the fruit of peace, and happiness and songs of praise shall be sung by all those who live and pray for the peace of our Zion. As in the 26 chap[ter] of Isaiah, 1 verse: In that day shall this song be sung in the land of Judah: we have a strong city. Salvation will God appoint for Walls and Bulwarks of our religion. Again at the 4 verse: Trust ye in the Lord forever, for in the Lord Jehovah is everlasting strength. He is the rock of ages, and the only sure foundation, even Jesus Christ himself the chief cornerstone. There is not one of the prophets speaks so fully of the coming of our Saviour as Isaiah, and he describes more beautifully the blessings of peace under the Christian dispensation at the 12 verse of the same chap[ter]. He saith, Lord, thou wilt ordain peace for us, for thou has wrought all our work in us; thou has magnified thy work in us in preserving us in a most wonderful man-ner in safety thro' all the cruel and bloody wars in which the Jewish Nation was continually involved. He then goes on to describe the blessings of the Gospel in chap[ter] 27 verse 6: He shall cause them that come of Jacob to take root. Israel shall blossom and bud and fill the face of the earth with fruit. Let us, my Christian friends, rejoice with thanksgiving and praise that we live under that blessed dispensation and enjoy, free from all persecution, the benefit and happiness the Jew-ish nation was so infatuated as to reject, altho' it has pleased God to permit as a scourge for our faults the rage of evil men to involve us in a cruel war.

Oh sacred and blessed shades of our pious ancestors, [as?] your Spirits hover over this your beloved country, look with pity on your degenerate children and gently cast Elijah's mantle on every Elisha of these New England states. Let me entreat you all to return unto the good old way.[11] Let us all on this day of Jubilee rejoice in the Lord, not in word only but in deed; and in truth and sincerity, let us shew our gratitude to our heavenly parent by benevolence and charity to our fellow creatures. If heaven has blessed us largely with his bounty, let us impart freely to those who many stand in need; remember the Widow and Fatherless;[12] and do good unto all, but especially to those who are of the household of faith.

Wherefore comfort ye one another, teach the word of truth to them that err. Commit all your affairs and the cause of your country to him that ruleth among the nations and he shall reprove kings for your sakes, that is, if you will be humble and reform and become his willing and obedient people. We must determine to do justly and love and shew mercy,[13] and the God of peace and righteousness will bless and keep us in and for the sake of our Saviour Jesus Christ. Finally, my Brethren, let me exhort you with the exhortation of our revered Apostle Paul. I will close with the words of the text: Be careful for nothing, but by prayers and supplications with thanksgiving make known your request unto God. And he will in his own time send a most gracious answer of peace to all your supplications. And the praise and glory shall be given to him who is the same yesterday, to day, and forever.

An Humble Address to the Reason and Wisdom of the American Nation

By Increase Mather Jun. of the inner Temple

From those words
Kings first. 9 chap[ter], 26, 27 verses
And king Solomon made him [a] navy of ships in
Eziongeber, which is beside Eloth on the Red Sea in
the land of Edom. And Hiram sent in the navy, his
servants shipmen that had knowledge of the sea, with
the servants of Solomon.

My August Hearers,

It ought to be the wisdom of Solomon to address such an Audience, but as we read in the second of Corinthians, 4 chap[ter], 7 verse, we have this treasure in earthern[1] vessels. However, the beauty of the passage is lost, in some degree, by our translation as you may find it is in the original Hebrew: We have this treasure as in an oyster shell, alluding to the pearl found in the oyster. And it is a very beautiful metaphor of Saint Paul's, who was a scholar, and he wished to compare the gospel to the richest pearl for its value. And our Saviour himself is styled the pearl of great price.[2]

Now, my hearers, as an earthern vessel, or as the shell containing the pearl, or as the weaker vessel, I am called in providence to address you this day. Therefore, supposing the wisdom of the Nation united in this august body, I have thought proper to bring into your view the wisdom of Solomon in building a Navy. I shall consider his Character in a religious, moral, civil, and political light and shall display his wisdom and make a suitable application to our own government.

We find him as soon as he is appointed king, or ruler, seeking for wisdom. We do not find him seeking for riches, honour or popularity, no; but we find him praying for an understanding heart to judge thy people, that I may discern between good and bad, for who is able to judge this thy so great people? How amiable he appears and how meek, when he says now I am a king instead of my Father David. I am but a little child. I know not how to go out, or come in.[3] He sensibly feels the importance of his situation at the head of a great Nation. Here his wisdom is displayed in that he is not puffed up with pride and ostentation. No, but he is humble, fervent, and sincere and commits himself to the guidance and direction of Jehovah, who is wisdom. And we read at the 10 verse the thing pleased the Lord, and he gave him wisdom and an understanding heart, of which we see him making a wise improvement by his sincerity in his religious sentiments. For we find him agreeable to his Father's wish, ready to set about building a house for to worship the only living and true God in. His Father David had intended to have done it long before, and this his son knew: his Father's heart was in the cause, but the continual wars the Israelites were engaged in prevented him from attempting to do it.

As they had no continuing city or place of refuge long enough to build a house in, so they bore about an ark, or tent, as a place to worship God in. And the most high God was pleased to own and bless the sincerity of David by establishing his covenant with him that his seed should be blessed. And we find the promised blessing made good to him in his son Solomon. We see this wise young man, as the first step to the happiness of his subjects, negotiating peace with all Nations, well knowing war a bane to all morality, virtue, and religion. As soon as he finds himself at peace, he sends to Hiram for materials to build a house to worship the God of his Father in, which he could not have done while in a state of anarchy, or war. What a charming instance of filial duty is here shewed to his Father David, that he not only holds his promise sacred but fulfills it in the most sacred manner by devoting himself and the cause of his people to the wisdom and direction of the infinitely wise disposer of all the events of mankind.

He is found next settling the dispute between the two Ladies respecting the Child. He must indeed have well studied the human heart and feelings so soon to determine who was the right mother by her heart's yearning and being willing to give up her own Child rather than have it hurt. He was evidently directed by his God in the righteous decision. Tis plain he must have been habitually under the influence and direction of divine grace in all his conduct. Next, to compleat his religious Character, as soon as the house for divine worship is finished, he has it dedicated to the service of the most high God and appoints him priests, not of the lowest of the people, but of the tribe of Levi: men of good education and strict morality, such as were proper persons to go in and out before the people, and by their good life and conduct teach them every moral and religious duty.

Here we have a striking instance of his wisdom and policy in a political view, that when he was at peace with all nations, he built him a Navy—he did not raise a standing army in the time of peace, tho', but in his great wisdom he built him a

Navy, well knowing it to be the bulwark of every commercial Nation. We soon see the consequence of his having a Navy, for Hiram, who was abounding in riches, sent his servants, good seamen, to join with Solomon's servants in navigating the vessels. And it is very plain he united with Hiram, for in the 10 chap[ter], 22 verse, we read he, the king, had a Navy at sea, that of Tharshish united with that of Hiram's, and once in three years came the Navy of Tharshish bringing gold and silver, ivory, apes and peacocks.[4] So king Solomon exceeded all the kings of the earth for riches and wisdom,[5] for by his having a fleet united with Hiram his fame was wafted over the vast Atlantic. Had it not been for the spreading sails of his Navy, perhaps the queen of Sheba might never have heard of his wisdom. And we find she was a very rich princess, and I rather think a pretty artful one. For, we are further informed, she questioned him with hard questions[6] that required the wisdom of Solomon or a master mason to solve. However, he gave her satisfaction and reason to exclaim with rapture, one half of his wisdom was not told me,[7] tho' she came prepared to laud him with riches and honour, and she gave him an hundred and twenty talents of gold, spices and precious stones[8] and the Navy of Hiram brought him gold from Ophir, and great plenty of Almug trees and precious stones.[9] And besides that he had the traffick of the Merchant Men, and the traffick of the spice merchants, and of all the kings of Arabia, and of the governors of the Country, here we see his grandeur and how he rose to dignity. It was by his having a well-manned and respectable Navy, by which means he was enriched at home and respected abroad; happy, happy people who have such a wise head or ruler over them.

We, my respected hearers, have had such a ruler at the head of this Nation, whose fame with his Navy has spread over the vast Atlantic. From the south even to the north pole, from the capes of Virginia even to the Cape of Good Hope, the name of our Washington has sounded, even on the barbarous shore of Algiers, but alas, our glory has departed. The die is cast. Ceasar has passed the Rubicon the very day our wise Administration under the reign of their wise Philosopher, whose wisdom cast our Navy into dry dock, our shipping oeconomized into gunboats as coffins for our youths, and graves for the American honour. Such, such, my respected hearers, is the state and a gloomy one of our beloved Country. If there is any virtue or honour yet to be found in the head government of this nation, open your ears to the truth; hear now the voice of the prophet speaking peace. Turn then your hearts from war to the best offers for an honourable peace. We find the wisest of kings ready to negotiate for peace on honourable terms. For heaven's sake, don't let us have to sue for it in the rear of a ragged and defeated Army, but let us like men demand it at the head of a victorious Navy.[10] This, this, would be the glory of the American Constitution.

And Solomon, with all his glory was crowned with riches and honour by the respectability of his Navy. To you who talk of your internal policy and agriculture, let me ask you, What can you do with your corn, wheat, and rye, when you have raised them, and every other article called for by the belligerent powers, without commerce? Your grain must rot in your granary,[11] your sturdy oaks must crumble down with age. Your enterprising Youth, will prove sluggards for want of proper intercourse with other Nations thro' the medium of Commerce. Ye Southerners, how inconsistent to vote for your own destruction. Without commerce your slaves will rise for your destruction, for they tread out your corn, and cultivate your rice, and your cotton; and without exportation you cannot support the very objects of your Tyranny. To you my friends and hardy Northern Yeomanry, who cultivate your own soil and fell the stately oak, let me say you will find but a scanty meal for your fine little rugged family without the help of commerce to vend your stores of grain. Let me then remind you, my Southern and Northern friends, we are formed by Nature as mutual[12] helps and, I wish I could say, comfort to each other tho' our interest and views may differ as much as the climate we live in.

We ought to bear in mind, we are formed in one federal band for the joint interest of the whole body politic. And the very Name of democracy ought to be annihilated in this land, [if] it is in other terms anarchy, or many-headed monster; worse than Polyphemus with his one eye, for it has many heads, with august eyes ever open for the destruction of the very government that protects them. But a true republican government is a free and honourable one and, while there is virtue enough in the people to support it, is a happy one. Such, my hearers, is ours. We are a number of distinct republics, formed and united under one federal band for the mutual support of the whole body politic. Now can it be possible, any one Member can be so weak or wicked, as not to glory in the honourable Name and Character of being a true federal republican? No, my respected friends, when we had our Washington at our head and a Navy at sea, the federal name and Character was respected thro' all the powers of Europe. We are now from folly, or Ignorance, in a very depressed state, but the God of our Fathers has not given us wholly up tho' he has, for some wise purposes in providence, permitted us to be chastized with the scourge of war for our transgressions which have been many. Let me entreat this august assembly to take into view the life and conduct of the wisest of beings that we have had this day set before us. Heaven grant it may have proper influence on the hearts of you all—that you may follow the example and seek for wisdom as for hid treasure, that the influence of divine grace may direct your counsels at this important period. It is indeed a day to try men's souls.[13]

You must bear in your mind there is an higher tribunal than I now address to whom you in high office must account for the lives of your fellow creatures who have already fallen, or may fall, should the war continue long. We don't find Solomon trifling with the lives of his subjects. No, he is found seeking wisdom from God to direct his counsels, and what is the result? Why tis this: he negotiates a peace with all nations. In the next place he builds an house for them to worship the God of peace in, knowing it the best mode to secure the happiness of his subjects. We have had a display of his wisdom, honour, riches, and prosperity and the tender regard he had for his people at all times. And we, my hearers, may in a great measure enjoy like comfort, and happiness, if the things that belong to our peace are not hid from the eyes of our rulers. May the very God of peace open your ears and your eyes to the truth, and grant you all wisdom to go out and come in before this great people. For wherefore go we forth, except the God of our Fathers go with and bless us. May he ever dwell with our American Israel as a shield and buckler of the whole United States. May he, as in the burning bush, be a continual light to our feet and shining light to our path.

Amen.

Antiquarian Researches, Pleasant and Easy

By an Original Antiquarian

Search the Scriptures, Search all nature,
Up to Nature's God.

Bring out of your treasury hidden
mysteries as Antiquarians:
[it] is a duty with diligence to perform.

Having often been asked the question: what utility an Antiquarian society can be of to mankind, or what can influence
a Lady to take any interest in promoting such an institution,
with a desire of gratifying many friends, I now take my pen
with the most fervent wish that I may be ever able and ready
to give a reason for the hope that sustains me. Though I acknowledge myself singular in being an advocate for Masonry
and a warm enthusiast in the cause of antiquarian researches,
but as I was admitted from a child, I may say, to sit at the feet
of Gamaliel,[1] I was soon charmed with hearing the tongue
of the wise and learned. I heard them talk of ancient days,
and learning, and what great advantage might be obtained by
resorting to the original languages. I then imbibed the sentiment that if we wish to obtain knowledge, we must press on
to the extent of this short life that we may treasure up a fund

of learning and knowledge that shall fit us for some important station in a future state, as no rational being can suppose the wise governor of the universe has created and placed us in this world to perform only the common duties of this life. If we do no more, in what do we excel the animal creation, for they perform all the duties required of them by Man.

There is a line of difference must be drawn. Man has a reasoning power or faculty of mind, and as my respected Watts says, we must be measured by the soul: The mind's the standard of the man.[2] And that mind should be always improving in something valuable for the benefit of society and dignity of human nature, for the activity of the human mind is such that if it is not engaged in some valuable pursuit, it will resort to some evil habit for want [of] a regular employment. The best means to prevent the evil will be to engage the mind in historical, literary, and scientific improvement. To those who possess an inquiring disposition, antiquarian researches will afford a large field for the expanded mind. In these researches may be found the authenticity of ancient history: by the establishment of such a society much good may arise to you, America. By their exertion, many hidden treasures may be restored to light, for your resources are almost inexhaustible. And there is some reason to suppose the original inhabitants of this country sprang from one of the tribes of ancient Israel, as the Indians now retain the same customs, manners, symbols, and traditions of the ancient Jews: they number, name, and go forth by tribes; they continue the phylacteries engraven on them the memorable feats of their departed sires which they still hold sacred; they continue the earrings and nose jewels with an humble imitation of all the gaudy trappings that adorned the ancient Jewish Ladies as far as they can obtain in their present state of obscurity.[3] But it must be left for the antiquarian to prove the authenticity of prophecy;

by their researches and care shall be developed all ancient literature and scientific knowledge which shall be handed down to the latest posterity. And future generations shall bless the memory of the antiquarian who has preserved from oblivion the accounts of the rise and progress of the arts and sciences as well as many valuable articles that the corroding hand of time must have entirely destroyed had they not been renovated by their softening care. Some of the first Characters that were ever drawn are still preserved and may be seen at this very day. And from them came the art of writing, and in time arose the still greater art of printing. And that is one of the greatest blessings ever bestowed on man.

What a privilege may be enjoyed by this art through the channel of Books, that when recluse from society we may in a manner converse with the whole expanded globe. We can privately discuss every point in Theology, Law, Physick, Astronomy, Geography, and cultivate the pleasant science of Chymistry, and make up our own opinions and hurt no one's feeling. We can celebrate the praises of the historian who has handed down to posterity the rise and progress of the arts and sciences, and the rise and fall of empires, nations, and states. It is for the antiquarian to preserve, and record, the documents that shall give authenticity to ancient history. By this means, this institution must be of great utility and infinite value to future generations. For children not now on the stage of action shall ask of their parents the way of knowledge; and they shall answer, look to the rock from whence you was [sic] hewn, though not literally so, but look to the learned and wise of every age. Seek for wisdom as for hid treasure, look to the rock of ages as [the] source and fountain of all wisdom, follow the example of the wisest king there is on record. And he asked wisdom from Jehovah himself as recorded in sacred writ, and a blessing attended his administration. And thanks are due to the historian for recording his wisdom in rebuilding the temple as well as his wisdom in building a respectable navy as a safe ground for his country.

Let it still be recorded for an example to future governments. And his Father David shewed great wisdom and prudence not only as a wise mason but as an antiquarian in preserving the manuscripts, parchments, and documents with the first records made and kept by him. During the whole Jewish captivity he committed them to the care of his son Solomon with direction to have them preserved in the holy of holies as a safe deposit, as none but the high priest was allowed to enter there; either of the first or second temple, we cannot say, but perhaps the queen of Sheba might be admitted to view it. However, it is recorded he withheld nothing from her. Perhaps that means with the exception of his Masonic knowledge that has ever been held too mighty for the female comprehension, though some of the ancient Fathers celebrated the praises of women. The learned Jerome with all his austerity has some handsome encomiums on women.[4]

The ancient Jewish rabbis held a tradition from their Fathers that Moses, when he in wrath destroyed the first table of commandments, he prudently saved the grand secret, as they term it, and deposited it in the sanctum sanctorum; and that has ever been held sacred by the ancient Jewish rabbis agreeable to the account given by the Jewish writers.[5] From the very able and learned addresses delivered before the antiquarian society, there is reason to anticipate with raised expectation that the institution will progress and extend its influence to the utmost boundary of the American regions; and that by the magnetic power of attraction, much fire will be extracted from the flint, and the compass of genius will direct the wise mariner safe to the cabinet of the antiquarian where they may find a safe deposit for every article worthy of preservation.[6] Here many ancient families that appear to be extinct shall become renovated by their softening care; and in some future day a branch shall spring from the root of Jesse, and many respectable families shall outlive the rack of time.

Many advantages must arise from an institution of such extensive nature and founded on such liberal principles as it controls no man's sentiments in any point of religion or politics. It embraces the man of science and literature. A combination of such a class of men must certainly have a tendency to promote, preserve, and extend much useful knowledge and information in every branch of science and literature.

Much good may accrue from extending the gospel among the heathen nations as light will eventually spring out of darkness. The forming of literary and benevolent societies may have a happy effect on the whole Christian world by forming one general bond of friendship and harmony, but it is for the antiquarian to trace and retrace till they discover deity in all its attributes of wisdom, rectitude, justice, and mercy in sending his son Jesus Christ as a sufficient saviour for the Children of men.

The antiquarian society must have a tendency to harmonize the feelings of mankind, as it consists of no particular party or sect. It has no interest to seek but that of preserving and extending knowledge to future generations; therefore, such an association must be of universal utility. For should it continue from age to age, it will still move up. Even old age will enhance the value of the institution. It is not, as may be the vague opinion of some, necessary to be an odd or antiquated animal to be a proper member of such a society. No, for the more liberal, enlightened, and expanded the mind, the more pleasure and beauty will be discovered in antiquarian researches.

When commenced early in life, they may anticipate living many lives in one. That is, by retracing former ages, we may look forward with a pleasant prospect that future generations shall retrace our steps, and thus the inquiring mind will be continually improving in useful knowledge.

Much may be obtained by diligence and perseverance. This institution must be productive of universal benefit by giving credit, and confidence, to the historian that might have been doubted had not the facts been recorded by the antiquarian. By prudence and assiduity much learning may be preserved, and great information may be communicated. Most of the knowledge and information obtained depends on the assiduity of man. Had not the Jewish artist engraven on the hardest substance and most valuable and durable stone the names of the 12 tribes of Israel intended to adorn the Breastplate of the high priest,[7] perhaps the model would not have continued to posterity as a guide for the high priest of the present day. By preserving the pattern of the ark, the artist received the first clue for building a vessel. The pattern of Solomon's temple having been preserved and handed down to posterity by the prudence and skill of the Master Mason now serves as a guide for all the dignity and splendour of the architecture of the present day.

Perhaps even the pattern of a tunick might have been forgotten had not Hannah prudently have saved that of Samuel's as a relick, or pattern. Even the skill of the wheel and distaff might have been left in obscurity had it not been recorded by the wisdom of the preacher in sacred writ: that the mother of king Lemuel[8] sent for her son a wife well skilled in spinning and industrious in seeking wool and flax and prudent in all her domestic economy.[9] By the prudence of even a matron, a nation may be saved by her preserving the records and certain documents that shall be sufficient evidence to prove the boundaries of the nation; and the ancient land marks shall be restored, and the original proprietors shall recover their right. By the preserving care of the antiquarian shall be recovered treasures of ancient knowledge that have long been hid in dark obscurity. Many valuable requisitions[10] shall be obtained by their exertions in literary and scientific researches.

The happy time may come when knowledge shall run to and fro in the earth, and righteousness flow like a mighty stream[11] and that happy period arrive when all nations shall know the Lord. And Father Abraham with the whole Jewish nation by seeking shall find out and acknowledge Jesus Christ as the just and righteous saviour of the Jews and the Gentiles also. Then shall the antiquarian produce from his cabinet documents and proof to a demonstration of the authenticity of ancient prophecy. Then shall the most obdurate sceptic stand abashed and fully convinced that there has been but one chain of events from creation, and all governed by infinite wisdom and goodness. And the belief of this is a continual consolation to the calm, reflecting mind of the real Christian. And every person may derive comfort and happiness from a firm belief in the just government of a wise and gracious providence who guides and directs the affairs of the Children of men, and that not even a sparrow falls but by divine permission,[12] and that he who rules among the nations of the earth can take into one view the whole system of the human race.

One[13] of the most pleasant and sublime ideas the human mind can possibly entertain is that in a future state shall be revealed to our senses the inscrutable and to us the incomprehensible wisdom of God in his dispensations to the children of men in this present world. Then shall be unfolded the whole mysteries of divine providence to his intelligent creatures that now seem dark. Then shall the mind be expanded in proportion to the talents, and the improvement made of them in this probationary state. Here indeed may commence, literary, and scientific researches. But while the spirit is clogged with this earthly tabernacle, we can make but small attainment in that wisdom that is from above. But when the spirit once shakes off the shackles of this clay and is allowed to expand in regions as yet to us unknown, though I trust in a world where there will be no clog or end to improvement throughout a boundless eternity, and there shall the antiquarian satisfy his thirst for knowledge; and the historian shall find full scope to complete his history. Then shall be unfolded, the hidden mysteries that now perplex and gall our shackled spirits while we continue in this world.

Every association formed for benevolent or literary purposes has a happy tendency to make man mild and sociable to man.[14] It must consequently be laudable to encourage every attempt to alleviate the miseries incident to human life, and there can be no means devised more likely to dispel the glooms and sorrows of human life than to engage the mind in literary and scientific researches, and none can have a better effect than the antiquarian researches. From the vast variety of pleasing instruction they afford to those who engage in them with vigour, they may expect to enjoy a continual feast of rich viands. From these considerations I acknowledge myself a warm advocate for forming associations for literary and scientific improvement. The advantages arising from such societies must be great and have a happy effect on the whole order of the community. And they will reap a rich harvest of information, but they must not expect to reap grapes of thorns or figs of thistles, but may reasonably expect to reap pleasure and knowledge from the preservation of all ancient learning.

To the antiquarian[s] we must repair, for they will produce specimens of the first fruits of ancient literature and science. And from those may be produced modern refinement and improvement.

As this generation may improve on the past, so shall future generations improve on the present as one generation passeth away and behold another cometh.[15] Then it plainly is our duty to encourage all efforts to preserve documents, manuscripts, patterns, and exhibitions of every kind as guides and directions for future generations to improve and refine upon. These considerations, I trust, will convince all rational beings of the propriety and utility of an institution formed for the preservation of the most minute article that shall in some future as well as the present day prove to the eye of the beholder the value once set on the gold Brocade, and the embroi[der]ed Tablet. And from viewing the ancient painting that once adorned the royal courts in former ages, the sculptor shall improve and refine his art. And from some relic[16] of a hero slain, the present hero shall renew his strength and courage too. And from some relic of departed worth, some pious, learned, virtuous sire shall naturally arise this ardent, virtuous, pious prayer: Oh, may Elijah's mantle[17] gently fall and rest on thy descendant child. And every member of the society who has preserved the precious relic of departed worth, be blessed and covered with the mantle of charity.

An humble imitation of Dwight's "Columbia"

Columbia, Columbia, to glory arise,
Let thy virtues ascend with our hymns to the skies.
For thy genius commands thee, they sires behold,
With learning and knowledge thy splendours unfold.
Your empire's the last on the annals to rise.   5

Your wealth is immense, and fair freedom you prize.
Your sires assemble this day to proclaim,
With grateful remembrance the much rev'd[18] name
Of Columbus the great, the faithful and wise,
Whose fame with his virtues re-echo the skies.   10
Antiquarian researches no longer shall rest.
Your Sires will press on from east to the west.
They'll press on with vigour and ardour of mind,
Till America's strength and resources they find.
Wise men from the east bent their course to the west   15
By the pole star directed, asylum for rest.
Now the day star arises, bright prospects appear
For the call of the gospel the heathen now hear,
The day, fast approaching, when all shall unite
To join the same anthem of praise and delight: 20
When all shall unitedly sing and record,
The saviour is Christ, our King, and the Lord.
Till time is no more our praises shall arise,
Like incense ascend with perfumes to the skies.
They mantle, Columbus, transfer to each sire,   25
From ages to ages their ardour inspire.
For your fame is recorded on every heart,
And your name has a charm that shall courage impart.
Then Columbia, Columbia, to glory arise,
Let your virtues ascend with our hymns to the skies.   30

Isaiah Thomas Esqr.
Worcester.
Belonging to the
Antiquarian Soc[ie]ty.[19]

II

Becoming an Advocate, 1815–1819

A Series of Letters on Free Masonry

By A Lady of Boston

BOSTON:

PRINTED BY JOHN ELIOT, 1815

TO the protection and patronage of the M.W.[1] Past Grand Master, the Past Grand Chaplain, and the present Officers and Members of the Grand Lodge of Massachusetts, this little work is now humbly dedicated, by the author, with the most ardent wish of benevolence, that every worthy member may square his conduct by the line of integrity.

P. Americana.

PREFACE

HAVING been indulged with the perusal of the following Letters, I was so pleased with their ingenuity, and so gratified with the candour and liberality of sentiment which pervades them, that I solicited the consent of the writer to a publication of them. The Brethren of the Fraternity are obliged to her for the permission, and will feel highly honoured by the opinion of one, who, superior to all jealousy on account of the exclusion of her sex, and all prejudice from any other source, has so fairly estimated, so freely allowed, and so happily stated the merits of Free Masonry; while readers in general will find here additional reasons for approving an Institution which has met with such an advocate.

T. M. HARRIS[2]

July 7, 1815.

LETTERS, &c.

Boston, Sept. 7, 1810.

My Friend,

YOU often solicit my opinion on the subject of Masonry.
From what motive you can wish for the ideas of a lady on
such a topic I cannot fathom, and must leave it in your
own breast to solve. I am ready, however, to express my
sentiments. As a prelude to the subject, I send you a few
extracts I made from Maurice's *Indian Antiquities*, taken
by him from M. Basnage.[3] He says, "the perfections of
God are the pillars which support the Universe; *Mercy*
illumines *Justice*, and Beauty decorates *Strength*."[4] The
old Jewish rabbis did believe the three *Sephiroths*, or
Splendors, to shine with intrinsic luster [Comment;
from whence perhaps may originate the ancient
Masonic light and knowledge which few Masons of
the present day know much about.][5] "The names of the
Sephiroths are Gedular, *Strength* or Severity; Gebutah,
Mercy or Magnificence; Thipherath, *Beauty*; Nersah,
Victory or eternity; Hod, *glory*[;] Jehod, the *foundation*;
Melcuth, the *kingdom*."[6] This is the order in which
they are arranged on an engraving in the old works of
M. Basnage, which I have seen.[7] The Circle, being the
most perfect of figures, denotes the perfection of Deity
and its attributes.[8] Now[,] my friend[,] it is clear in my
mind, from every circumstance, that the Jewish rabbis
did believe in a trinity of some kind. I cannot say what
their ideas were respecting the trinity; but this[9] much I
will venture to say, it is plain from many ancient records I

have seen, that they invented triangles, and were the first that introduced the rule of three, in arithmetick.

The Jews were a very cunning, artful people, and tis[10] plain from some of the rabbinical writings that the rabbis did meet in consultation and formed a plan or lodge, long before their dispersion; and gave each other certain signs and tokens. This was of great advantage to them after their dispersion, when scattered among strangers and in different parts of the world. They found it necessary for the safety of their property to establish funds in different places of resort, and thus when they wanted money they would give some respectable person an order on their treasurer, who, as their property was in his hands[,] would answer the order, or bill[,] on sight; and by that means they held good credit in many parts of the globe. And it was this plan that first gave rise to drawing bills of exchange; by which mode a great part of our business is now transacted, and the buying, selling, and transferring bills of exchange has become a very large branch in the broker's line. I think, you'll say, "this is not answering my question. I solicited your opinion respecting the Masonic institution." My friend, you might with the same propriety have asked my ideas respecting the Mosaick dispensation.

I suppose, indeed, that you knew, in the younger part of life, I did investigate some of the principles of Masonry; not from any wish of prying into hidden mysteries, but from motives of benevolence, if possible, to quiet the minds of several of my female friends, who were very anxious, on account of their husbands joining a lodge, lest it should injure their moral and religious sentiments; and as the hour of their retiring to rest was much later than usual, and infringed on domestick quiet and happiness.

For my own part, I ever respected the Brotherhood, as a society formed for the most benevolent purposes of charity, and friendship; and, from an ardent wish to promote the quiet and happiness of a friend, I was first influenced to examine some of the rules and regulations of the society.

To my great joy I soon restored peace of mind to my anxious friends; and satisfied them respecting the value of the institution, if supported on the original plan.

I have no doubt the principles are good, the Corner Stone well laid, and ought to be supported by Wisdom, Strength, and Justice. If they conducted with prudence, they might diffuse that universal benevolence, which would promote "peace on earth and good will to men." The original principles are said to be a compound of Wisdom, Strength and Beauty.[11] There is, however, some reason to fear that many young Masons, grasp the shadow only.

A good Mason ought to be a good man. He ought to be three times more circumspect in his life and conversation than those who have never taken the same oath. He ought to be thrice three times more vigilant than those who have never bent the knee within due Square;[12] having bound himself by the most solemn vow. He having obtained more light, ought to impact knowledge to those who are yet blind and ignorant; and by a virtuous life do honour to the profession.

I had the honour some years ago to preside as Mistress of a *similar institution*, consisting of females only; we held a regular lodge, founded on the original principles

of true ancient masonry, so far as was consistent for the
female character.[13] We recognized the Brotherhood
as preeminent, as may be seen from several Addresses
and Songs that were printed in the *Centinel*, and other
papers. One or two of them gave umbrage to a few
would-be-thought Masons; but by the most respectable
part of them we were treated like Sisters. The prime
inducement for forming the lodge, was a desire for
cultivating the mind in the most useful branches of
science, and cherishing a love of literature; for at that
period, female education was at a very low ebb. If women
could even read and badly write their names it was
thought enough for *them*, who by some were esteemed as
only "mere domestick animals."

But the aspiring female mind, could no longer bear
a cramp to genius. They roused to thought, and clearly
saw they were given by the wise author of nature, as
not only helps-meet, but associates and friends, not
slaves to man. I have reason to think this institution
gave the first rise to female education in this town, and
our sex a relish for improving the mind; as a few even
then, dared to study the languages under the auspices
and patronage of the benevolent Dr.[14] M.[15] He was
good, learned, and a great scholar. His easy manners,
pleasing address, and the calm serenity of mind which
he possessed, in a very eminent degree, made instruction
pleasant and gratifying; and under his directing eye and
patronage, we agreed to unite as a society. Our sole aim
was friendship, and the improving the mind; that by
Strength, and *Wisdom*, we might *beautifully* adorn the
female character, and shew to the Brethren that we had
obtained the grand secret, of securing the affections of

our best friends by performing every domestick duty
with ease and harmony. We had our *tokens, signs,* and
word; and within *due Square* we marked our lives by
the parallel line of integrity. Most of the old members
of the lodge, are now, I trust, gone to join the Grand
Lodge above in the realms of bliss and happiness. I hope
to see a revival of this, or a similar institution, on the
same principles, for cultivation of the mind, and acts of
charity and benevolence. There are a number of societies
now formed by ladies for beneficent purposes; and many
poor children are instructed under their patronage.[16]
I pray heaven may reward the good undertaking with
a blessing!— Surely, then, it is to be wished that some
respectable ladies would join in a society, and by their
presence and patronage promote Science and Literature.
I think many hours might be redeemed that are now
spent in frivolous calls, or trifling with some foolish
novel to craze the brain, or contaminate the heart.

If the society introduce history, let it be read and
explained. The history of our own country first. Make
youth early acquainted with the virtues of their ancestors,
as an incitement to the love of virtue. Then let such other
works be read and lectured upon as will tend to enlarge
the mind, refine the taste, and perfect them in all female
accomplishments.

I think I hear you say, "this letter is rather a little essay
on female education, than your ideas of Masonry." I own
I have rather begged the question, but will now give you
my opinion of Masonry, as far as may be consistent for
a lady to give, on a subject we are indeed debarred from
investigating. I suppose, indeed, that it will be thought
by many, a bold attempt for a female to even dare enter

on the subject at all; but a truly independent mind will rise above the fear of man. I will then venture to say so much as this — I think the foundation good, the chief Corner Stone is laid with Wisdom, Strength, and Beauty and ought to be adorned with *honour, truth,* and *justice,* and *universal benevolence.* The principles, well improved, might lead the mind to the most sublime contemplations of the great architecture of the universe. It is[,] however, to be feared, that the members, like those of many other institutions, have deviated from their original plan, and many errors have crept into the system: so it is also to be feared that the Christian system is greatly adulterated by many corrupt members that never practise the right principles.

Let me entreat you[,] my friend, if you join a Lodge to Square your conduct by the plumb line of the ancient principles.[17] We may *in theory* be a Mason, Philosopher, or a Christian, but if we do not *practise* the moral virtues, our theory will never lead us to join the Grand Lodge above, where our heavenly Master completes the source of all perfection and blessedness, and is ever ready to receive all his faithful servants to the perfect *Sanctum Sanctorum* of bliss and happiness forever[.] Act your part well in this life, and heaven bless and keep you, is the ardent prayer of your friend.

With sentiments of affection,
A. P. Americana.[18]

———

[Answer.][19]

Montpelier, Sept. 21, 1810.

Dear Madam,

ACCEPT my warmest thanks for your letter. With the
sentiments on Masonry, I feel almost ready to exclaim
as Agrippa did when forcibly struck by the energy of
Paul's preaching, almost though persuadest me to be a
Mason,[20] which is, or ought to be a *Christian*, agreeably
to your ideas. Though I owe it staggers my faith, when
I see many members sally forth after the lodge is closed,
in a very imprudent way. It makes me have my fears, of
the effects it will have on the morals; as the influence
of others, will operate on the mind of youth, very often.
Now, dear madam, let me ask you this one question,
"How far such an institution may tend to promote a life
of dissipation?" Let me beg you to consider the question
and give me your opinion, so far as you think competent;
and you will add another obligation on your friend,

And humble servant,

Enquirer.

Boston, Sept. 30, 1810.

My Friend,

I FEAR I have said more on the subject of Masonry
than may be consistent for a female. But as I have really
a pretty good opinion of the Institution, and a wish to
oblige you, I will endeavour to take off any prejudice you
may have imbibed, from the observation you make on

some irregular members. That appears to you rather a stumbling block. I own my sensibility is often wounded at observing the immorality, not only of many Masons, but of many members of the Christian Church. But surely *that* can be no reason for my neglecting to comply with any known duty. If any member of the same Church is irregular or immoral, it can be no reason for my quitting that Church, if I perform *my* duty. I once belonged to a literary society. I was often wounded in my feelings when I observed how few had, or paid any attention to literature, or science; yet there was enough to form a society for promoting useful knowledge and improvement, for all those, that wished to obtain it. Now I could see no good reason for my withdrawing from the society, though some of the members knew and cared very little for any thing more than to take a cheerful glass.[21] That was not the fault of the society, but of the individual; for the institution was a very good one, and designed to promote learning and external knowledge; and if any of the members did not make improvement the fault was their own, and not any in the institution.

It is not for us to judge the heart, as we can form just judgments only by the known life and conduct. If any one sits up all night to pray and tell his experiences, and the inward working of the spirit; now, if that same man, by noon next day wrong his friend, or prove guilty of any other immorality, I must think that person does not conduct becoming the Christian character. Yet that surely can be no reason why I should restrain prayer, but ought to be an incitement to me, to pray that I may be more circumspect in my own life and conversation.

I am sensible[,] my friend, that the imprudence of some who style themselves *Masons*, has been a stumbling

48

block to many; but in the light I view it, any other society, might as well be productive of immorality as the [M]asonic. The fact is, if the members would retire as soon as the lodge was closed, as many worthy members do, there would be nothing unseemly or disorderly heard or thought of. The chief danger, is, from so large a number uniting in one social band of friendship. Some of your jolly souls may take the advantage of being assembled, to carry their mirth to an unreasonable degree; though I am of the opinion that some classes of men would form a circle for riot and dissipation, if no lodge had been formed. There are also some political clubs, that only meet to breed a ferment; but that surely can be no reason why the inhabitants of a Town or State should not meet in a regular manner to transact the business of their community. The truth is this, I do not think the institution of Masonry tends more to produce immorality than any other society formed for social intercourse; on the contrary, from the universal benevolence it extends to the Brotherhood, it has a tendency to make man mild, and sociable to man.[22] I think, every benevolent institution has a happy effect on society at large.[23] The more we form circles for literary disquisition, if only for benevolent purposes, it has a tendency to enlarge the mind and expand the heart; and by that means promote the happiness of mankind in general. Every humane, charitable, religious, political, or literary society, if founded on a rational plan, has a tendency to promote the general utility and happiness of our fellow creatures. But every person ought to consult his own finances, and not by his benevolence infringe on his domestick happiness or comfort. Charity should begin at home, but not be retained a prisoner there.[24]

A liberal mind should devise and give, in proportion to the abundance heaven has blessed him with. We should be always ready to help the necessities of our fellow creatures. Every benevolent institution must promote the happiness of individuals in this way, by making us acquainted with the circumstances of many poor persons, that without the aid of such an institution might have continued unknown, and consequently unassisted. I must think there can be nothing immoral in joining any benevolent society. Then surely it is clear there can be no immorality, in joining the Masonic society; for they stand preeminent on the list, for charity and benevolence. I wish virtue and integrity may be added to the list, that if you see your way clear, to join a Lodge, you may be able to say, "it is good for me to be a Mason; as I really find it gives me a greater relish for every Christian duty, and leads me more sensibly to contemplate on the benevolence and mercy of the Grand High Priest of the Christian profession, and is a new source of all hope, comfort, and happiness." May a full portion of the divine influence and grace, direct your path,

Prays most fervently your friend,
A. P. Americana.

————————

Montpelier, Oct. 9, 1810.

Madam,

PLEASE to accept my acknowledgment and gratitude for your candid opinion on Masonry. So far as respects the morals, I now fully imbibe your sentiments; admitting, that it is not from any fault in the Institution, but of the individual who belongs to the society, that this has ever been questioned. And any other institution might with as much propriety be condemned as the Masonic, was it to be judged only from the imprudence of some irregular members. You have further convinced me that every benevolent society, formed for charitable purposes, must have a happy effect on the whole system of social order. Pardon me, madam, if I again solicit your opinion, how far you think the Masonic institution may affect, not only the moral, but religious sentiments of the members. My question is this, "Can Masonry have any good effect on our religious sentiments, and from what source?" If you will gratify me with an answer to this question, you will add another obligation to

Your friend, and humble servant,

Enquirer.

Boston, Oct. 20, 1810

My Friend,

DO you still persist in soliciting my opinion of Masonry? and surely the most important part of the Institution? If we admit the principle, that the foundation is laid on the rock of ages, and that the Corner Stone is laid with Wisdom, Strength, and Beauty, it certainly should impress the mind of every member with the most exalted ideas, of the Great Supreme Architect of the universe. No one can be admitted to a lodge till he has made himself acquainted with some parts of the Old Testament, that perhaps he might never have comprehended, had it not been from an ardent wish to join a lodge. How many are there, who view with wonder and admiration, *the magnificence of Solomon's Temple*. Many who never would have thought of a *Sanctum Sanctorum*, had they not seen it engraven on the post of the door of the holy of holies, agreeable to the old Jewish superscription. This must, I think, lead them to make some enquiry respecting the Jewish nation, and why they are distinguished as God's peculiar people. The answer will be this: they were the first nation to whom Jehovah was pleased to reveal his mind and will, and gave them commandments and laws, by his called and faithful servant Moses. Some of the Jewish rabbis boast, to this very day, that when Moses, in his anger, destroyed the first table, there was a part of second law saved, and kept by Moses; which is recorded in some of their rabbinical writings. They say it has been deposited in the inner sanctuary behind the veil, in the ark of the covenant of the first and second table; and none but the High Priest was allowed to enter there. Now this may still lead to a further investigation respecting this people; and for what purpose laws and commandments were given them; and why they are held a distinct people, though dispersed over all parts of the globe. These enquiries may tend to direct the mind to the most sublime contemplations, where there is such a display of Wisdom, Strength, and Beauty as is most plainly seen in the whole order of creation. And when all the attributes of divine majesty and perfection are brought to view, can man alone be mute, when all creation sings his praise? No: every rational being must acknowledge an infinitely

supreme power, who in wisdom has created and sustains
the universe.

I think the basis by which the pillars of Masonry are
supported, may serve to strengthen the minds of men in
contemplating the divine perfection and benevolence in
creation; and by further searching, they may discover the
wisdom of God in the plan of redemption, by his Son
Jesus Christ, who is *the chief Corner Stone* of the Christian
profession. From the very benevolence of the Masonic
institution, they must, they will, certainly, be induced
to trace the origin of the Christian religion; and, by a
train of thought, and concatenation of ideas, from the
first Jewish dispensation to the building the Temple by
Solomon, with all the curious utensils, by the handcraft
of their Grand Master Hiram, and with all the light and
knowledge that illumines the Masonic art, trace farther
the grandeur of the system. The aspiring mind of man
will not rest here, but press on till it discovers the bright
and shining light of the gospel, through the many types
and figures[25] of the old Jewish ceremonies. I cherish the
pleasing idea, that in this point of view, it will have a
happy effect on the religious sentiments of many of the
members of the Masonic society.

I wish still to impress on your mind, that every
benevolent institution has a tendency to spread universal
good will to men, which is one of the blessings of the
Christian religion. If there was no Corner Stone, and
the foundation was not well laid, the fabrick must soon
fall. And we know, that the Masonic institution is of
very ancient date, and has stood the test of ages. That
it has, cannot be doubted, any more than the Jews have
remained a distinct people even to this present day,
though dispersed among all the nations of the earth. And

this very people, most probably, were the first founders of the Masonic institution. Now different lodges may naturally be incited to investigate the reason, why this ancient nation are [*sic*] in such a deplorable state, from the coming of the Messiah to the present day; and why they are still preserved a monument to this truth; namely, that they were so infatuated as to refuse the chief Corner Stone, even Jesus Christ himself, who was the founder of the Christian system.[26] They must be convinced of the beauty and order, by which the Christian religion has been established. The situation of this infatuated nation, ever since the destruction of Jerusalem, has kept them a living witness to the truth of the Christian religion; for, had they not have crucified the Son of God, they might still have continued a happy nation.

The Masonic Institution may have a good effect on the members, if they will make a wise improvement of their boasted light and knowledge; if they will contemplate the divine attributes in their order and perfection. It may have a happy effect in promoting those religious sentiments that shall effectually produce the fruit of true holiness, and a good conversation among the Brethren. Heaven grant, that true religion may spread and prevail throughout the whole world, till that happy period arrive, when all nations shall be blessed in Jesus Christ, in another and better world, and all unite in one Grand Lodge; where, I trust, even females will be admitted to join in celebrating the praises of him who died that we might rise to bliss and happiness!

May eternal happiness be your portion.

A. P. Americana

Montpelier, Oct. 31, 1810

Dear Madam,

YOUR last letter has settled my mind entirely. I have enlisted my name on the records of Masonry, with a full determination to become a master workman, and hope I shall prove myself one, that shall not be ashamed.[27] To you, madam, I feel indebted for the satisfaction I have obtained. I expect soon in person to acknowledge, with gratitude, every obligation you have conferred on your friend

And humble servant,

Enquirer.

————

Boston, 1778,

First printed in the *Centinel,* headed thus:

Brother Russell,[28]

The following lines were actually written by a lady of this town, who imagines she has some insight into the mysteries of the Craft, how far I will not say; the fraternity may judge from the composition. Please insert the lines, and oblige yours,

W. S. B.

[B. William Shattuck.][29]

A SHORT ADDRESS.

By the Mistress of St. Ann's Lodge.

COME Ladies fair,
Within due Square
Let each renew her vow,

No timid maid
Need be afraid,   5
Her Sacred Knee to bow.

Since Sheba's queen
The first was seen,
To gain this wondrous art;
She made the vow   10
We all do now,
And gain'd the wise king's heart.

Let none disclose
To secret foes,
Our *tokens*, *words*, or *signs*.   15
May Beauty grace
Each lovely face,
And Wisdom guide our minds.

May we have Strength
To join at length,   20
The heavenly Lodge above,
Brothers there meet
Though none here greet,
There join in mutual love.

That sacred plan,   25
Held here by man,
As far above our reach,
Shall to each fair
Within due Square
Their love and duty teach.   30

In sacred love
We'll join above
The widow's son and mother,

With one accord
We'll join the word,   35
To hail each sacred brother.

———————

A SONG.

By the Mistress of St. Ann's Lodge.

PRINTED IN THE *CENTINEL*, 1778.[30]

COME Ladies all
Attend the call
Come join with one accord,
Let each agree
To join with me   5
Keep *token*, *sign*, and *word*.

Our lodge within
Admits no sin,
But Wisdom, Strength, and Beauty
Adorn each air,   10
We welcome here
All well perform their duty.

Each act their part
With cheerful heart,
With fervency and zeal,   15
And all agree
To join with me,
No secret to reveal.

Our brothers rare
Within due Square   20
May try our skill in science;

57

We'll clearly prove
To them our love,
And on them place reliance.

But then we'll be,   25
As Masons free,
To think, and speak, and reason;
We'll act our part
With skill and art,
And never think it treason.   30

No idle tale
Shall us regale,
Of widow's son, or mother;
But each at ease
Shall strive to please   35
Their husband, friend, and brother.

———————

*On seeing the solemnities of the Grand Lodge in Boston, in com-
memoration of General Washington. By a lady, who sat in the east
gallery of the Old South meeting, to view the procession and hear
the Eulogy by Brother Bigelow.*[31]

FROM north to south I chanc'd to roam,
Well seated in the sacred dome
Within due form; I took my seat
The eastern corner to complete.

Well form'd around the sacred Square,   5
With wonder view'd each lovely fair.
With out stretch'd neck, and piercing eyes,
There *Wisdom*, *Strength*, and *Beauty* lies.

Here Jachin well establish'd stand,
There Boaz strengthens every hand.[32]   10
In *faith*, and *hope*, with *love* divine,
May every faithful brother shine.

Hail sacred lodge, 'tis my desire,
To tune my harp, new string my lyre
To give due praise, could it be given,   15
Till we join Washington in heaven.

Here *Strength* appears, in every youth,
With *Beauty* shines each sacred truth;
Here Sheba's queen as once of old,
Might say, "one half has not been told."   20

Here every widow's heart, with joy
Must view the lovely sleeping boy,
Well placed upon the sacred urn;
Each heart with holy fire must burn.

Each hand a spring of *cassia* bring,   25
With loud applause, each valley ring!
Accept most worshipful and true,
The praises, that are justly due.

Oh may that sacred Arch arise,
To realms of bliss above the skies;   30
Where you, with *token*, *sign*, and *word*,
May join the choir, with one accord;
The Holy Lodge of saints above,
In friendship pure, and fervent love!

[PRINTED IN THE *CENTINEL*.][33]

The School of Reform, or Seaman's Safe Pilot to the Cape of Good Hope

By the Seaman's Friend, H. M. Crocker

It is not in man that walketh to direct his steps;
neither can the mariner steer the right course,
if the compass is out of order.

BOSTON:

PRINTED BY JOHN ELIOT.

1816

School of Reform

Cast thy bread upon the waters;
for thou shalt find it after many days.
Ecclesiastes xi. 1.

Sir,

FROM some philanthropic sentiments you expressed the other day, respecting the fellow craft, seamen, and coasters, I fully imbibed your sentiments, that if the necessity of a regular course of living was pointed out to them in a pleasant manner by a female, it would be well received, and, probably, have a happy effect on the sensibility of that class of men, who have ever been celebrated for paying respect to the opinion of females. Impressed with this idea, I now say, bear a hand, messmates, as I have taken passage for the Cape of Good Hope, in the fast sailing ship Time; owner, Columbus;[1] commanders, Fortitude, Perseverance; Wisdom and Reason helmsmen; the hard arms all manned with skill and prudence, sound hearts and clear heads. Directed by the compass of genius, they shall steer safe to their destined port or haven of rest. Let your stores be head matter, and your ballast sound principles, founded on the chief corner stone of pure vital religion. Honour and friendship must cement the whole. Thus manned, freighted, and equipped,

> Brave seamen, you may safely sail,
> And never fear a sudden gale.
> You ev'ry storm shall safely brave,
> Though sea run high and rough the wave,
> For reason guides the helm, you know,   5

And wisdom baffles ev'ry wo[e].
The port you sail for is Good Hope,
The capes you'll clear, by fathom rope:
Now dowse your topsails, anchor cast,
At cable length make anchors fast;   10
All hands on deck, my worthy crew,
Let all this solemn vow renew;
We'll drink no more, to drown old care,
Wisdom shall pilot, foul or fair;
Reason our future lives shall steer,   15
With honest hearts, and heads quite clear;
No more to loggerheads we'll go,
Nor stake our lives against a throe;
Reason shall guide our future lives,
To bless our children, and our wives;   20
Heaven's wonders on the seas we'll tell,
While grateful hearts each bosom swell.
With gratitude and sacred love,
We'll raise our hymns to God above.

Worthy and respected Friends,

We know that of ourselves we can do nothing. But if there are sincere desires of heart, and a clear head, heaven will bless the efforts of men to keep them so. Many vessels have been lost in consequence of the pilot's not keeping his head steady, while guiding the helm. We find it just so in every occurrence of human life; if reason is not at helm to steer and guide the turbulent passions of men, which, when inflamed by intemperance, are like the troubled sea, when tost [*sic*] by the great wind called Euroclydon,[2] or north-east gale, that drives all before it, till the vessel bilges on some rocks or shoals. Just so is the rage of man when bereft of his reason. I well remember some years ago hearing the great and wise philosopher, Dr. Franklin, make this observation: "That mother Nature had furnished her children with sufficient spirits to support them through the voyage of life, if they would not forsake their animal spirits for the more ardent spirit of the dram shops, which soon debilitates the whole system, produces an inflammation of the liver, that eventually proves a fatal decay of nature. My children," said the philosopher, "beware how you quit the path of nature and rectitude."[3] Here he paused. Let me, then, as having treasured up the advice, say to all who now read it, Take heed, and improve the warning before it is too late. If any have commenced the career, oh, quit it! for the love of God, before it becomes a fixed habit, as all are, more or less, creatures of habit.

The good order of society depends much on the citizens forming virtuous habits. A person intoxicated is not able to guide himself, and, therefore is incapable of directing another. He has rendered himself unfit to protect his family, or property, from the hand of the spoiler. A habit of intemperance originates often from taking the morning cordial to invigorate the debilitated frame, which the morning air, and moderate exercise would soon restore, without the aid of cordial. Some may fall into the fatal snare, by taking too often the social glass, with the circle of his acquaintance. From the real spirit of benevolence he joins with his friends till the constant practice becomes second nature. From the late forming a society for the suppression of intemperance, may be anticipated great utility. Such an institution may be the means of restraining the passions of many, and check any disposition to the vice before it becomes a fixed habit. Take a retrospect of the world from the creation till the present day[,] it will be seen that most of the evils of life have arisen from the rage of men when inflamed with liquor. By indulging a sensual appetite, human nature is degraded, and they lose that rank in society they once were an honour to. This one vice is often followed by many others, till men are sunk in all the miseries incident to human frailty, and the human being is no longer the man, as he has dethroned the reasoning powers and mental faculties which constitute the whole man.

And now, what art thou, oh man! Reason has deserted the helm, and your rudder is lost, and you have not even an anchor of hope to support you; for alas! you know not what you do.[4] Awake, then, ye inhabitants of the earth, awake from your lethargy; let not the snore of intoxication be heard in your dwellings. Awake then, oh man! For such is the active mind of man, that, if not engaged in some valuable pursuit, it will resort to some evil propensity for want of regular employment. Hearken, then, oh man! for the day is approaching when he, whose right it is, shall take to himself his great power, and reign.

If, then, the righteous shall hardly dare appear in the divine presence, where shall the drunkard and ungodly hide their heads? Stop your career for one moment; let reason resume her throne; consider and know the day is approaching, when all nations shall know the Lord, by the extensive spreading of his gospel, even to the uttermost ends of the earth. From the exertions now making in Europe and America, there is reason to suppose that happy day is not far distant, when there shall be peace on earth and good will to men, by the influence of divine grace on the human heart. Let me remind those who do business on the mighty waters to consider his wonders in the depths of the sea. Let it remind you that his omnipresence is extended to every region: his scrutinizing eye views the inmost recesses of the human heart. He knows the governing principle, by which men are actuated. By intemperance every virtuous principle of the mind becomes blunted. From the many hardships that seamen are exposed to, may originate the almost invariable habit of too free use of ardent spirit. Cannot some way be devised that shall remedy the prevailing evil? Yes, worthy friends, you have a remedy in your own breast, if you will exert yourselves to resist temptation. Enterprize, resolution, and fortitude are characteristical traits of the true seamen; armed with such weapons, you are equal to combat with this worst of enemies and destroyer of the peace and harmony of the human species; the flame of inebriating liquor can be repelled by the more sparkling and brilliant fire of the flint, and most seamen partake a large share of that fire, which will be sufficient to resist the evil spirit, or propensity to evil. Put on the new man;[5] and by divine assistance you can work out your own salvation.[6] You must, by an active faith in the gospel promises, stretch forth the withered hand, as the good man in the gospel did.[7] He made the necessary exertion, and by faith he was restored. Now by the exercise of that same kind of faith, the spirit of divine grace will enable you to continue firm in the performance of every moral and Christian duty. You will find the ways of wisdom are ways of pleasantness, and all her paths are peace. Our heavenly parent requires no more of his dependent children than a reasonable service.[8] He says to every one, my son, or my daughter, give me thy heart; that is, devote yourself, your time and talents to my service and the good of your fellow creatures, and that is but a reasonable service due to God, as our Creator, and Jesus Christ, as our Redeemer and Saviour. Those who deprive themselves of reason by intoxication, are rendered unfit to offer a reasonable sacrifice, or even perform the common duties of life. The consequence is, harmony and peace are destroyed, and calm serenity of mind, that alone can alleviate the rigid cares of life, are fled forever from the happy mansion, and the destroying angel of discord has taken possession of the unhappy family. What can prevent the spreading of this evil in our country[?] The most likely mode of prevention is to increase schools for the education of poor children; schools of industry for males and females. Get youth an early habit of industry, for idleness will not only clothe a man with rags, but multiply many other vices; and that of drinking to drown sorrow, which eventually will increase a tenfold misery. Now while the human feelings are alive to sensibility, and all Europe and America are called on to aid in measures devised for promoting the conversion of the Jews, let the wealthy and benevolent take into consideration the situation of the Gentiles in our own remote parts of the country.[9] Societies are now combining in Europe; let Americans improve the blessings of peace by joining with them in extending the gospel of peace to the most remote regions of the heathen nations; and let it remind the wealthy and benevolent, of the almost total ignorance of the inhabitants of many obscure places of this country.[10] Friends of humanity, send missionaries from north to south, and from east to west; impress on their minds the necessity of industry, not only to cultivate the land, but to cultivate the mind. Spread true gospel principles among them, not only by precept, but by an example of every moral and Christian virtue. Let your light so shine[11] before the unenlightened, that it shall make them seek for knowledge by the bright example of their respected missionary. Our venerable ancestors laid the foundation for learning by early establishing schools, churches, and colleges. Do not let any forget the rock from whence they were hewn; but remember our churches were originally founded on the rock of ages, and Jesus Christ was the chief corner stone,[12] and the power of death shall not prevail against it.[13] The human mind and frame must be civilized before it can be Christianized.[14] We must be rational to prepare us for Christian beings. Arise, then, like human beings, and exert all the mental powers of the mind to resist temptations of every kind. It will be found, that from indulging a depraved appetite, and from a propensity to ardent spirits, has arisen most of the miseries in human life. Take a retrospect of the horrid scenes that daily occur, as may be seen from the printed accounts, in the publick papers; and, when traced to their covert,[15] can be proved to have been committed in a paroxysm of liquor.

The too free use of ardent spirits will keep the body in a continual fever, and inflame the mind, and produces most of the political altercations that arise among the citizens. Most of the political squabbles and frenzies of the brain originate in this obnoxious practice, which produces an heated imagination that ends in a fever on the spirits; then medical aid is resorted to for relief, and the whole train of prescriptions must follow, from letting the vital blood till the last fatal blister on the head.[16] But all prove vain; for all human help has failed.

Fellow citizens, recall your wanderings before it is too late; particularly let it remind that class of men who steer through life on the mighty ocean, to steer clear of the fatal infusion, that will produce a fatal confusion among their ship's crew, and perhaps frustrate the most prosperous voyage.

When you commence life apply to the same pilot that steered the ship safe to the Cape of Good Hope. Carefully avoid the rocks and shoals incident to human life. Let Wisdom and Prudence direct, Reason Steer, Fortitude and Perseverance command, and the compass of Genius guide. You must continue firm and steady as the north pole.

Steady! Boys, Steady!

Has ever been the seaman's motto; and it must be supported by temperance, sobriety, and manly fortitude. If then, brave men, you will improve these qualifications to correct any evil propensity, you cannot fail to conquer. Take the divine guide of religion for your pilot, as it is that alone can steer you safe through the stormy sea of life, and afford you a safe passport to the haven of bliss and perfect happiness, which is the Cape of Good Hope. You must carefully avoid all the quicksands and shoals that surround your passage; and these are intemperance, vice, and immorality of every kind.

Support, surmount, subdue your fate,
And quit destruction ere too late;
Let reason guide, religion sway,
Your head to govern night and day.
Whether at home or on the main,   5
From drinking hard,[17] good friends, refrain.
Drink not too deep to drown old care,
Let your resort be daily prayer,
That fortitude, on sea or shore,
May never leave you any more;   10
But you, from stem to stern may view
Your honest, steady, happy crew.
All hands on deck! with hearts sincere,
Well man the yards, with heads quite clear,
Then steady, steady boys you'll see   15
Return with bless'd prosperity.
That future bliss may you attend,
Will pray the seaman's fervent friend.

Prudencia Americana.

Observations on the Real Rights of Women, with Their Appropriate Duties, Agreeable to Scripture, Reason and Common Sense

By H. Mather Crocker

And God saw it was not good for man to be alone;
and he made him an help meet for him. — and Adam
said she is bone of my bones, and flesh of my flesh,
therefore she shall be called woman.

BOSTON:

PRINTED FOR THE AUTHOR

1818

DEDICATION.

TO MISS H. MORE.[1]

MADAM,

YOUR writings on moral and religious subjects are held in the highest estimation by one, who thinks your Comparative View of the Sexes[2] is indeed worthy of yourself.

To your patronage allow me to devote the following pages. Your approbation of the sentiments will be the most distinguished palm the author wishes to obtain.

Though personally unknown, permit me to subscribe myself, with sentiments of the highest esteem and respect,

Yours,

H. M. CROCKER.

AUTHOR'S PREFACE.

———

Proposals for printing the following pages were issued more than a year since. The author, having been afflicted with sickness, has unavoidably been unable to collect subscriptions till the present time.

The publishing has therefore been suspended. To those who first subscribed let me say, I hope when they receive the work, they will have reason to say, patient waiters are no losers; and she sincerely wishes those who peruse the work may find reason to say, the author has not spent her strength for nought, neither have they spent their time in vain, who have read the work.

With this wish the work is now devoted to the public notice; with a hope, that the work will receive the candour and patronage of a free, enlightened, independent, federal nation.

CONTENTS.

———

CHAP. III.

CHAP. IV.

CHAP. V.

CHAP. VI.

CHAP. VII.

CHAP. VIII.

INTRODUCTION.

———————

THIS little work is not written with a design of promoting any altercation or dispute respecting superiority or inferiority, of the sexes; but the aim will be to prove, in a pleasant manner, and, we hope, to even demonstration, that though there are appropriate duties peculiar to each sex, yet the wise Author of nature has endowed the female mind with equal powers and faculties, and given them the same right of judging and acting for themselves, as he gave to the male sex; although it is plain, from scripture account, that the woman was the first in the transgression, she justly forfeited her original right of equality for a certain space of time, and a heavy and humiliating sentence was passed upon her, that her sorrow should be multiplied, and that under the Jewish dispensation, the man should rule over her; and she was under the yoke of bondage, till the birth of our blessed Saviour, which, according to the promise given, was the seed of the woman, that should bruise the serpent's head.

We shall consider woman restored to her original right and dignity at the commencement of the Christian dispensation, although there must be allowed some moral and physical distinction of the sexes agreeably to the order of nature, and the organization of the human frame, still the sentiment must predominate, that the powers of mind are equal in the sexes. We shall produce examples, both from sacred and profane history, of the great abilities and exertion of many females, when called into action, either on political or religious account. For the interest of their country, or in the cause of humanity, we shall strictly adhere to the principle and the impropriety of females ever trespassing on masculine ground: as it is morally incorrect, and physically improper.

We shall therefore state in a plain manner the beauty and order that must arise, from each sex performing their appropriate duties with mutual fidelity and harmony; a plan or theory, or a Christian system will be drawn, by which means the mutual happiness of the sexes may be promoted; and the rights, liberties, and independence of a brave and free people shall continue secure to them by the mutual virtues and integrity of the sexes; the plan must be reduced to practice, by mutual agreement, and the mantle of charity be drawn over every little imperfection, that peace and harmony may prevail.

May the same mantle be extended to the following pages by the candid reader.

RIGHTS OF WOMAN, &c.

CHAP. I.

Of the creation and fall of our first parents.

THE foundation stone[3] of the present work must be laid in the first creation of the human race. When the great Jehovah had created the earth, and all things therein, he created man; male and female created he them, in his own image, so far as he endowed him with intellectual powers and faculties, and gave him an immortal and rational soul, and powers of mind capable of reasoning on the nature of things. And the Lord God said, it is not good for man to be alone; I will make him an help meet, for him: And the Lord God caused a deep sleep to fall upon Adam, and he slept: and he took one of his ribs, and closed up the flesh instead thereof. And the rib, which the Lord God had taken from man, made he a woman: and brought her unto the man, and Adam said, this is now bone of my bone, and flesh of my flesh: she shall be called woman, because she was taken out of man; as she partakes of my original nature, she shall therefore partake of my name; therefore shall a man cleave unto his wife, and they shall be one flesh: See Gen. ii. [18–]24.

It seems, says an able commentator,[4] to have been the Creator's design to have inculcated the lesson of perfect love and union, by forming the woman out of the man's body, and from a part of it so near the heart, as well as to make woman of a more refined and delicate nature, by thus causing the original clay to pass, as it were, twice through his refining hand.[5] Now it is consistent to say, if they are become one flesh, there should be but one and the same spirit operating equally upon them both, for their mutual happiness. Adam, having given her a name, and placed himself as her guardian, became in some measure, responsible for her conduct, as the rightful protector of her innocence. It should be recollected, as a small palliative for Eve, that the command, respecting the tree of knowledge and forbidden fruit, was before the woman was made: see Gen. ii. 16 and 17. And the lord God commanded the man, saying, of every tree of the garden thou mayest freely eat; but of the tree of knowledge, of good and evil thou shalt not eat, for in the day thou eatest thereof, thou shalt surely die. She must therefore have received her information from Adam, if she knew of any command; as she probably had heard of it, by her answer to the serpent. Perhaps Adam communicated it to her as the injunction of their Maker, but possibly with such mildness and indifference, that she was not fully impressed with the importance of the command.

It seems, that, in an unfortunate hour, these then pure and happy beings, were separated. Oh, fatal hour! Oh, inconsiderate Adam! How couldst thou leave the friend of thy affection to wander in the garden, unaided by the support and strength of thy arm, and the pleasure of thy conversation. Didst thou for one moment feel the supreme dignity and full consequence of being placed lord of the lower creation? Didst thou walk forth to survey the animals created for thy use, and subjected to thy dominion? No, no; we say pride had not then polluted the human heart. Thou wast not then puffed up with the idea of knowing good and evil; but thou might have had tenderness enough for thy 'rib, that was taken from thy side,' to have kept near enough to her to protect her innocence from the wiles of the tempter. Nothing can justify Eve's imprudence in parlying[6] with the serpent at all; and she is condemnable for holding any converse, or supposing knowledge was ever desirable, that must be obtained in any clandestine or dishonorable manner. No one can approve of the asperity of Adam's answer to his Maker, when called on to answer how he knew that he was naked. He answered evidently with a very indignant air: The woman thou gavest to be with me, gave me of the fruit of the tree, and I did eat.[7] It does not appear, from his own account, that Adam withstood the temptation with more fortitude than Eve did; for she presented the fruit, and he received it without hesitation; but it is plain she did not yield immediately, though the most subtle agent of the devil told her that her eyes should be opened, and that she should be like a god. When indeed she saw that the tree was good for food, and that it was pleasant to the eyes, and a tree to be desired to make one wise, she took of the fruit thereof, and did eat. It appears her desire was to obtain knowledge, which might be laudable, though her reason was indeed deceived.

And reason is quickly deceived, says the eloquent Saurin, when the senses have been seduced. It was already yielding to the temptation, to hearken so long to the tempter.[8]

By the joint transgression of our first parents, sin, misery and death were introduced into this present world: They appear equally culpable; yet God, who is ever wise and just in his dealings, passed the most severe sentence on the woman, as she was told her sorrows should be multiplied. And a still harder fate attended her. She was reduced, from a state of honorable equality, to the mortifying state of subjection: Thy desire shall be to thy husband, and he shall rule over thee.[9] Heaven never intended she should be ruled with a rod of iron; but drawn by the cords of the man, in the bonds of love. It is however evident, Adam was placed over her as her lord and master, for a certain period, and by the express will of his maker, and was taught to appreciate his own judgment, as every creature was brought to him to give them names; and whatsoever names he gave them, they were called: And he gave his rib the name of woman, and displayed some judgment in the reason given for calling her woman: For she is bone of my bone, and flesh of my flesh, and therefore she shall be my equal. She shall have equal right to think, reason and act for herself, with my advice corroborating. He should therefore have resisted the temptation with manly fortitude, and, not only by precept, but by example, strengthened her resolution to resist the evil spirit: but he fell a prey to his own credulity, and sunk his posterity in depravity.

However strange their conduct may appear to the human understanding, we fully believe, in the great scale of divine providence, it was perfectly just they should be left to commit sin and folly, to convince the human race of their insufficiency, when left to act for themselves; and, from their example, shew to their posterity, the propriety of placing their dependence on Him, who alone is able to keep us from falling.

There is a very beautiful description of our primeval parent's first interview, in Miss Aikin's epistles on women.[10] We give the extract in her own style:

> "See where the world's new master roams along,
> Vainly intelligent, and idly strong;
> Marks His long listless steps and turpid[11] air,
> His brow of densest gloom, and fix'd infantile stare.
> No mother's voice has touch'd that slumb'ring ear, 5
> Nor glist'ning eye beguiled him with a tear.
> Love nurs'd not him with sweet endearing wiles,
> Nor woman taught the sympathy of smiles.

Ah! hapless world, that such a wretch obeys,
Ah! joyless Adam, though a world he sways.   10
But see they meet, they gaze, the new born pair,
Mark now the youth, and now the wond'ring fair.
Sure, a new soul that moping idiot warms,
Dilates his statue,[12] and his mien informs.
A brighter crimson tints his gloomy cheeks,   15
His broad eye kindles, and his glances speaks."

From this description, there appears to commence a sympathy of nature, or mutual affection, inherent in nature, which perhaps might operate on Adam's sensibility, and cause him insensibly to partake of the forbidden fruit that proved their fatal fall, and her deepest humiliation; as she is placed under subjection to the man: And the command was put into full force under the old Jewish dispensation, as they bought and sold their wives and daughters, and made trafficks of them as they did their cattle. But blessed be God, the bonds are dissolved, the snare is broken, and woman has escaped by the blessing of the gospel.

CHAP. II

*Woman is restored to her original rights of equality
under the Christian dispensation.*

HERE, indeed, is the love of God manifested to the disobedient children of men. Though by the fall of our first parents misery and death was the consequence; yet the promise is made good to man, that the seed of the woman should bruise the serpent's head, and that in her seed, all mankind should be restored to peace and happiness. And at the appointed time Jehovah was pleased to over-shadow the espoused wife of Joseph: and there was more than a common presence of the divine eradiator[13] attending at his birth. The wise men or astrologers of the east, had calculated a new star that would appear about that time, and it forboded some great event to take place. Agreeably to their calculation, at the very time they were gazing for the stranger, behold it did appear agreeable to their expectation, and by the bright and effulgent light of this new and till now unknown star, the wise men of the east were directed till the star reflected on the menial place of the birth of our Saviour. And here was the degraded woman found; exalted to the highest honour of embracing in her maternal arms the Son of God himself in human nature. What an interesting scene it must have been to the wise men that had been looking for some great event to take place! What a scene it must have been to the man of sensibility! The amiable, the devout Mary, apparently degraded, is now exalted to the highest honour among men; and life and immortality are brought to light, by the divine influence of the gospel, under the dispensation of grace. She, who was condemned to servitude, is now, by the blessing of the dispensation, restored to her original privileges: As the woman was first in the transgression, and in some measure, the cause of their fall, she is now, by divine goodness, made the instrument of bringing life and future happiness to mankind.

The prophecy is accomplished, that in her seed all nations shall be blessed: Herein she is exalted, and fully restored to her original dignity, by being the mother of our blessed Lord and Saviour Jesus Christ, according to his human nature. This, surely, must place her equal with man, under the Christian system. Since the Christian era she is no longer commanded to be the slave to man, and he is no longer commanded to rule over her.

The offers of divine grace are equally tendered to both male and female; and all have equal right to accept the blessing; and if any judgment can be formed from the visible church, there is reason to conclude that women embrace the privileges of the gospel, with as much, or more energy, than men. If we trace throughout the known world, it will be found that there are more open professors of religion amongst women, than there are amongst men. And they have an undoubted right to this distinction, as their powers of mind are not inferiour, and their sensibilities are certainly greater, or as keen. There must be a moral and physical distinction of sexes, from the organization of the human frame, as well as from their different modes of life and education, as from their different appropriate duties; and women for the most part are not called to make the same exertions in life; yet there are frequent instances of women, when called in providence to the trial, have made as great exertions as men; and have stemmed the torrent of human misery, with equal fortitude to any man, under like circumstances. They can claim no superiority of opinion, only an equal right of judgment with the bolder sex. They are not called to plough on masculine grounds, from the moral distinction there is in nature.

It must be the appropriate duty and privilege of females, to convince by reason and persuasion. It must be their peculiar province to soothe the turbulent passions of men, when almost sinking in the sea of care, without even an anchor of hope to support them.[14] Under such circumstances women should display their talents by taking the helm, and steer them safe to the haven of rest and peace, and that should be their own happy mansion, where they may always retire and find a safe asylum from the rigid cares of business. It is woman's peculiar right to keep calm and serene under every circumstance in life, as it is undoubtedly her appropriate duty, to soothe and alleviate the anxious cares of man, and her friendly and sympathetic breast should be found the best solace for him, as she has an equal right to partake with him the cares, as well as the pleasures of life.

It was evidently the design of heaven, by the mode of our first formation, that they should walk side by side, as mutual supports in all times of trial. There can be no doubt, that, in most cases, their judgment may be equal with the other sex; perhaps even on the subject of law, politics or religion, they may form good judgment, but it would be morally improper, and physically very incorrect, for the female character to claim the statesman's birth, or ascend the rostrum to gain the loud applause of men, although their powers of mind may be equal to the task.

We find among men, that their powers of mind are not equal in all cases;[15] if the wise author of nature has been graciously pleased to endow all men with the same powers of mind, they do not all improve them to the same advantage; or, from some imperfection in the organization of the human frame, the powers or faculties cannot operate on all alike. Some minds are so enfeebled that they are rendered incapable of judging right from wrong; therefore it appears necessary, from the very order of nature, that there should be a distinction in society, and that those whose minds are more expanded should be looked up to, as guides, to the general mass of the citizens. Females have equal right with the male citizen, to claim the protection, friendship and the approbation of such a class of men. As she is now restored to her original right by the blessing of the Christian system, no longer is she the slave, but the friend of man. From the local circumstances, and the domestic cares in which most females are involved, it cannot be expected they should make so great improvement in science and literature, as those whose whole life has been devoted to their studies. It must not be expected that the reputable mechanic will rival the man of letters and science, neither would it well suit the female frame or character, to boast of her knowledge in mechanism, or her skill in the manly art of slaughtering fellow-men. It is woman's appropriate duty and peculiar privilege to cultivate the olive branches around her table.[16] It is for her to implant in the juvenile breast the first seed of virtue, the love of God, and their country, with all the other virtues that shall prepare them to shine as statesmen, soldiers, philosophers and Christians. Some of our first worthies have boasted that they imbibed their heroic principles with their mother's milk; and by precept and example were first taught the love of virtue, religion, and their country. Surely they should have a right to share with them the laurel, but not the right of conquest; for that must be man's prerogative, and woman is to rejoice in his conquest. There may be a few groveling minds who think woman should not aspire to any further knowledge than to obtain enough of the cymical[17] art to enable them to compound a good pudding, pie, or cake, for her lord and master to discompound. Others, of a still weaker class, may say, it is enough scientifically to arrange the spinning-wheel and distaff, and exercise her extensive capacity in knitting and sewing, since the fall and restoration of woman these employments have been the appropriate duties of the female sex. The art of dress, which in some measure produced the art of industry, did not commence till sin, folly and shame, introduced the first invention of dress, which ought to check the modest female from every species of wantonness and extravagance in dress;

cultivate the mind, and trifling in dress will soon appear in its true colours.

To those who appear unfriendly to female literature[,] let me say, in behalf of the sex, they claim no right to infringe on any domestic economy; but those ladies, who continue in a state of celibacy, and find pleasure in literary researches, have a right to indulge the propensity, and solace themselves with the feast of reason and knowledge; also those ladies who in youth have laid up a treasure of literary and scientific information, have a right to improve in further literary researches, after they have faithfully discharged their domestic duties. With maternal affections, when her olive branches have spread forth to form new circles in society, the maternal mind has become satiated with the common concerns of life, and the real Christian wishes for peace and retirement, for contemplation; and this is the most convenient season for [her] to take a retrospect of past scenes, and this is a fully ripe season to read, write, meditate and compose, if the body and mind are not enfeebled by infirmities. The well informed mind, if still in full vigour, is now fully ripe for composing; and females of that class must have a right to unbend their minds in well digested thoughts for the improvement of the rising generation;[18] and if they can by well digested sentiments, implant in the youthful breast, by precept and their example, the seeds of virtue and religion, it will fully compensate, for a long life of toil and study. The furrows of age shall be cheered with the expectation of a rich harvest of mental improvement and satisfaction; and where religion sways, the whole deportment will be calm, serene and placid, and the infirmities natural to the decline of life, will be alleviated in the bright prospect of immorality, to which both sexes are equally entitled to aspire.

Women have an equal right, with the other sex, to form

societies for promoting religious, charitable and benevolent purposes. Every association formed for benevolence, must have a tendency to make man mild, and sociable to man;[19] an institution formed for historical and literary researches, would have a happy effect on the mind and manners of the youth of both sexes. As the circulating libraries are often resorted to after novels by both sexes for want of judgment to select works of more merit, the study of history would strengthen their memory, and improve the mind, whereas novels have a tendency to vitiate the mind and morals of the youth of each sex before they are ripe for more valuable acquisitions. Much abstruse study or metaphysical reasoning seldom agrees with the natural vivacity or the slender frame of many females, therefore the moral and physical distinction of the sex must be allowed; if the powers of the mind are fully equal, they must still estimate the rights of men, and own it their prerogative exclusively to contend for public honours and preferment, either in church or state, and females may console themselves and feel happy, that by the moral distinction of the sexes they are called to move in a sphere of life remote from those masculine contentions, although they hold equal right with them of studying every branch of science, even jurisprudence.

But it would be morally wrong, and physically imprudent, for any woman to attempt pleading at the bar of justice, as no law can give her the right of deviating from the strictest rules of rectitude and decorum. No servile dependence on men can be recommended under the Christian system, for that abolished the law of slavery, and left only a claim on their friendship; as the author of their nature originally intended, they should be the protectors of female innocence, and not the fatal destroyers of their peace and happiness. They claim no right at the gambling table, and to the moral sensibility of females how disgusting must be the horse-race, the bull-bate, and the cock-fight. These are barbarous scenes, ill suited to the delicacy of females.

It must be woman's prerogative to shine in the domestic circle, and her appropriate duty to teach and regulate the opening mind of her little flock, and teach their juvenile ideas how to shoot forth into well improved sentiments. It is most undoubtedly the duty and privilege of woman to regulate her garrison with such good order and propriety, that the generalissimo of her affection, shall never have reason to seek other quarters for well disciplined and regulated troops, and there must not a murmur or beat be heard throughout the garrison, except that of the heart vibrating with mutual affection, reciprocally soft. The rights of woman displayed on such a plan, might perhaps draw the other sex from the nocturnal ramble to the more endearing scenes of domestic peace and harmony.[20] The woman, who can gain such a victory, as to secure the undivided affection of her generalissimo, must have the exclusive right to shine unrivalled in her garrison. There is no distinction of sexes in heaven, which may be found agreeable to scripture in our blessed Master's answer to the Sadducees[21] when they interrogated him respecting the woman who had been the wife of seven brethren, Matthew xxii. 29, 30. Jesus answered and said unto them, ye do err, not knowing the scriptures, nor the power of God. For in the resurrection they neither marry nor are given in marriage, but are as the angels of God in heaven.

It is a pleasant and most sublime idea, that we shall know and be known to each other in this state of bliss and happiness, and perhaps agreeably to Dr. Watts'[22] enlarged ideas, though there is no marriage, nor giving in marriage, nor any distinction of sex, yet those who have lived in a state of celibacy here, may, in the expansion of the celestial regions, find the twin soul that, though lost upon the road, had joined the general choir of perfected spirits; and that may account for some continuing single in the present world.

The following extract from Watts' *Indian Philosopher*, perhaps, he intended should be a handsome apology for his own living in a state of celibacy.

> "The mighty power, that form'd the mind,
> One mould for every two design'd,
> And bless'd the new-born pair;
> This be a match for this, he said,
> Then down he sent the souls he made,   5
> To seek them bodies here.
> But parting from their warm abode,
> They lost their fellows on the road,
> And never join'd their hands;
> Ah, cruel chance, and crossing fates,   10
> Our eastern souls have lost their mates,
> On Europe's barren lands."[23]

This possibly may account for some cross matches, or be a sufficient reason for some continuing single, which the sexes have a right to do. It must be left to their mutual decision. There is reason to suppose the mental powers of the sexes are about equal, though their bodily habits, from constitution or mode of living, are different; and both moral and physical causes may be ascribed for it. Alexander, in his history of women, says, the notion of woman's being addicted to witchcraft,[24] had taken deep root, and spread itself all over Europe; it had been gathering strength from the days of Moses,[25] and had subsisted till the inquiring spirit of philosophy demonstrated by the plainest experiments, that many things supposed supernatural, were really the effects of natural causes, though it was always old women most suspected.[26]

This idea of the inferiority of female nature has drawn after it several others most humiliating to the sex, as well as absurd and unreasonable; but such is the pride of man, that wherever the doctrine of immortality has obtained footing he has confined that immortality to his own genius, and has considered it much too exalted for any other being, and only their prerogative.[27] Where this opinion first began is uncertain; it could not however be of very ancient date, as the belief of the immortality of the soul never obtained much footing till it was revealed in the gospel.[28] The Mahometans both in Asia and Europe, and a great variety of writers, have entertained this general opinion. Lady Montagu[29] has opposed this general opinion, in her letters, of the writings concerning the Mahometans: She says, they do not absolutely deny the existence of the female soul, but only hold them, inferior to men, and that they enter not into the same, but an inferior paradise, prepared for them on purpose.[30] But the religion of the gospel teaches better things; and shews plainly our God is no respecter of persons or sex.

My respected Miss H. More observes in her comparative view of the sexes,[31] "whatever characteristical distinction may exist, whatever inferiority may be attached to woman from the slighter frame of her body, or the more circumscribed powers of her mind, or from a less systematical education, or from the subordinate station she is called to fill in life, there is one leading circumstance, which raises her importance, and even establishes her equality. Christianity has exalted women to true and undisputed dignity in Christ Jesus. As there is neither rich nor poor, bond nor free,[32] there is neither male nor female, in the view of that immortality which is brought to light by the gospel.

"Woman has no superiour. To borrow the idea of an excellent prelate, women make up one half of the human race, equally redeemed by the blood of Christ. In this their true dignity consists; here their best pretensions rest, and here their claims are allowed. All the disputes for preeminence between the sexes have only a few short years, the attention of which would be better devoted to the duties of life and the interest of eternity. As the final hopes of the female sex are equal, so are the present means perhaps more favourable, and their opportunities less obstructed than those of the other sex. In the Christian warfare, women have every superiour advantage,[33] though it is the main object of this little work rather to lower, than raise any desire of celebrity in the female heart, yet I would awaken it to a just sensibility for honest fame. I would call on women to reflect, that our religion has not only made them heirs of a blessed immortality hereafter, but has raised them to an eminence in the scale of beings unknown to the most polished ages of antiquity. The religion of Christ has bestowed a degree of renown on the sex, beyond what any other religion ever did. Perhaps there are hardly so many virtuous women, (as I reject the whole catalogue of those whom their vices have transferred to infamy, and who are named in all the pages of Greek and Roman history) as those handed down to eternal fame, in a few of those short chapters with which the great Apostle of the gentiles has concluded his epistles to his converts of devout and honourable women. The sacred scriptures record not a few. Some of the most affecting scenes, the most interesting transactions, and the most touching conversations which are recorded of the Saviour of the world passed[34] with women: They are the first remarked as having administered to him of their substance; they appear to be the last at his tomb, and the first in the morning, when he arose from it. Theirs was the praise of not abandoning their despised Redeemer when he was led to execution; and under all the hopeless circumstances of his ignominious death, they left him not a moment: and theirs was the privilege of receiving the earliest consolation from their risen Lord. Theirs was the honour of being first commissioned to announce the glorious resurrection to the world, and even to furnish heroic confessors, devoted saints, and unshrinking martyrs to the church of Christ, which has not been the exclusive honour of the bolder sex."[35] — *Miss More.*[36]

There is a natural desire in women to be agreeable, and they no doubt would wish to model themselves to what they think will please. If, therefore, those who take the lead in society would set the fashion to be wise and virtuous, others would follow.[37] Villemert says in *The Friend of Women*,[38] Wisdom and reason are found much oftener united with the graces, than the detractors of the sex conceive them to be endowed with.[39] As well as us with a soul and heart, they ought to labour to enlighten one, and regulate the other. The mind, to perfect itself, only requires a moderate degree of study, which may be ranked among the class of pleasures.[40] A woman of real good sense, only makes herself noticed by that which deserves to be so; she is independent of all those trifles which cause to weak minds a joy or affliction equally ridiculous. Free from those alterations of good and bad humour that disconcert friendship, she preserves a continual pleasing gaiety, which sets her charms off better than the most studied decoration.[41] The empire of beauty is short, but the dominion of virtue, and triumphs of religion, are great and eternal;[42] and since the promulgation of the gospel, it has been fairly proved, even to demonstration, that the female powers and faculties are equal with the men; but their mode of education often checks their progress in learning.

There appears a chasm in the history of women till the time of [43] Moses; and he speaks of singing men and singing women. Among a variety of the nations, the Egyptians, however, were in this respect, different and singular. The same reason that determined other nations to teach women that pleasing art, determined the Egyptians to debar them from it, because, said they, it softens and relaxes the mind, as it was found that music would often soothe even the savage breast. Therefore it was probably the opinion of the legislator, that too much softness and delicacy would disqualify them for managing the affairs of trade and commerce, and that certain softness of sex, which was encouraged in other nations, would ill suit the Egyptian women, who were generally employed in the same manner as was destined to the men. However, when we survey the account given by the ancients, of the arts, sciences, laws, and above all, the culture and wisdom of the Egyptians; and when we consider the high estimation in which women were held, and the powers with which they were invested; when to this we add the literary fame of the nation, there is the strongest reason to conclude that though we are at this period unacquainted with their opinion of female education, it certainly must have been such as suited the dignity of so wise a people, and of a sex, so beloved and respected.[44] Whatever moral or physical distinction they allowed is uncertain; but there is no doubt they fully appreciated the judgment of the female sex. In any region a superior[45] genius will soar above the common level.[46] Even two women, grinding at the same mill,[47] will rise or soar above each other, not only in their mode of work, but in their mental powers and faculties. These kinds of mills are in use, at this very day, all over the Levant, and in the north of Scotland, where they have a song composed on purpose to divert their attention from thinking of their hard fate, and to alleviate the female mind.[48]

It has been observed, that men, secluded from women, have become more slovenly in their persons and manners;[49] but women secluded from men are generally more neat and particular than other women are.[50] If the observation is just, men must reap most advantage from the company of women. In former times, the greatest philosophers were seldom fit company for women, or enjoyed their conversation. Sir Isaac Newton hardly ever conversed with any of the sex,[51] though he allowed each sex were equally subject to the power of custom, and civil and religious compacts were equally binding on the sexes.

Therefore, with Watts, we say, the mind must be the standard of the man or woman.[52] And shall proceed to give some account of illustrious females and their writings, which have appeared in almost every age of the world.

CHAP. III

Of the strength of mind, and writings of many illustrious females, both in sacred and profane history.

FROM Dr. Hunter's *Sacred Biography*,[53] which places females in a very desirable point of light, the following character of Deborah is extracted:

He says, And whither are our eyes turned or directed at this time? To hold the Saviour of a sinking country, behold the residue of the spirit is on the head of a woman: The sacred flame of public spirit smothered and dead in every manly breast, yet glows in a female's bosom; and the tribunal of justice, deserted by masculine virtue and ability, is honourably and usefully filled by feminine sensibility, discernment, honesty and zeal.

Deborah was a prophetess, the wife of Lepidoth, she judged Israel at that time. She was a wife and mother in Israel; and such a wife is a crown to her husband, and the pride and glory of her children; but her capacious soul, embraced more than her own family; she aimed at the happiness of thousands; she sweetly blended public, with private virtue. It is not unreasonable to suppose, the discreet and wise management of her own household first procured her the notice and esteem of the public; and the prudent deportment of the matron passed by an easy transition to the sanctity of a prophetess, and the gravity of a judge. Certain it is that the reputation which is not established on the basis of personal goodness, is like a house built on the sand, which must soon sink and fall. Hitherto we have seen only holy men of God speaking as they were moved by the Holy Spirit. But the great Jehovah is no respecter of persons or sex: The secrets of the Lord are with them that fear him, and he sheweth unto them his holy covenant. The simple dignity of her unadorned and unassuming state is beautifully represented.

She dwelt under the palm tree of Deborah, between Ramah and Bethel, in mount Ephraim, and the children of Israel came up to her for judgment. Behold a female mind exalted, above the pageantry and pride of external appearance, not deriving consequence from the splendour of her attire, the charms of her person, or the number of her retinue: but from the affability of her manners, the purity of her character, and sacredness of her office; the impartiality of her conduct, the importance of her public services; not wandering from place to place, panting after little empty applause, but sought unto of all Israel, from the eminency and extensive ability of her talents and virtue.

Her canopy of state was the palm tree, her rule of living God, her motive the inspiration of the Almighty, her aim and end the glory of God, and the good of his people, her reward, the testimony of a good conscience and the respect of a grateful nation, the admiration of future generations, and the smiles of approving heaven.[54] In her, united poetry and musical skill, fervent devotion, heroic intrepidity, and prophetic inspiration.

A combination how rare! how instructive! how respectable![55] To her life is affixed an historical note, short indeed, but highly interesting and important. And the land had rest forty years. This is the noblest eulogium of Deborah, and the most honourable display of her talents and virtues. If there are feelings worthy of envy, they are those of this exalted woman.[56] How lasting and extensive is the influence of real worth! There is one way by which every person may be the saviour of his country, that is, by cultivating the private virtues.[57]

I now proceed to illustrate the female character, its amiableness, usefulness, and importance, in persons and scenes of a very different complexion; in the less glaring, but not less instructive history of Ruth the Moabitess, and Naomi her mother.[58] Let us wait her appearance in silent expectation, and muse on what is past.[59]

She had a soul capacious and capable of fond respect for departed worth and living virtue: She had magnanimity to sacrifice everything the heart held dear to decency, friendship, and religion.[60] In Ruth we have this higher principle likewise beautifully exemplified, rational, modest, and unaffected piety.[61]

We proceed to unfold from sacred history, the character and conduct of Hannah.[62] Every thing, of any importance for us to know respecting Hannah, is what related to her son Samuel, and to that, accordingly, the scripture account is confined. She is the fourth, as far as we can recollect, recorded in the same similar case; and she is not the least respectable.[63]

The manner in which Elkanah and Hannah lived together was exemplary and instructive. They have one common interest, they have one darling object of affection, they express one and the same wish, in terms of mutual kindness and endearment.[64] Hannah's song of praise, possesses all the majesty, grace, and beauty of ancient oriental poetry. It is one of the happiest effusions of an excellent female heart, labouring under a grateful sense of the highest obligation.[65]

From the sacred records in the New Testament, we find many females celebrated for virtue, religion and true holiness; and some were admitted to the highest dignity and honour, in attending on, and having the friendship and blessing of their Lord and Saviour Jesus Christ.

Russell[66] says, The courage of the Christian women was founded on the noblest principles and motives, and animated by the glorious hopes of immortality. Those to whom the church assign the compound title of saint and orator, recommended to admiration the Christian women.[67]

But he who speaks of them with most zeal, is St. Jerome,[68] who, born with a soul of fire, spent twenty-four years in writing, combating and conquering himself. The manners of this saint were probably more severe than his thoughts. He had a number of illustrious women at Rome, among his disciples. But, though surrounded with beauty, he escaped weakness

without slander, and flying the world, the women, and himself, he retired to Palestine, where all which he had quitted
pursued him, and still tormented him, under the penitential
sackcloth, and in the midst of solitary deserts, reechoes in his
ears the tumults of Rome.

Such was St. Jerome, the most eloquent panegyrist of the
Christian women, of the fourth century. That warm and pious writer, though harsh and austere, softens his style in a
thousand instances, to praise the Marcelas, the Paulas, and
many other Roman women, who, at the capital had embraced
Christianity, and studied in Rome the language of the Hebrews, to read the books of Moses.

When the Roman empire, like some venerable column, was
pushed from its basis, and broken into pieces by the myriads
of the north, Christianity passed from the conquered to the
conqueror by the zeal of the women, who at the same time,
diffused the gospel, and softened the manners of the savages.
It has been observed in every age, that Christian women have
been more anxious to make proselytes, than men have been.
However just this observation may have been, or from what
motive they were actuated, the world has been obliged to them
for their ardour. It was women,[69] who, making the charms
of their sex subservient to religion, raised to thrones by their
beauty, drew over their husbands to their opinion, and spread
Christianity over the greatest part of Europe. It was by their
means that France, Germany, Bavaria, Hungary, Lithuania,
Poland and Russia, and for some time, that Persia, received the
gospel. By the same influence Lombardy renounced the opinion
of Arius;[70] women were then desirous of attaining every species of learning, and some have succeeded in every age of the
world.[71] In former ages what has since been called society, was
not then known. Luxury and the want of occupation had not

introduced the fashion of sitting five or six hours at the glass to invent fashions. Some use was then made of time, and hence the languages and sciences were acquired by females.[72] If the women of those ages were ambitious of arraying themselves in the knowledge of men, the men were at all times ready with their panegyricks to return the compliment.

It was the sequel of the general spirit that carried gallantry into letters, as it had introduced it into arms.[73] Greece was governed by eloquent men, and the influence courtezans had held in public affairs was by the influence [that] the celebrated courtezans held over the orators. There was not one, but they had some influence over; even the thundering, the inflexible Demosthenes,[74] so terrible to tyrants, was subjected to their sway. Of that great master of eloquence, it has been said, what he had been a whole year in erecting, a woman overturned in one day.[75]

The illustrious Zenobia,[76] though not of Roman extraction, presents herself to view, as a widow who reigned in great glory for some time. The celebrated Longinus[77] was her preceptor and secretary.[78] Not being able to brook the Roman tyranny, she declared war against the emperor Aurelian, who took her prisoner and led her in triumph to Rome, and butchered her principal nobility,[79] and among others the excellent Longinus, who taught her to write as well as to conquer. She was afterwards unfortunate with dignity, and she consoled herself for the loss of a throne with the sweets of solitude and the joys of reason.[80]

Jane of Flanders[81] is highly celebrated by Rapin[82] and other historians. When John was taken prisoner and sent to Paris, which misfortune must certainly have ruined his party, had not his interest been supported by the extraordinary abilities of his wife, Jane of Flanders, a lady who seems to possess all the excellent qualities of both sexes. Bold, daring and intrepid, she fought like a hero in the field; shrewd, sensible and sagacious, she spake like a politician in the council; and endowed with the most amiable manners, and winning address, she was able to draw the minds of her subjects by the force of her eloquence, and mould them to her pleasure. She happened to be at Rennes when she received the news of her husband's captivity. But that disaster instead of depressing, raised her native courage and fortitude. She assembled the citizens, and holding her infant son in her arms, recommended him to their care and protection, in the most pathetic terms, as the male heir of their ancient dukes, who had governed them with lenity and indulgence, and to whom they had ever professed their zealous attachment. She declared herself willing to run all hazards with them in so just a cause. She pointed out to them the resources that yet remained in the alliances with England, earnestly beseeching them to make one vigorous effort against the usurper, who being forced on them by the intrigues of France, would, as a mark of gratitude, sacrifice the liberties of Britanny[83] to his protector. The people, moved by the affecting appearance of the princes, vowed to live and die with her in defence of the rights of her family.[84]

There have[85] been many eminent and distinguished writers in almost every age of the world. In 1643, a piece appeared at Paris, under this title, *The Generous Woman*;[86] who shews her sex are more noble, more patriotic, more brave, more learned, more virtuous and economical than men. In 1665, another lady published at Paris, a book entitled, *The Illustrious Dames*,[87] where, by good and strong reasoning it is fairly proved that women surpass the men. In 1673, a performance appeared, entitled, *The Equality of the Sexes*,[88] shewing the importance of divesting ourselves of prejudices.[89] These discourses were philosophical and moral. Madam De Gournay wrote upon her sex; but being more modest, she confined herself and pretensions, and was contented with equality.[90]

Mary Schurman,[91] born at Calona, is extolled for extraordinary capacity in learning. She was a painter, musician, engraver, sculptor, philosopher, geometrician, and understood nine different languages.[92]

Elizabeth,[93] queen of England, is noticed by some historians, for the great strength of mind she discovered in her youth. Mr. Ascham, her tutor, in a letter to his friend Sturmius, says, I am reading Greek with the princess.[94]

The orations she understood at first; not only the meaning of the orator, but the whole force of the language, and the whole system of the laws, customs, and manners of the Athenians.[95] Some historians say, the reign of Elizabeth was justly esteemed as one of the most shining periods of English history; and for purity of manners, vigour of mind, vigour of character, and personal address, it is perhaps unequaled. The magnificent entertainments which that illustrious princess so frequently gave her court, and at which she generally appeared in person, with a most engaging familiarity, rubbed off the ancient reserve of nobility, and increased the taste of society, and even of gallantry.[96]

Some historians assert that the reign of queen Anne was the summer, of which William was only the spring.[97] Every thing was ripe and nothing was corrupted. It was a short, but glorious period of heroism, and national capacity, of taste and science, learning and genius, gallantry without licentiousness, and politeness without effeminacy.[98]

Lady Jane Grey[99] is described by Dr. Fuller,[100] as possessing the innocency of childhood, the beauty of youth, the solidity of maturity, and the gravity of age.[101]

In the character of Sir Thomas More[102] are found blended the perfections of the male sex, as neither his religion, or learning, blunted or soured his temper, or his taste for society. His love, affections, and ideas of the female character would do honour to any gentleman of the present day. In an elegant Latin piece to a friend[103] on the choice of a wife, he writes, May you meet with a woman not stupidly silent, nor always prattling nonsense. May she be learned, if possible, or at least capable of being made so. A learned and accomplished woman will be always drawing sentiments out of the best authors. She will be herself in all the vicissitudes of fortune, neither blown up by prosperity, or broken down by adversity.[104] She will be your friend at all times. You will spend your time in her company with delight. You will be always finding out new beauties in her mind. She will keep your soul in continual serenity,[105] agreeably to these delicate sentiments. It is virtue, learning, and religion, which constitute the real felicity of the connubial relation.

From history we shall furnish a few more instances of exalted characters that have shone as bright luminaries, in different ages, for virtue, learning, and for filial and maternal affection.

Cornelia, the illustrious mother of the Gracchi, after the death of her husband, who left her twelve children, applied herself to the care of her family, with a wisdom and prudence, that acquired her universal esteem; only three lived to maturity, one daughter named Semphronia, who was married to the second Scipio Africanus;[106] two sons, Tiberius and Caius,[107] whom she brought up with so much care, that, though they were generally acknowledged to have been born, with natural talents and happy dispositions, it was judged that they were still more indebted to education, than nature. The answer she gave a Campanian lady concerning them, is very famous, and includes in it great instructions for ladies and mothers. That lady who was very rich, and still fonder of pomp and shew, after having displayed in a visit to her, her diamonds, pearls, riches, and jewels, earnestly desired Cornelia to let her see her jewels also. Cornelia turned the conversation to another subject, to wait the return of her sons, who were gone to the public school. When they returned and entered their mother's apartment, she said to the Campanian lady, pointing to them with her hand, these are my jewels and the only ornaments I admire. And such ornaments are the strength and support of society, and add a brighter lustre to the fair, than all the jewels of the east.[108]

Valerius Maximus relates a singular fact of a woman of illustrious birth, who had been condemned to be strangled. The Roman praetor delivered her to the triumvir, who caused her to be carried to prison in order to her being put to death. The gaoler who was ordered to execute her, was struck with compassion, and could not resolve to kill her; he chose therefore to let her die of hunger, besides which he suffered her daughter to see her in the prison, taking care, however, that she brought nothing for her to eat. As this continued many days, he was surprised that the prisoner lived so long without eating; and suspecting the daughter, upon watching her, he discovered that she nourished her mother with her own milk. Amazed at so pious, and at the same time so ingenious an invention, he told the fact to the triumvir, and the triumvir to the praetor, who believed the thing merited relating in the assembly of the people. The criminal was pardoned. A decree was passed that the mother and daughter should be supported for the rest of their lives at the expense of the public, and that a temple sacred to piety should be erected near the prison.[109]

The same author gives a similar instance of filial piety, to a young woman named Xantippe,[110] to her aged father Cimonus, who was also condemned to die, and in prison, and which is universally known by the name of the Roman charity. Both these instances appear so extraordinary and uncommon to that people, that they could only account for them, by supposing, that the love of children was the first law of nature. — Pliny, *[Natural] Hist[ory].* 1, 7, 36.[111]

Lady Burleigh is noticed in English history as an amiable example of beneficence. She was wife of the famous Lord Burleigh, lord high treasurer of England, and privy counselor to queen Elizabeth.[112]

Madame Maintenon, Madam de Sévigné and Madam Chapone, rank high in history, as letter-writers, in their day.[113] Miss Wollstonecraft[114] mentions some ladies with energy. Of Mrs. Chapone she says, I only mention her letters, as they are written[115] with such good sense and unaffected humility, and contain so many useful observations, that I notice them to pay the worthy writer a tribute of respect.[116] The word respect, reminds of Mrs. Macaulay,[117] a woman undoubtedly of the greatest abilities this country ever produced, and yet this woman has been suffered to die without sufficient respect having been paid to her memory; posterity will be more just, and remember Catharine Macaulay was an example of intellectual acquirements, supposed to be incompatible with the weakness of her sex. In the style of her writing, indeed no sex appears, for it is like the sense it conveys, strong and clear.[118] Her judgment is the profound mature fruit of thinking; she writes with sober energy.[119]

Mary Wollstonecraft was a woman of great energy and a very independent mind; her *Rights of Woman*[120] are replete with fine sentiments, though we do not coincide with her opinion respecting the total independence of the female sex.[121] We must be allowed to say, her theory is unfit for practice, though some of her sentiments and distinctions would do honour to the pen, even of a man. Her distinction between modesty and humility is certainly very ingenious. She says, modesty, sacred offspring of sensibility and reason, true delicacy of mind, may I unblamed presume to investigate thy nature, and trace to its covert the mild charms, that, mellowing each harsh feature of character, renders what would only inspire admiration, lovely.[122]

Milton[123] was not arrogant when his suggestion of judgment suffered that to escape, which proved a prophecy.[124] Nor was General Washington,[125] when he accepted the command of the American forces. The latter had always been characterised a modest man. Had he been merely modest, he would have probably shrunk back irresolute; and afraid to trust himself with the direction of an enterprize on which so much depended. A modest man is steady, a humble man is timid, a vain man is presumptuous; this is the observation many characters have led me to form. Jesus Christ himself was modest, Moses was humble, Peter was vain.[126] — Vol. II. p. 314.[127]

These questions are put to the higher class of ladies, who have been weak enough to consult old gypsies[128] for the knowledge of future events. Do you believe that there is but one God, and that he is powerful, just, and good? Do you believe that all things were created by him, and that all things are dependent on him? Do you rely on his wisdom, so conspicuous in his works, and in your own frame; and are you convinced, that he has ordered all things, that do not come under the cognizance of your senses, in the same perfect harmony, to fulfil his designs? Do you acknowledge that the power of looking into futurity and seeing things that are not as if they were, is an attribute of the Creator? And should he see fit, by any impression on the mind of his creatures, to impart any event hid in the shades of time, to whom would he reveal the secret by immediate inspiration? The opinion of ages will answer this question — to reverend old men, distinguished for eminent piety.[129]

Impressed by their solemn, devotional parade, a Greek or Roman lady might be excusable to inquire of the oracle, when she was anxious to pry into futurity. — Wollstonecraft's *Vindication*.[130]

In this enlightened age, it seems almost impossible that any one, either in Europe or America, can be so infatuated as to encourage such a class of artful vagrants, who pretend to reveal future events. Be not deceived by their juggling tricks, but put your trust in the All-wise Disposer of the affairs of human life, and know that it is not in man that walketh to direct his steps, neither is it wise or prudent for any person to pry into the hidden mysteries of futurity, but trust in Providence, that what we know not in this state, shall be revealed to us in another.

There are few females at the present day, that would wish to claim the Otaheite's strength, as represented by Capt. Wallis.[131] He says that Obereah, queen of Otaheite, lifted him over a marsh with as much ease, as he could a little child.[132]

For strength of mind, and real virtue and dignity, we must now introduce queen Isabella, whose influence in the court of Spain determined them to support Columbus, in his voyage to America. Had it not been for her energy, the plan must have been frustrated, and perhaps the continent not discovered till this present time. She offered to pawn her jewels to defray the expenses, rather than the voyage should fail. The court were so impressed with the magnanimity of her conduct, that they resolved to support the cause without the aid of her jewels.

It certainly is not beneath the dignity of the female character, to aid, assist or advise, when any thing of importance labours, either in church or state. They have a right to even pawn their jewels, or any other ornament, for the general good of the community.

———

CHAP. IV.

*The female character and writings are equal in
the present day to any former period; and some
miscellaneous sentiments respecting the sex.*

MADAM DE STAËL,[133] for strength of mind, true magnanimity, patriotism and independence, as well as her literary talents and acquirements, shines unequalled. Her late work of *The Influence of Literature upon Society*,[134] would do honour to the able pen of a man. She can have no rival.

For poetic fancy and genius few have ever excelled Lucy Aikin.[135] Her *Epistles on Women*, and other poems, do honour to her pen.[136] We give a further specimen of the general spirit of the author:

"Does history speak; drink in her loftiest tone
And make Cornelia's virtues all thy own.
Thus self endow'd, thus arm'd for every state,
Improve, excel, surmount, subdue your fate;
So shall enlighten'd man at length efface,   5
That slavish stigma, sear'd on half the race;
His rude forefather's shame, and pleas'd confess,

Tis yours to elevate, tis yours to bless.
Your interest, one with his, your hope the same,
Fair peace on earth, in death undying fame,   10
And bliss in words, beyond the species general aim,
Rise shall he say, O woman, rise, be free,
My life's associate, now partake with me.
Rouse thy keen energies, expand thy soul,
And see and feel, and comprehend the whole.   15
My deepest thoughts intelligent divide;
When right confirm me, and when erring guide;
Soothe all my cares, in all my virtues blend,
And be my sister, be at length my friend."

EPIST[LE] ON WOMEN.[137]

Many other authors could be produced who have done honour to the female pen and character in their writings.

We must now say of the amiable Miss H. More, "many daughters have done virtuously, but thou hast excelled them all."[138] Her works from the smallest grade to the most important, are all calculated to improve the mind, and mend the heart.

AMERICAN CHARACTER NOTICED.

America, though as yet but young in the arts and sciences, will not long remain in the background, as she can now claim the birth-right of many respectable female writers, both in prose and verse.[139]

The lovely Morton[140] may vie with many in Europe for her sublime and poetic fancy. She, with many other respectable writers, who have not been sufficiently appreciated, still shine with the lustre of the aurora borealis in the northern hemisphere.

Among the most distinguished historians are seen a War-ren,[141] and an Adams,[142] who have done honour to themselves, their country and sex, as faithful compilers of history. Mrs. Warren, in her *History of the American Revolution* (vol. I. page iv) observes, There are appropriate duties assigned to each sex, and surely it is the peculiar province of masculine strength, not only to repulse the bold invader of his country's rights, but in the nervous style of manly eloquence, describe the blood stained field, and relate the story of slaughtered armies.[143]

In vol. II. page 30, she mentions Mrs. Ackland, who was a British officer's lady, as a pattern of female heroism and con-jugal affection. She came with her husband to America, and shared with him all the hardships of the camp life; he was badly wounded and taken prisoner by the Americans; she knew his situation, and left him not a moment, but joins herself a prisoner, and by her fortitude supported him, as she lost not her resolution or usual spirits. The American commander, pleased with her firmness, gave orders that she should have attention paid to her rank, character, and sex.[144]

There might now be recorded a number of American la-dies, who left domestic peace and retirement, to share with the partners of their affections, all the trials and fatigue of a camp life; suffice it to notice two in particular, Mrs. Wash-ington, and Mrs. Jackson, who with six little boys, left her rural retreat to accompany the Colonel to the field of battle. She partook with him in the fatigues and inconveniences of the camp life; he was soon commissioned as a general officer: Under her own guardian eye she had these sons trained and disciplined, till they were efficient to become respectable of-ficers, which they all were in the American army.[145]

Mrs. Washington shone a bright example of female excel-lence; she followed the foot paths of her beloved hero, by her firmness and Christian fortitude; with affection she soothed every care of his long war-worn life. She has left a bright example, of every virtue that adorns the Christian or female character. Mrs. Warren says, Having personally known her I can say, her whole deportment was blended with such a sweetness of manners, that she not only engaged the affection of her intimates, but of all who had the felicity of knowing her, and even strangers were captivated with her mild and affectionate address. To every child of sorrow and affliction, she lent a listening ear, and often extended the hand of meek charity, to alleviate the cruel anguish of poverty. She shone as the patriotic wife, the meek Christian, and the truly upright in heart. She was like her Fabius, modest, but not timid. She may with propriety be esteemed a model of female perfection, and highly worthy the imitation of the American fair.[146] May her memory, with her virtues, be engraven on the tablet of every female's heart. She has erected a temple of virtue and fame, for the female standard.

By the mutual virtue, energy, and fortitude of the sexes, the freedom and independence of the United States were attained and secured. The same virtue, energy, and fortitude, must be called into continual exercise, as long as we continue a free, federal, independent nation. The culture and improvement of the female understanding will strengthen the mental faculties, and give vigour to their councils, which will give a weight to any argument used for their mutual defence and safety. No nation nor republic ever fell a prey to despotism, till by indolence and dissipation, it neglected the arts and sciences, and the love of literature. They then became effeminate and degraded; and by them the female character was degraded. As long as the German women were free and honoured by the men, it acted as a stimulus to their ambition. On the value and integrity of both sexes their success and independence very much depended.[147]

If we take a retrospect of the world, from the creation, it will be found, that in every age where ignorance prevailed most, women were most degraded. Before the Christian era, and through the dark ages, very little light was thrown upon their characters. They were supposed to have the command of Pandora's iron box, which contained all the accumulated evils incident to human nature. Some authors say, from the circumstance attending this box, at that period, that age was called the iron age, and has been known by that name ever since.[148]

There are some excellent sentiments respecting women in a small treatise, entitled, *The Friend of Women*, by Villemert in French, translated by Morrice.[149] He says, every one speaks of women according to the disposition of his heart; and the most vicious men are most disposed to paint them in the most odious colours. He says, whatever we meet with in the different opinions of men with regard to women, the lively interest they regard them with, is always the principal.

Every thing which this lovely half of the human race does, has a right to interest us;[150] we are born the friends of women, and not their rivals, still less their tyrants.[151] Let women then, who lead in our first circles, condescend to cultivate their minds, and encourage useful reading; their merit will cause a swarm of thoughtless beaux to disappear from their presence, and men of more merit will form a circle about them, more worthy the name of good company; in this new circle they will join on the score of friendship, without losing any thing in point of cheerfulness; merit is not naturally gloomy, on the contrary, there is generally found among polite people, who are well bred, a mild serenity far preferable to bursts of stupid and ignorant merriment.[152] Happily for us, the day is past that condemned women, as well as the nobility, to rustic ignorance, though there [have] always been some women found, who dared to think, and speak reasonably. We have in the present day, many who do not blush to be better informed than many of our court gentry, or petit-maitres are.

But of all studies most necessary and most natural to women is the study of men; as their government must be that of persuasion, it is necessary for them to know the main springs by which men are actuated.[153] If any thing can add to the pleasure derived from a select society, it is the charms of friendship. The injustice they have done women by excluding them [from] the privilege of being friends, they cannot account for on any principle, as women are born with more sensibility than men, and are as capable of being friends.

I shall not enlarge on the advantage of friendship, which may be called a double life, as each lives in his friend.[154] I shall give you Pliny's receipt for making friendship. From Pliny's *Natural History*[155] we find this curious receipt, for making a Roman friendship.

The principle ingredients were, union of hearts, a flower that grew in several parts of the empire, sincerity, frankness, disinterestedness, pity and tenderness, of each an equal quantity; these made up together with a rich oil, which they called perpetual good wishes, and serenity of temper, and the whole was strongly perfumed with the desire of pleasing, which gave it a most grateful smell, and was a sure restorative against vapours of every kind. The cordial thus prepared was of so durable a nature, that length of time could not waste it. What is more remarkable, says our author, it increases in value the longer it is kept.[156]

That women are capable of friendship there can be no doubt.

There is no deficiency in the female mind, either as to talent or disposition.[157] Women are more sensible than men to all moral distinction: They do not indeed class the virtues in the same order, but they give the highest importance to the comprehensive virtue of temperance.[158] But it is Christianity, undoubtedly, which has seated woman on her true throne. Bound to the same duties, and candidates for the same happiness,[159] as soon as a woman wishes to raise herself above all the trifling objects that debase her, her mind will find itself capable of the same strength as that of men. Mind has no sex, and women cannot be made too frequently to recollect this truth, to preserve them from all those frivolities in which they place too much happiness. Oh, that women would but keep their rights, and improve them to their and our advantage.[160] For women have not degenerated; there are many among us at this time, whose success has made them sufficiently known, without my naming them; and who comparatively with us, have reaped the golden harvest in the fertile field of history and philosophy.[161] Their powers and intellects are equal with the men, but their mode of education often checks their progress in learning. — *So says Villemert.*[162]

We must join with him in thinking their powers of mind are very equal. Still it might be thought an unequal right, to profess or claim any knowledge of the Masonic art; for it seems really man's prerogative to bear the hod, or mould the mortar.

But females may erect a temple of fame, and support it by virtue, wisdom, strength, and beauty, and perfect rectitude. Let then the mysteries of the craft remain profoundly secret to the female ken, till time shall unfold the hidden mysteries of all ancient knowledge and science. Then may the master mason display his skill and talent in architecture, and lay the corner stone in rectitude and justice, and by his skill draw the parallel line correct, that shall encompass the views of the sexes to their mutual satisfaction and happiness. It cannot be expected the views of females will exactly correspond with the men, respecting the Masonic art, as they are debarred the investigation of its principles in some measure.[163] Yet in the present day, there ought to be that harmony and mutual confidence, respecting the system, as shall effectually eradicate any old prejudices respecting the powers of females being unequal to comprehend the incomprehensible mysteries of the Masonic art. Let females then retire within the veil, and in the Sanctum Sanctorum, study the beauty of holiness, and endeavour to follow the example of their kind and master, Solomon, by praying for an understanding heart, and seeking that wisdom which is from above, and can direct our moral and religious course, through life.

CHAP. V.

From observation on characters sacred and profane may be drawn a theory, or plan of rights and duties as agreeable to scripture, reason and common sense.

AGREEABLY to scripture, the corner stone for permanent happiness must be laid in vital piety, or heart religion, reduced to practice. As much of the happiness of nations depends on the domestic economy of individuals, oftentimes the trials and perplexities of families arise from the trifling way some women spend their time, and gratify their eyes and ears only, instead of improving their mental faculties. It may be said the same of some men. There are triflers of both sexes, who do not consider time is a jewel that every one bids largely for, when they want it, and often spend it very foolishly when they have it. They are indeed to be pitied, who spend themselves and misspend their time in doing nothing. For the most part ceremonious visits are an intolerable consumption of time, unless regulated with more than common prudence. They are often spent in vain and frivolous conversation, or a pack of cards must fill up the vacancy of time; whereas, if the mental faculties were cultivated, the mind would be enriched, and capable of communicating mutual information and pleasure, of the most rational kind, from sex to sex. Let those who move in the first circles shew the sacred right they have to set an example of purity or manners, mutual harmony of sentiments and reciprocal union of soul. There can be no doubt but the same harmony, and good order will extend itself throughout all classes of society, as the force of example has much greater effect than precept. Nothing can contribute more to the happiness of mankind than a well regulated community, which must commence in personal agreement and mutual compact, founded on love and friendship; for love is the life and soul of every relative duty— the powerful enlivening principle, which alone can inspire us with vigour and activity in the execution of it.

Without love, even diligence is ungrateful, and submission itself has the air of disobedience. Mutual trust and confidence are the great bonds of society, without which it cannot possibly subsist.[164] Mutual love must be founded on the basis of mutual friendship, without which life will have but few charms. The only things which can render friendship sure and lasting, are virtue, purity of manners, and perfect integrity of heart. With an elevated soul, it is highly proper that we should distinguish the friend from the companion. A conformity of taste for pleasure, and for any thing besides virtue, may constitute a club, but cannot make a society of friends.[165] We must commence life with a religious determination, that "as for me and my house, we will serve the Lord";[166] and by a mutual agreement and sympathy, cemented by friendship, secure the right of mutual affection, on which connubial happiness very much depends.

The surest foundation to secure the female's right, must be in family government, as without that, women can have no established right. This must be the touchstone of the matrimonial faith; and on this depends very much the safety and happiness of a free republic. Family government should, in some measure, resemble a well regulated garrison; there should be sentinels continually on the watch-tower, and general orders should be given for the day, and these should be attended with the morning and evening orisons, that should ascend like holy incense, with gratitude of soul, for the divine care and protection. Women have a right to join in the family prayer and praise. Family worship must be mutual, as any jar or animosity will disorder the whole garrison, and a mutiny may ensue and throw the whole into confusion, and thus frustrate the cause of religion and virtue, and the demon of discord may enter, with all the accumulated miseries of Pandora's box, and perhaps storm and carry the garrison. For want of mutual skill and judgment to defend the fortress, there must be a fixed principle in the mind, that no real happiness can be attained, but in a religious course of life, and that will give a calm serenity, and peace of mind, that will afford us real satisfaction in every situation of life. We must believe there is no situation so permanent but it may have some alloy; and there is no one so happy, as might warrant our changing with them at all hazards; for what would make one person apparently happy, might not suit another. Our ideas are so very different, that what would consummate one person's happiness, would prove to another complete misery.

I must think the wise Author of our nature has distributed human happiness much more equally than the generality of mankind will allow: therefore they must determine in their own minds what sort of happiness they are in pursuit of, and what use they intend to make of it, when their desires are obtained. It is to be feared, we may say, without pretending to much superiour sagacity, that few people know themselves. The only sure resource of real happiness, is to obtain peace of mind, arising from a pure conscience, with principles founded on real vital religion. The Christian hope has always sustained the Christian women, and reconciled them to their many privations, which they always sustained with Christian fortitude. Many instances might be produced of both sexes, who have stemmed the torrent of human misery in support of Christian principles. In support of the rights of women, the only wish is to analyze, harmonize and equalize the sexual rights, as far as the human organization will admit.

There can be no doubt but there is as much difference in the powers of each individual of the male sex, as there is of the female;[167] and if they received the same mode of education, their improvement would be fully equal. All mankind are not born to be heroes or heroines. The constitution and habit of body has a very great effect on the mind of either sex, allowing for the moral and physical distinction. A morbid, or bilious habit of body,[168] will have pretty much the same effect on the constitution. Those, who are much afflicted with a bilious complaint, are often of a gloomy turn of mind, and view the dark side of every event that happens in the course of divine providence: On the contrary, those who are more free from such complaints, are generally more vigorous and animated, and for the most part cheerful, and willing to make the best of even a bad bargain.

From the gloomy habits of the ancient monks, may be traced all the austerities of the monastic life; when disappointed in life, many poor females have immured themselves in the solitary cell of a convent.[169] But this is not the pure vital religion of the heart, which works by love, and is pure and peaceable; which produces good fruits and is replete with good works. A gloomy religion generally originates in the gall of bitterness, and is seated in an affection of the liver; real religion expands the heart with every sentiment of affection for our fellow-creatures. This is the religion our blessed Saviour taught, and exemplified in his own life. This religion is not confined to any particular party or sect. It is extended to all who will accept the offered blessing. There will be no distinction of sex. There will be no distinction of climate or religion, in another and better world. As all mankind do not look alike, neither can they think or act, exactly the same. Still in essential points all may unite. Women have an undoubted right, agreeable to scripture, to think, reason and determine on all points relating to religious principles; that by a union of sentiments, they may lay the foundation for mutual peace, and assist each other in the Christian warfare to eternal bliss and happiness. This is the Christian plan, and real right of woman.

CHAP. VI.

Reason will dictate that a regular Christian course of life will have a tendency to promote future happiness, and is but a reasonable service.

REASON surely must dictate to common sense, that women have a right to join in every reasonable service, for the mutual security and happiness of the female compact. As the care of children naturally devolves on the women, and is one of the important duties annexed to the female character, this relative duty may afford forcible arguments in favour of female education. To strengthen their understanding, and fit them, if necessary, to obtain their own living, only let it be properly considered. How much more respectable is the woman, who earns her own living, than the most accomplished beauty, who depends on her friends for support? Heaven has bestowed on all its rational creatures the faculty or power of reasoning; the reflecting mind will reason on the nature of men and things; females have a right to study the ways of man, and the dispensation of divine providence, in its dealings towards the children of men, agreeable to the dictates of reason. Men will act or forbear; many of the evils of this life might be prevented was reason always at the helm. To guide the fractured bark through the stormy sea of human life, reason is undoubtedly a good director; but without the divine guide of religion to pilot our frail bark, the earthly vessel may founder for want of proper ballast. It is religion alone that can direct and guide us safe to the haven of bliss and perfect happiness.

There must be a reasonable allowance made for the moral and physical distinction there is in nature, as well as constitution and habit of body; as also different climate. It is plain a very warm climate has a great effect on the human constitution, and has a tendency to produce a general debility of the whole animal system, which often degenerates into a complete lassitude of body and mind, which prevents any mental improvement.

Let these very same persons remove into a colder climate,

they will soon recover strength, and find themselves renovated, animated, and able to engage in making further mental improvement. So nearly are the body and soul allied, that when the whole head is sick, the whole heart is faint.

So nearly are the soul and body connected, that it requires a constant supply of rational Christian philosophy to balance the scale, and poise a proper equilibrium. The powers of the human mind have often been weakened, by a continual pain of the body, and vice versa, the body has often been greatly emaciated and even crumbled to dust, from some secret affliction of the soul, concealed in the human heart. From the preceding suggestions may be seen the many advantages that may accrue from having a rational companion; not only a help meet, but a woman capable of reasoning and giving advice for mutual happiness. This is woman's reasonable right.

As there is a sympathy between the human frame and soul, there is also a natural, or mutual sympathy of the sexes. There is a natural affection, implanted in the human breast, by the wise Author of our nature, which gives the sexes equal right to partake with each other, in the cares and trials, as well as the pleasures of this life. There cannot be a doubt that many of the serious squabbles in the matrimonial life might be prevented, by the woman's showing her right, and by giving up the point contended for in a reasonable manner; but never assent merely to please a tyrant, for that betrays a servile mind; nor ever contradict merely to vex, for that shows an ill temper, and bad breeding.[170] There should be not only love, but that mutual friendship and confidence in each other's fidelity, that nothing ought to be concealed from each other but the secrets of another friend.

The necessary advantages of friendship are mutual confidence and benevolence; the purse and the heart ought to be open for the use of a bosom friend. There can be no hazard in trusting a well chosen friend with your secrets, or your strong box;[171] for where true friendship subsists, their mutual interest is one and the same; and as it is the lot of mankind to be happy or unhappy by turns, and divine wisdom sees fit it should be so for our mutual advantage, that by the mediation of this mixture we have the comfort to support us in affliction, and the apprehension of change to keep a check on us in the height of our grandeur; so by this vicissitude of good and evil we are kept steady in our philosophy and religion; as one puts us in mind of God's omnipotence and justice, the other of his goodness and mercy; the one tells us there is no trusting to our own strength, the other preaches faith and resignation in the government of divine providence.

It is woman's reasonable right to partake with man in all the vicissitudes and changes of life, and faithfully support their mutual interest, as by the reciprocal exchange of kind attentions they will secure that love and affection, which will eventually constitute the permanent love of our neighbour as ourselves, agreeably to the golden rule of equity, which implies that love, which will produce the affection of benevolent and generous sympathy, that shall interest the heart in the misfortunes of our fellow-creatures.

It must be allowed that these fine feelings are most particular traits in the female character; every habit of their lives inclines them to a generous sympathy for others' woes. Very few women have ever been wanting in commiseration for the patient sufferer; and there is reason to believe, very few men of any sensibility have ever been unwilling to aid and assist them in their benevolent intentions. The mutual and reasonable right of the sexes may be handsomely displayed, by the males supplying the means to help the needy; and the females, who were the first susceptible of the fine feelings of benevolence for the sufferer, shall have the right and privilege to distribute relief and comfort to the destitute and afflicted.

From the same principle of benevolence, women may reasonably become equal with men in patriotism and disinterested love of country, which embraces all its citizens, and produces that universal benevolence and philanthropy, which extends its influence to all nations. This idea leads us to an important subject, that is, the moral and political, which Russell says, consists in regulating ourselves and others. He says, to compare the advantages and disadvantages of the sexes, with regard to this object, it would be necessary to observe the same talent in society, and as applied to government, the women in society being continually upon the look-out. From the motive of curiosity and policy they must have perfect knowledge of men; they must be able to disentangle all the folds of self-love, and discover all their secret weaknesses; the false modesty, and the false grandeur; what man is, and what he should be. They must know and distinguish character. They must know the diffidence which proceeds from character or vice; from misfortune or from the mind; in short, they must know all their sentiments and all their shades. As women set a high value on opinion, they must reflect much on what will produce it: They must know how far one can direct without appearing to be interested, and how far one may presume upon that art after it is known; in what estimation they are held by those with whom they live, and to what degree it is necessary to serve them, that they may govern them, in all cases of business. Women know the great affairs which are produced by little causes; they know how to captivate by praises those who deserve them, and sometimes raise a blush by bestowing them where they are not due.

These delicate sciences are the leading strings by which women conduct the men; men have less time for observation and can hardly be possessed of such a crowd of little notices, and those polite attentions, which are every moment necessary in the commerce of life. Therefore men's calculations in society must be more slow and less sure than women's, as applied to government.[172] It seems, in consequence of the character of women, that their religion must be more tender, and the men's more sincere, as one consists more in practice, the other more in principle. The women are more liable to superstition; and the men are liable to fanaticism. The domestic virtues are intimately connected with religion, and doubtless common to both sexes; but the advantage seems still to be in favour of women; at least they have more need of virtue, which they have more call to practice.[173] He says, these are some of the subjects, which should be considered in settling the dispute respecting the superiority or equality of the sexes. To treat the subject properly, it would be necessary to be at the same time a philosopher, a physician, an anatomist; and to be equally rational and sentimental, and above all these singular attainments, we must be perfectly disinterested.[174] — Russell's *History of Women*.[175]

The writer of this little work cannot pretend to attain to the stated qualification here mentioned, but hopes to be so singular and disinterested, as to convince the reader she has the mutual interests of the sexes very much at heart, in drawing the line of equality as impartially as the nature of the subject will admit, after consulting the most approved authors who have written on the subject.

As a philosopher we would wish to reason on the nature of men and things, the nature, causes, and effects of all moral distinction of every created being; as a physician would consult, advise, prescribe and administer rational, quiet, and pacific medicine, as best for all rational beings; and as an anatomist would dissect the brain, and analyze every fiber of the human heart, to harmonize the sexual right, to the mutual satisfaction of the sexes. Certainly scripture and reason appear to be on the side of the just equality of the sexes.

This orthodox doctrine can be proved by plain philosophical reasoning on the nature of men, and may be demonstrated as clearly as any problem in Euclid.[176]

CHAP. VII.

Treats of the beauty and good order that may accrue to society, by the united fidelity of the sexes in performing their appropriate duties.

AS[177] it appears from scripture and reason there is a just, and right equality of the sexes, common sense must teach the propriety of a union of the sexes in sentiments and opinions respecting the rights of women. Very little has been written on the subject in America; and perhaps it has not been necessary in a land where the rights of women have never appeared a bone of much contention. It may naturally be supposed, the ideas of a free[,] independent people, will be more liberal and expanded respecting the sexual rights.

Under this impression, the writer has ventured to pen this small system or statement of the mutual rights and appropriate duties of the sexes with the most philanthropic wish, that the parties concerned may mutually agree to support the real orthodox principle of a mutual dependence on each other, which will promote peace, harmony and happiness; for without harmony and affection subsist between the sexes, society must soon become a mere nuisance to itself.

Our venerable ancestors, soon after they came to this country, framed laws and regulations for the general utility, and made ample provision for the happiness of every class of the citizens, including equal rights for the female sex. They soon as possible instituted schools, churches, and colleges, as the best mode of promoting the interest of their country; and females partook of the advantage of education, and some made a wise improvement of it.

Among some of the early instructors of writing may be found Mrs. Sarah Knight,[178] in the year 1706. She was famous in her day for teaching to write. Most of the letters on business, and notes of hand, and letters on friendship were written by her. She was a smart, witty, sensible woman, and had considerable influence at that period.

The first characters for learning and knowledge at that time certainly had an exalted opinion of the female character and abilities, and fully appreciated their rights and judgment, as they were often consulted on important subjects both in church and state. From that time they have often been consulted on important occasions.

In the important struggle for the independence of the American States, some females embarked in the cause of freedom, both by their writings and advice; and ever since the establishment of independence, it has been an invariable fixed principle in the female character to pray for the peace of our American Israel.[179] And they must have an equal right to enjoy, with mutual satisfaction, all the blessings, [that] tranquility, freedom, and peace can bestow on a free and happy people.

It is almost impossible that those, who reside under a despotic or monarchical government, can imbibe as liberal sentiments as those, who reside under the more temperate zone of a free, federal,[180] republican government, which admits of free discussion of sentiments among all classes of the citizens. Such a government requires more sense and judgment to preserve it from disorder and disunion; therefore the union and right understanding of the sexes will have a tendency to strengthen, confirm and support such a government, and common sense must allow women the right of mutual judgment, and joining with the other sex in every prudent measure for their mutual defence and safety.

It may be seen by the fatal fall of Greece and Rome how much depends on public faith and confidence in the government, which must commence in the private faith and confidence of individuals.

From the universal benevolence, conspicuous in every section of the union, there is reason to anticipate our future greatness and respectability. The various institutions, for benevolent and charitable purposes, have a tendency to promote the kind affections, and make man mild and sociable to man; women shine preeminent in most of them, and have an equal right to establish schools of industry and economy, which must have a happy effect on the community. There is nothing can make better subjects for a republican government, than to give children an early education, and train them in habits of prudence and industry. Every day produces some proofs how much we are the creatures of habit; the juvenile mind requires continual occupation, for the vivacity of youth is such, that if not constantly employed in some valuable pursuit, there is danger of their resorting to some evil propensity, for want of regular occupation; for such is the natural depravity of the human heart.[181] As women generally have the forming of the infant mind, it is necessary their own minds should be cultivated, that they may be capable of enlarging the mind of their pupils; as the first seeds implanted in their breast, if virtuous and noble, will prepare them for some important station in life. Children's constitution and capacities differ so very much, that it requires the affection, tenderness and care of a prudent woman to mould and model the tender olive-branch, as there is hardly a human being, though of very inferiour abilities, but will discover a genius for some particular employment, and that ought to be cultivated, and the bent of their genius should be always consistent; for of those, who set out wrong in life, there are few who ever clear the rocks and ledges, and very seldom arrive at plain sailing; the whole voyage of life will prove rough and boisterous, if it is not commenced right. This may often be seen in the common course of human life, if the compass of genius is not regulated by learning, prudence, discretion and religion.

A religious, steady, rational course of living will be found the safest pilot[182] to the haven of rest and perfect happiness. It is faith in the divine promises that can alone give peace of mind and great joy in believing. It is that which only can give that calm serenity of mind, which will support us under all the vicissitudes of this transitory state. There is no path can be pursued more likely to promote this calmness and serenity of mind, than to appropriate a certain space of our time every day for meditation; as every rational being, who reflects at all, must be sensible there is a wise governing providence that superintends the affairs of men, kingdoms, nations and states. It is most undoubtedly the duty of every individual to commit every event of their lives to his care and disposal, for he who can take into view and comprehend the whole plan of creation, must know what is best for his dependent creatures.

Therefore unerring wisdom can do no wrong. We may safely

trust in his protecting care, and when called to affliction in the course of divine providence, if we receive the chastisement with the spirit of meekness, and bear it with Christian fortitude, it may prove the brightest epoch in human life.

The minds of the sexes are equally capable of making a wise improvement of the various dispensations of divine providence; they all have equal need, and equal right, to seek the divine favour, aid, protection and consolation; and without the support, hope, trust and confidence in the promises of divine grace, they must both be equally unhappy. How vain and inconsistent are those, who flee from trouble to drown sorrow in dissipation! Oh foolish and inconsiderate mortals, why will you involve yourselves in greater troubles and ten-fold misery, by adding to your sorrow the bitter sting of perhaps a too late death-bed repentance!

But let us turn the scene, and view the calm[,] sedate Christian, who, through the whole passage of life, is resigned to the divine direction and guidance, in the firm faith, that all the dispensations of providence are perfectly consistent with divine rectitude, and goodness. Under such impressions, the real Christian will most fervently say, not my will, but thine be done, heavenly Father.[183]

Scripture, reason and common sense dictate the divine right is in women, to promote those fine sympathetic affections that will have a tendency to assist, harmonize and sweeten a religious course of life. The power of friendship can soothe the cares of this transitory state, and meliorate the greatest miseries of human woe. Love is the sacred bond of mutual friendship, and promotes a reciprocal intercourse of kind affection.

Good humour, Dr. Johnson[184] says, may be defined a habit of being pleased; a constant and perennial softness of manner, easiness of approach, and serenity of disposition, like that which every man perceives in himself, when the first transports of new felicity have subsided, and his thoughts are only kept in motion by a slow succession of soft impulses. Good humour is a state between gayety and unconcern, the act or emanation of mind at leisure to regard the gratification of another.[185]

It has been justly observed that discord generally operates in little things. It is inflamed to its utmost vehemence by contrariety of talk oftener than of principle; and might therefore commonly be avoided by innocent conformity, which, if it was not at first the motive, ought always to be the consequence, of indissoluble union.

The great remedy which heaven has put in our hands is patience; by which, though we cannot lessen the torments of the body, we can in a great measure, preserve the peace of the mind, and shall suffer only the natural and genuine force of an evil, without heightening its acrimony or prolonging its effects. When patience has performed its perfect work, it is the right of every female to have ready the mantle of meek charity, to gently cover the faults of her domestic circle.

CHAP. VIII.

*Let the mantle of charity make allowance for,
and shield every human imperfection.*

THE hand of meek charity should be extended to every object of our affections. It is the soft hand of an affectionate female that can best soothe the pillow of dissolving nature, and meliorate the passage to the grave, by constant expressions of that love and mutual friendship, which never shall be dissolved.

Although the king of terrors shall arrest this earthly frame, yet the friendly spirit, still hovering over the pensive brow, shall kindly whisper in the ear, thy friend and lover is not dead, but only sleepeth. The spirit must ascend to the realms of bliss, where we shall meet again, and be renovated and prepared to join the sacred lodge,[186] where the refined soul shall partake of love, friendship and uninterrupted happiness, never to suffer change, or any mixture or alloy.

As there is no spiritual distinction of sexes, the twin[187] soul shall there join the general choir of all those who are equally redeemed by the precious blood of Jesus Christ, the Lamb of God. Such will be the advantage of forming sacred love and friendship here, that it shall be the foretaste of our future bliss, and temporal death will not dissolve the sacred tie, and there the sexual rights will be mutual; our God is no respecter of persons or sexes.[188]

From what has been here offered on behalf of female rights, it appears plainly, virtue, harmony, love and friendship, religiously improved, will be the surest passport to the realms of bliss and happiness. And may the voice of philanthropy unite to embrace in the arms of her affection the whole human race, which the sexes have equal right to extend to every individual person throughout the whole order of society.

It is hoped that this treatise or small system of the sexual rights will meet the mutual approbation of the sexes. Allow the author to say, it was written with the best intention; of communicating some pleasure with instruction to the candid reader. Let the philanthropic peruser then, gently draw the mantle of charity over all its imperfections.

APPENDIX.

TO shew real impartiality, it is but just to give some account of illustrious men, as a sequel to illustrious women, as our wish is the mutual happiness of the sexes, for the well being and good order of society.

In every age of the world, from creation to the present day, there has been recorded many illustrious characters, both in sacred and profane history. Moses was first legislator and lawgiver, and he was a wise one, as he received his laws from Jehovah himself. His mother, it seems, shewed[189] great prudence in concealing him in the ark of bulrushes, and she was blessed of heaven for her faith in the preserving care of a gracious providence, and he was preserved and made an instrument in the divine hands to lead his people Israel through all the Egyptian bondage, and conduct them safely through the Red Sea, as on dry land. We find many great and illustrious characters among the kings and prophets of ancient times. Job is recorded for patience, Solomon for wisdom, and he asked that of the Almighty. Isaiah, among the prophets, stands preeminent, as giving the most correct prophecy respecting the Messiah. Isaiah and Daniel, more especially, seem rather to describe the past, as historians, than to anticipate the future as prophets. We know that multitudes of the Jews, who had diligently studied the prophecies from their youth, and acknowledged their divine authority, felt the force of their application to our Lord, and were converted to his religion. And not to appeal to other instances, we know the fifty-third chapter of Isaiah, so circumstantially descriptive of the suffering Messiah, effected the conversion of the Eunuch of Ethiopia mentioned in the acts of the apostles,[190] and contributed greatly to produce a conviction in the mind of the profligate Lord Rochester.[191] This fact is recorded by Bishop Burnet.[192] To him Lord Rochester held open with great freedom the tenor of his opinion and the course of his life, and from him he received such conviction of the reasonableness of moral duty, and truth of Christianity, as produced a total change both in his manners and opinions. The account of those salutary conferences is given by Burnet in a book, entitled, Some passages in the life and death of John, Earl of Rochester.[193] The critic ought to read it for its eloquence, the philosopher for its argument, and the saint for its piety. — Johnson's *Life of Rochester*.[194]

Christians can appeal to an independent train of witnesses, to Jewish and profane writers, for circumstantial accounts of the fulfilment of his and our Lord's predictions. The historian Josephus[195] descended from the family which bore the sacred office of high priest. A distinguished general in the early part of the last Jewish war has given a particular and exact confirmation of every circumstance. With singular care he has avoided to mention the name of Christ, and yet with singular precision he has illustrated his prediction relative to the destruction of Jerusalem. The important service he has thus rendered to Christianity is wholly unintentional. What he relates is drawn from him by the power of irresistible truth, and in a testimony far more unexceptionable than an explicit mention of the name of Christ, and a laboured encomium of his words and actions. Josephus' *History of the Wars of the Jews* is confirmed by Tacitus, Philostrates and Dion Cassius.[196] It is probable they were all of them unacquainted with the works of the Jewish historian, and yet they all corroborate his account, and all unite to illustrate the prophecies of our Lord;[197] and when we contemplate on the character of our Lord and his apostles, we are lost in wonder and admiration at the strength of mind and energy of the apostle Paul, after his conversion. We cannot help exclaiming, surely he must have been inspired with divine grace. But if the infidel will not believe Moses and the prophets, neither will he be persuaded though one come to him from the dead.

A due attention to ancient history might have a good effect on many, who are wavering in mind.[198] Where can we find persons of such profound understandings and inquisitive minds as Bacon, Locke and Newton; where of such sublime genius as Milton; where of such extensive learning, exhausting all the literary treasures of the eastern as well as western literature, as Sir William Jones, who at the close of life recorded his conviction of the truths of divine revelation, and celebrated the excellency of the holy scriptures.[199] To compare the race of modern infidels in point of genius; to compare Voltaire, Hume, Gibbons, Godwin and Paine,[200] with such men as these, were surely idle, and as absurd as to compare the weakness of infancy with the maturity of manhood, or the fluttering of a butterfly with the vigour and soaring of a[n] eagle, or the twinkling of a star with the glory of the sun, illuminating the world with his meridian brightness.[201] — See Kett's *Elements.*[202]

We wish to give an impartial account of illustrious characters that have been conspicuous in different ages of the world, both male and female, as the author's wish is to equalize the mutual rights of the sexes, and to harmonize the whole by the bright examples of the most amiable and virtuous of both sexes, as collected from sacred and profane history.

Pliny is recorded as one of the most finished gentlemen and the politest writer of the age in which he lived; and one of the best husbands in the whole Roman empire.[203] He did

not think it below him to treat his wife as a friend, companion and counselor. He has left us in his letter to Hispulla, his
wife's aunt, one of the most agreeable family pieces I ever met
with; conjugal love is drawn with a delicacy which makes it
appear an ornament as well as a virtue.[204] The following extract is from the letter, and we refer the reader to the Beauties
of History for the whole.

PLINY TO HISPULLA.

As I remember the great affection which was between your
excellent brother, and know you loved his daughter as your
own, so as not only to express the tenderness of the best of
aunts, but even to supply that of the best of fathers, I am sure
it will give you pleasure to hear that she proves worthy of
you, and of yours, and her ancestors;[205] accept, therefore, our
united thanks: mine, that you have bestowed her on me, hers
as a mutual grant of joy and felicity.

The same amiable disposition and conjugal tenderness is
seen in his letters to his wife, when he was at a distance from
her. — See *Beauties of History, 1st vol.*[206]

Cicero[207] was in all respects as good a man as Pliny, and has
written whole books of letters to his wife. They are full of
beautiful simplicity, which is altogether natural, and is the
distinguished character of the best ancient writers. Some of
his letters to his wife were written when he was banished from
his country by a faction that then prevailed at Rome.[208] After
reading them, it gives pleasure to see this great man in his
family, who makes so different a figure in the forum, or sen-
ate of Rome.[209] Every one admires the orator and the consul,
but for my own part I esteem the husband and the father. His

private character, with all the little weaknesses of humanity, is as amiable, as the figure he makes in public is awful and majestic. The writer says it would be ill-nature not to acquaint the English reader that his wife was successful in her solicitations for this great man, and saw her husband return to the honours of which he had been deprived, with all the pomp and acclamation that usually attended the greatest triumph.

From the foregoing example, it appears incontestably evident, that a happy marriage has in it all the pleasures of friendship, and all the enjoyments of sense and reason, and indeed all the sweets of life; and to make it so, nothing more is required than discretion, virtue and good nature.[210] The poet says,

"They know a passion, still more deeply charming,
Than favour'd youth e'er felt, and that is love,
By long experience mellow'd into friendship."[211]

The character of a good husband, may not come amiss after the foregoing account. A good husband is one, who, not wedded by interest but by choice, is constant, as well from inclination as from principle; he treats his wife with delicacy as a woman, with tenderness as a friend. He attributes her follies to her weakness; her imprudence to her inadvertency. He passes them over therefore with good nature, and pardons them with indulgence; all his care and industry are employed for her welfare; all his strength and power are exerted for her support and protection; he is more anxious to preserve his own character and reputation, because hers is blended with it. Lastly, the good husband is pious and religious that he may animate her faith by his practice, and enforce the principles of Christianity by his own example, that, as they join to promote each other's happiness in this world, they may unite to secure eternal joy and felicity in that which is to come.[212]

To equalize, we give the character of a good wife from the same author. The good wife is one, who, ever mindful of the solemn contract which she hath entered into, is strictly, conscientiously virtuous. Constant and faithful to her husband, chaste, pure and unblemished in every thought, word and deed, she is humble, modest from reason and conviction, submissive from choice, and obedient from inclination; what she acquires by love and tenderness, she preserves by prudence and discretion. She makes it her business to serve, and her pleasure to oblige her husband, conscious that every thing that promotes his happiness must in the end contribute to her own; her tenderness relieves his cares, her affection softens his distress, her good humour and complacency lessen and subdue his afflictions. "She openeth her mouth," as Solomon says, "with wisdom, and in her tongue is the law of kindness. She looketh well to the way of her household, and eateth not the bread of idleness; her children rise up and call her blessed, her husband also, and he praiseth her."[213] As a pious and good Christian, she looks up with an eye of gratitude to the great dispenser and disposer of all things, as the husband of the widow, and the father of fatherless, entreating his divine favour and assistance in this, and every other moral duty, well satisfied that if she punctually discharges her several offices in this life, she shall be blessed and rewarded for it in another. "Favour is deceitful, and beauty is vain, but a woman that feareth the Lord she shall be praised."[214]

We here see drawn the character of a good husband and a good wife on a plan worthy of imitation. It may not be amiss to mention some traits of a good father. The good father is ever tender, humane and affectionate to his children; he treats them with lenity and kindness, corrects with prudence, rebukes with temper, and chastises with reluctance. He is prudent that they may be happy; industrious that they may be rich; good and virtuous that they may be respected. He instructs by his life, and teaches by his example.[215] Parents repeat their lives in their offspring, and their concerns for them is [*sic*] so near, that they feel all their sufferings, and taste all their enjoyments, as much as if they regarded their own persons. However strong the fondness of a father for his children, yet they will find more lively marks of tenderness in the bosom of a mother. There are no ties in nature to compare with those that unite an affectionate mother to her children, when they repay her tenderness with obedience and love,[216] which has been seen in some of the most exalted characters in every age of the world. Some of the ancient fathers have owned they loved a mother, and some have written in praise of the sex. Jerome has been noticed.[217]

All Europe have had their great and good men. Calvin, Luther, and Melancthon, were all great in the reformation.[218] Great Britain can boast of her great and good men. A Baxter, Howe, Owen and Burroughs, were great and good.[219] They all rank high in theology. In our own time we call to mind an Erskine, an Ogilvie, with half a score more, too many to mention.[220] Our respected Watts[221] must yet bring up the mighty rear. To equalize the sex allow us to say, he jointly with Mrs. Steele[222] we hear resounding with praises in our churches. As statesmen, politicians, and as heroes, Great Britain has her best and wisest men. Who ever rivaled a Pitt, Burke, or an Erskine; and for literary fame, no period ever exceeded that of Dryden, Pope, Prior, Addison, and Johnson.[223] For purity of style, harmony, blended with taste, chasteness, piety, and sweetness, none ever exceeded Addison; for strength of mind, and profound learning, and critical knowledge, few ever exceeded Johnson. It may be said he was a great man, with many eccentricities. See his life for proof. For law knowledge, they boast of a Coke, Bacon, Hale, and many others, who were great indeed.[224] Their warriors and seamen rank high in the annals of fame.

America has her worthies yet to claim.[225] Columbus,[226] to thee we owe the discovery of this vast region; and to those venerable sires, who sprang from British root, and branched forth into this then howling wilderness,[227] do we owe all our gratitude for their unbounded zeal and perseverance, under all the difficulties they had to combat with. The names of many great and worthy men could be collected. We shall only mention a few of the first worthies, among whom stands a Bradford, Winthrop, Bradstreet, an Allen, with the good old Brewster, and the enterprizing Standish, brave and daring.[228] America can boast of her great and good men throughout the union. New England can glory in her worthies, divines, statesmen and heroes. In theology and piety who ever excelled a Hooker, a Partridge, an Eliot, a Cotton, with the fourfold line of Mathers; a Chauncy too we name, for ancient learning, piety and virtue, all renowned in the annals of America.[229] Of more recent date, for purity of manners, meekness and piety, who can we name to excel our venerable Sewall; Prince stands the faithful chronologer of his country; in the elegant Colman we view the good man and the gentleman; and whoever surpassed the accomplished Coopers, predecessors to our respected friend Dr. Thacher; the harmonious voice of a Stillman yet vibrates on our ears.[230] As the friend, Christian and gentleman he lived and died unrivalled. We might add a Pemberton and a Lathrop to the list,[231] with a whole score of worthy divines, but we wish not to enlarge. We are led to say, our fathers, where are they?

As statesmen, politicians and heroes, we have our boast;

for philosophers our Franklin might be styled a Newton; for literary and law knowledge, who can vie with our Paine and Parsons; as historians, we may boast a Belknap and Minot, with many others; as statesmen, we have had an Adams, a Bowdoin, an Ames, and a Dexter.[232] Ames and Dexter have been compared by strangers to a Chatham and an Erskine, the pride of England.[233]

The United States can claim a Washington as their father, friend, protector, and saviour of his country. Here we might name a host of heroes, but he was indeed an host himself.[234] Gratitude demands the names of Warren, Lincoln, Hamilton and Knox, with many more whom we revere, but it will enlarge our work too much to name.[235] Should we name the catalogue of old Harvard, and the other Universities, it would swell our work to the frightful size of a huge folio; which, as a late elegant critic observes, few men dare combat with, though a recent female writer has had the hardihood to wade through folio after folio from Josephus, Basnage, and Turkish history, even to the *Magnalia of America*,[236] and all to compile *The History of the Jews*, for the benefit of those who dare not, or cannot wade through a folio.[237] In this day of duodecimos,[238] the writers have reason to acknowledge with gratitude, that they have their ancient learning to assist them in their abridgements, and from them we can collect sentiments worthy to be handed down to the latest posterity.

MISCELLANEOUS SENTIMENTS, MORAL AND RELIGIOUS, FROM VARIOUS AUTHORS.

Give me, says Quintilian,[239] among his excellent rules for instructing youth, a child that is sensible of praise and touched with glory, and that will cry at the shame of being outdone, and I will keep him at his business by emulation; reproof will afflict and honour will encourage him, and I shall not fear to cure him of idleness.[240] None can be eminent without application and genius. To become an able man in any profession three things are necessary, nature, study, and practice.

The Hon. Mr. Boyle[241] was a man of extensive learning, and one of the most exact inquirers into the works of nature that any age has known; and what reflects the greatest honour on himself and upon Christianity is, that while he was an accurate reasoner, he was a firm believer in the Christian religion. — See *Life of Boyle.*[242]

Marcus Aurelius tells us, that he could not relish a happiness that nobody shared in but himself.[243]

When Cato was drawing near the close of life, he declared to his friend, that the greatest comfort of his old age, and that which gave him the highest satisfaction, was the pleasing remembrance of the many benefits and friendly offices he had done to others.[244]

There is more satisfaction in doing good than receiving. To relieve the oppressed is the most glorious act a man is capable of! It is in some measure doing the business of Providence, and is attended with a heavenly pleasure, unknown but to those who are beneficent and liberal. Men of the noblest dispositions think themselves happiest when others share with them in their happiness.[245] We ought to consult the worth of the person whom we have chosen for our liberality. Let a present be ever so considerable, the manner of conferring it is the noblest part.[246]

The uncertainty of our duration ought at once to set bounds to our designs, and add incitements to our industry; and when we find ourselves inclined either to immensity in our schemes, or sluggishness in our endeavours, we may either check or animate ourselves, by recollecting, with the father of physick, that art is long, and life is short. —*Johnson.*[247]

When Lee was once told by a critic that it was very easy to write like a madman, he answered, that it was difficult to write like a madman, but easy enough to write like a fool; and I hope to be excused if in imitation of this great author I presume to remind my kind contributors, that it is much easier not to write like a man than to write like a woman. — See *Rambler*.[248]

Johnson says, as every writer has his use, every writer ought to have his patrons; and since no man, however high he may now stand, can be certain that he shall not be thrown down from his elevation by criticism or caprice, the common interest of learning requires that her sons should cease from intestine hostilities, and instead of sacrificing each other to malice and contempt, endeavour to avert persecution from the meanest of their fraternity.[249]

Seneca has attempted not only to pacify us in misfortune, but almost to allure us to it by representing it as necessary to the pleasures of the mind. He that never was acquainted with adversity, says he, has seen the world but on one side, and is ignorant of half the scenes of nature.[250] It was the wisdom, says Seneca, of ancient times, to consider what is most useful as most illustrious.[251] Johnson says, if this rule be applied to works of genius, scarcely any species of composition deserves more to be cultivated than the epistolary style, since none is of more various or more frequent use through the whole subordination of life.[252] The man whose genius qualifies him for great undertakings, must at least be content to learn from books the present state of human knowledge.[253]

Constancy of mind gives a man reputation, and makes him happy in despite of all misfortunes.[254] There is not on earth a spectacle more worthy the regard of the Creator intent on his works, than a brave man superior to his sufferings. What can be more honourable than to have courage enough to execute the commands of reason and conscience, to maintain the dignity of our nature, and the station assigned us, to be proof against poverty, pain and death. To do this is to be great above title and fortune. This argues the soul of heavenly extraction, and is worthy the offspring of the Deity.[255]

"He lives in fame, who dies in virtue's cause."[256]

From the many illustrious characters and sentiments we have before us, arises this reflection; it must be for the mutual happiness of the sexes to unite in sentiments, and endeavour to follow the precepts and examples of the wise and good of every age, and thus promote the equality and happiness of the sexes, agreeably to scripture, reason and common sense.

To conclude: we shall give our readers a short account of Aurelius and Prudencia,[257] from recent observation in real life.

Aurelius was the son of an eminent clergyman, possessed with a natural, amiable disposition, and strong powers of mind.[258] He soon made progress in his learning; at an early age entered the seat of science, and passed through with great honour, and soon after obtained a handsome settlement. At the age of twenty-five, he formed a connexion in life with the daughter of an opulent merchant. Prudencia was only eighteen when they commenced life in the marriage state.[259] She was a lady of a strong and well improved mind, which had been well cultivated by a mother's prudent mode of education. They commenced life with the same views. They had but one mind and but one heart, vibrating the same cord, and that was philanthropy to all mankind.

Aurelius was a great scholar, a hard student, a Christian philosopher, but the truly polite gentleman. He could unbend himself from the most abstruse studies, and in the most engaging manner enjoy the society of his friends in the circle of domestic life, with the pleasing gayety of the man of gallantry; but he always blended instruction with morality and religion, in his conversation. He was easy of access to every fellow-creature and nation, as he was often heard to say, "he hath made of one blood all the nations of the earth."[260] Being asked by an Irish soldier, in the time of the revolutionary war, if he was a Roman Catholic, he observed to him, he could not say he was a Roman, but he could say he was a Catholic, and wished every order of men well and happy. He was always happy in the bosom of his family. That he might have full scope for his literary pursuits, his prudent and amiable wife took from his mind every domestic care. She was a wife and mother indeed. Such an one as Solomon describes, for she looked well to the ways of her household, and never ate the bread of idleness. Prudencia was rather tall, and possessed all the dignity of ancient nobility; but with the utmost familiarity and kindness, she could accommodate herself to the most menial objects that often surrounded her. In her intercourse with society, she was an agreeable companion. She loved her friends, and would descend to the most menial duty, to assist a poor neighbour. He was often seeking objects of distress, and she was ever ready to aid and assist them. They had several sons and daughters.[261] Their sons were called to fill places of respectability at a distance from home; their daughters continued near them. Though several of them married, they settled near enough to be a blessing to them, in the decline of life. The worthy old gentleman and lady mutually aided and supported each other through all the various changing scenes of this life: they had their mutual trials and comforts, though they appeared to have but one general sentiment prevailing in their hearts; and that was, the interest and happiness of all around them.[262] They lived to communicate happiness to their friends. With a talent to please, and a heart ever open to generous acts, who could be more happy than this amiable and virtuous couple. They were guided by religious principles and practiced its precepts. They passed through life as ornaments to society to quite an honorable[263] old age. Ever resigned to the various dispensations of divine providence, their life on earth might be said to be a foretaste of bliss in heaven. After living nearly fifty years together, Prudencia departed this life.[264] We cannot say she closed her eyes in death, for she gently fell asleep in Jesus. Aurelius supported the trying scene with Christian fortitude and philosophy. He continued a few years after her, and then a short illness terminated his valuable life, when, like a shock of corn fully ripe, he quit[t]ed his clay, and like a triumphant saint, he was heard to articulate this sentence, "Now lettest thou thy servant depart in peace";[265] then he gently closed his eyes to sleep and wake with Jesus, as we believe, to hear that blessed sentence, "Well done thou good and faithful servant, enter thou into the presence of your Lord and Saviour."[266]

The design of giving the account of this virtuous, happy and wise pair, drawn from a known couple in real life, is with the most ardent wish it may have a happy effect on those who are commencing life, and all who peruse the account may determine and say, let me live the life of the righteous, that my end may be like theirs, peace and future bliss, and happiness in another, better, and more permanent world than the present.

> Here ends the mutual rights of all,
> Attend the summons and obey the call;
> Let reason govern, and religion guide,
> For soul and body are most near allied.
> Rise then to virtue, quickly rise,
> To join with saints beyond the skies.[267]

The Midnight Beau

May 2—1819.

DRAMATIS PERSONAE[1]

Characters all high Bucks
   Henry Philanthropus[2]
   Joseph Stripling
   Paulinus Random
   Thomas Ludicrous
   Patrick Oh Glee
   Puffendorf Daft
   Roland Nightramble
   Captain Spoilation
   Major Rantapole

Ladies
   Angelica[3] Bloomly
   Amilia Prudencia, a Matron
   Patty, a Maid

Scene: M. Street, Town B . . . Midnight.

The Midnight Beau
A Farce in 2 Acts

Act 1
Scene 1
A Hotel.

A large Hall. Bucks discovered sitting round a large table smoking. Bottles, glasses and cigars spread on the table. Enter Stripling.

STRIPLING: Well, gentlemen, at your request I come to join this happy circle. Pray, gentlemen, how do you intend to pass your time? I trust we meet here to eat, drink, sing, and be merry.

OH GLEE: Ar'ry and by my faith, dear hony,[4] I will answer you before I speak. For by my soul, dear hony, whilest our great little folks are often dreaming of war, do you see, we will steal a little bit of a quick step, march upon them. Do you see, honies, to kill, murder, and destroy time is the aim of our present meeting. Oh, by St. Patrick, tis fact.

LUDICROUS: Pray, Glee, what murder shall we set about first? Shall we attack cats, rats, or rather rob some old woman's hen roost? What can we this night make our prey? Shall we rove about and make some timid hare the chase? A female chase might suit your taste, and them attack and murder reputation. Is this your aim, ha,'[5] Boy?

[OH] GLEE[6]: No, and by my faith, my hony, you have not[7] hit the mark yet, but by the cigar in your mouth I see you aim to murder one. And do you see, we have met here to eat, drink, smoke, and kick up jack, do you see, honies, that is, to kill, murder, and destroy time. Now, sirs, if our wise government would let us arm our vessels and be off to fight our enemies, do you see, we might shake off the embargo.[8] We shall this night lay on our understanding, for most of us here shall, before we part, shall find an embargo on his heels.

DAFT: Well, Paddy, what need we care about embargo? We have met here to drink till we are happy as kings, or fools. Come, fill another glass. *Drinks*. Here's a health to our own constitution. Come, brave Boys, I intend to buy into the stocks. I think the sinking fund[9] most likely to suit my plan and the plan of all such jolly fellows.

CAPT SPOIL[ATION]: That's right, my Boy: I like your plan for the stocks, for I may catch you in my trap and that is the stocks. I buy, sell, and loan cash and notes. I will take your notes at fifty per cent Discount and soon put them in the sinking fund, just to show you how it is done by the way of modern friendship.

MAJOR RANT[APOLE]: Upon my soul, Spoilation, you are the very best fellow of us all for you will make your fortune by sinking us jolly souls. But I'll be d — m'd[10] if I care, for I will dance, sing, and be merry, drive away old care, run in debt, get endorsers. You may buy my notes and hack them up and down the exchange and, by G-d, I hope they will sink on your hands. Then I shall have bit the bitten.

RANDOM: Well, gentlemen, I don't like either of your plans. I intend to try traffick and live as I list if traffick fails me. Why, you know, I can then turn stock broker for my head is most ripe for speculation, and then I shall be everything, but good.

Enter N[ight]ramble.

[NIGHTRAMBLE]. Well, my jolly lads, what are you all about this fine night? Are you asleep over your glasses? No fine girls to raise your spirits? Come; come, brave Boys, let us begin the chase. Here's a chance to make our fortunes if girls is our aim. Let's have at them. *Sings.*

1[11]

At every corner I came by
I met some pretty Lass,
Who looked at me, so sweetly sly.
I hardly could them pass.

2

But here I am, brave Boy, you see
To rout you out I come.
Make me your Guide, then follow me.
With a row, dow, done and drum.

3

We'll kick up Jack, and knock down Sue,
Then rally pretty Cate.
For I'm the Man, that's stout and true,
Who loves to sing, and prate.

. . . .

OH GLEE: Ar'ra and by the Boderation,[12] hony. D—m, your prate. Ramble on, Boys, do you see, Patrick will be after coming before you.

Scene 2

They all sally forth [to] meet the watch.

WATCHMEN: Who goes there with all this racket?

OH GLEE: Ar'ra, and by my faith, honies, tis I and myself and my own dear friends whom I just left behind me. And do you see, brave honies? You had better, if you know what [is] good for you. Shut your eyes, and not see at all, at all.

CAPT SPOIL[ATION]: Well, N[ight]ramble, you have taken[13] us out to see some pretty girls. Where are they? I can't see for these d——m lamps. Dash them down.

They all strike at the lamps till the street appears dark.

MAJOR RANT[APOLE]: That's right, brave Boys, there shall be no rest in this town tonight. We'll kick up a d——m noise. Come, let's raise the dead, kill the sick and save the doctor the trouble. This my jolly souls, this is clear fun. Let's storm the watch.

RANDOM: Well, now I am once out, d——m me if I care what I storm. I am now ripe to storm H-ll itself.

LUDICROUS, *staggering*. Yes, yes. I think we are all most ripe for the gallows. If we keep up these night capers much longer, we shall grow so ripe as to rot in a prison, and this is the modern fashion of keeping it up. Ha,' lads, what do you think?

DAFT: Don't tell me of keeping it up. I came out to knock all down before me.

They meet the watch, knock them down. They all cry, Knock them down, *run and say,* Take that and go sleep snug while on duty. *They all take leg bail.*[14]

ACT 2
Scene 1

Changes to Philanthropus's quarters.[15] *Philanthropus and Angelica discovered seated on a sofa. Enter several of the Bucks in full glee.*

PHILANTHROPUS: Well, my young friends, I rejoice to see you even at this late hour. Better late than never. Pray, from whence came you, gentlemen?

[NIGHT]RAMBLE: From whence came we? Why I will tell you, sir. As our Grand Master[16] once said, from going to and fro, here and there, and everywhere, we have taken the circuit of the whole town, breaking all before us and, faith, we have now come to storm your quarters.

ANGELICA: Well, gentlemen, I hope you don't intend taking me by storm, as I resign on no conditions[17] but those of the highest terms of honour. Then on my terms will I capitulate for peace, and on those only.

[OH] GLEE: Ar'ra and by my St. Patrick, we will capitulate on your own terms, if you will comply with our Dear honys and for the peace of our souls. Shut your own bright eyes that you may see us sign the treaty properly.

STRIPLING: Permit me, Madam, on behalf of myself and

the rest of these Jolly fellows, to make some apology for this intrusion. You must perceive we [are] all very high, but I hope we shall not be guilty of any impropriety that may wound your feelings for I would readily sacrifice my life to ingratiate myself with your sex. Tis for them, I wish to live. They are the very loadstone that attract[s] the sole spring that binds my soul and this frail bark of mine together. They are my source of perfection.

ANGELICA: My dear sir, you are the very essence of politeness, a mere rara avis,[18] for tis indeed very unfashionable for the Bucks of the present day to speak or even think as they ought of our sex. And I fear the reason is that you associate too much with the vicious part of them, and that often to your injury, and disgrace. And Oh,[19] wretched, how much despised is an abandoned Woman. Tho' greatly to be pity'd, I fear their fall is often from placing too much confidence in your sex, who first gain their affections, then ruin and destroy their reputation. The too credulous fair one finds too late herself lost to virtue, her peace is destroyed, happiness has fled from her. And she seeks in dissipation some refuges till lost to every sense of shame she becomes a disgrace to that very sex of which she might have shone one of the brightest ornaments had it not been for you, oh faithless, deceiving Man.

STRIPLING: I really think, dear Madam, we are for the most part, the source and ostensible cause of the suffering of your sex. By heavens, my own soul is harrowed up when I think how much care, and pain, I give my good Mother. But by the Spirits of my ancestors and by the Spirit of all the just made perfect, I swear: I intend to quit these night capers, and be yet a comfort to the good old soul before she takes her flight to the realms of bliss. God grant she may be paid for all her sufferings here.

PHILANTHROPUS: That's right, my young friend, let me be the shepherd that shall conduct the stray sheep safe home to the fold of his benevolent dam.

LUDICROUS: By heavens, Philanthropus, you are the very man to restore lost sheep, as you style us good fellows. But, by G-d, I don't think one half of us should run astray so often if your cursed Philanthropy had not set us the example. What think you of it, Rantapole?

RANT[APOLE]: Think? Why, d—m me if I think at all. If I did, I should run crazy or turn Methodist preacher. Oh, no: no: I don't think, never think, bury thought.

> I sing, and dance, I rant, and play,
> Get drunk at night, then sleep next day.

[OH] GLEE: Ar'ra and by St. Avony,[20] who is the saint for the lovers, and by the great Dragon at the feet of St. Michael,[21] who was the saint poor Avony embraced for the lovers, now, by my soul, tis the only one I think could plead the cause for that order of men. Now, by all the saints and more too, now, do you see, master Philanthropus? I wish you would be setting the example before us by returning to your senses first. For, by Jasus,[22] I think tis high time and Patrick will be often coming before you.

ANGELICA: Then, my dear young friends, let me entreat you to return quietly home to the bosom of your families and under their protection seek that rest you never will find in your present line of dissipation.

STRIPLING: Dear Madam, convinced of our errour, I will be the first that shall return to quarters if you, Philan[thropus], will go home with me and pass the morning for the night is far spent.

One and all cry, To quarters! Allons, allons, Boys, *and exit quick step.*

Scene 2

Changes to the mansion of Madam Prudencia. She is discovered seated in a calling chair.

Enter Stripling, pulling in Philanthropus and staggering.

STRIPLING: Well, Madam, here I am at last, thank God and Philanthropus, or I am sure I should not have reached home tonight.

PHILANTHROPUS, *taking Prudencia by the hand*: My dearest Madam, excuse my intruding at this unseasonable hour, but you must know a number of us, have been very high this evening. And I thought it incumbent[23] on me and a duty as one of the eldest rakes, and as a Christian to see a stray sheep safe home to his fold. For I am a Christian, Madam, as true as I am a Sinner.

STRIPLING: Well, d—m you, Philanthropus, sit down, and don't keep my mother standing if you are a Christian.

PHILANTHROPUS, *still holding Prudencia's hand and seating himself*: My dearest Madam, was it not so late an hour, I should further intrude on your goodness by making you a long visit.

PRUDENCIA: Accept, sir, my most grateful thanks for your attention in seeing my little reprobate son safe home. I hope his heart is good tho' his head may err. Dear sir, excuse me if I make one remark before we part. I very much fear, you who are old in iniquity and hardened in your mode of living are a great injury to thoughtless youth, and they too often lost to their friends and society by the force of your bad example. Excuse my zeal, sir, for I am a mother and sensibly feel and fear for the rising generation.

STRIPLING, *rising and staggering*: Don't preach, dear Mother, for God's sake, don't preach, but give Philanthropus a glass of wine.

PRUDENCIA: No, sir, not at present. Your friend, and yourself have had quite wine enough for tonight.

STRIPLING: Well, Pat, I say bring us some beer. I say, Pat, bring beer quick, I say quick.

Enter Patty with tumblers of beer.

STRIPLING, *still standing and speaking*: Keep your seat, Philan-thropus. Why you told me a d — m lie, you Christian sinner, for you promised to lay with me.

PHILANTHROPUS: So I did, my dear fellow, but in the present

case I really thought a little deception necessary as a Christian duty was the only way to persuade you home to your parent whose goodness and benevolence will make every allowance for the frenzy of youth. To your tender compassion, I once more commit your returning Prodigal.

PRUDENCIA: Sir, I have a hand, and a heart, ever ready to receive the returning penitent by day, or night. My life, sir, ever since I was a widow has been a life of care, and trial, but, blessed be my God, I never sink under them and never happier than when by tenderness I can reclaim a child to a right sense of their duty. Oh, my dear sir, I am confident, could they but once know the feelings of the Mother, they never would willingly wound the feelings of the parent.

PHILANTHROPUS: With a parent possessed of so much benevolence, I rejoice to leave you a prisoner in her care, and may the guardian angel of the night protect you.

STRIPLING: D—m you, I don't care who will protect me. Sit down, take off your hat, and take one more glass of wine.

PHILANTHROPUS: No, sir, I will take no more wine tonight; however, I thank you for the hint. *Bowing to Prudencia*: Madam, I beg your pardon for keeping my head covered while in your presence.

PRUDENCIA: Sir, if the heart is but right I wish the head may always be covered from evil, especially in the time of battle. Dear sir, once more after wishing you safe to your quarters, I shall close my doors. They are always open to my friends at seasonable hours. After that, sir, I close them with the most fervent wishes of happiness for all mankind and ardent prayer that the rising generation may grow wiser and wiser, from the rising to the setting sun.

The curtain drops.

The scene has clos'd. The cast was real and gave rise to the fiction in hope a song may catch him whom a sermon flies.[24] Dr. Fran[klin].

III
Taking Stock, 1820–1829

Selections from "Reminiscences and Traditions of Boston, Being an Account of the Original Proprietors of That Town, the Manners and Customs of Its People"

Hannah Mather Crocker

ca. 1829

[Sarah Kemble Knight]

Capt. Kemble[1] came from England with goods, took a stand near [Frizel] Square, and opened an English goods shop, made considerable property: 1676 he built several houses, a large one for that day on Moon Street for his own mansion. In 1699 Kemble returned to England for more supply of merchandize. After being absent from his family two years and a half, he arrived at Scarlet's Wharf[2] on Sunday morning. At the foot of Moon Street, a short distance from his house, he quickened his steps on seeing his wife coming out of the door to go over the way to meeting. When he met her at the door, he saluted her with the warmth of long absence. He was fined five shillings, and ordered the next day to stand two hours in the stocks for unseemly conduct in saluting his wife in the open street on the Lord's day. This is the first instance of open punishment at North Boston that we know of. The house has been rather remarkable ever since.

His only daughter married one of his capt[ains], an Englishman who was in Kemble's employ. He died soon after, leaving her a widow with one child. She made a journey to

New York in 1704 to claim some property belonging to her husband.[3] She returned the next spring 1705 and opened a school for children in the same house as her Father was dead. D[r] Samuel Mather[4] and D[r] Franklin went to her school till they entered the Latin school. She was a woman of keen wit and humour in her day. On a pane of glass in her school room there was engraven, as with the point of a diamond, a few lines written after her return from her journey. The date was 1709. The lines follow:

> After many toils, and frights
> I have returned, poor Sarah Knights.[5]
> Over great rocks, and many stones,
> God has preserv'd from fractured Bones.

———————————————————————————————— 6

She sold the estate in 1714 to a capt. Papillion.[7] After his death his administrator John Wolcott[8] sold the estate to Thomas Hutchinson, Esq[r]. He gave the estate to his daughter Hannah, wife of the late D[r] Sam Mather. In the year 1721 the whole stack of chimneys fell into the cellars breaking and destroying much property. His daughter and family remained spared, monuments of saving mercy.

[Miss Betty Thornton, "Little Red Riding Hood"]

A singular man reminds us of a singular small woman, Miss Betty Thornton. She measured hardly three feet in height; her limbs from the hips down were very short. When sitting down, [she] appeared common size. Her head was rather large for her body. She was a woman of good understanding, a very constant attendant at the Old North meeting in all weather. In winter she drest in a red cloth riding hood and by that means obtained the name of Little Red Riding Hood. A number now living remember her.

[Praise of the Earliest Settlers and the City upon a Hill]

These few lines gave new life and courage to the young lady which never forsook her during the whole siege of Boston. According to faith, it did turn out all well. The British evacuated Boston March 17, 1776. The spring after on the 20th she was restored to the arms of her dear parents, who had not suffered equal to the children's tears. Though they had suffered many privations, their spirits kept good fa[ith] with D[r] Eliot's, and a number more continued strengthening and encouraging the remaining few in the town who continued firm in the cause of their country. Our venerable ancestors lived on the first coming to America on faith and clams to prepare the way for Boston to shine as a city upon a hill.[9] May they be conspicuous for virtue and piety as their Fathers were.

[Apparel of Men and Women Prior to the War of 1775]

Liberty and equality are the reigning principle of the day. We will give some account of the mode of dress prior to the war of 1775. The ladies never appeared to more advantage in dress than at the last queen's ball on February 22, 1775. A sack with a long trail petticoat handsomely trimmed with the same, or riband as fancy chose, a satin shoe with a paste buckle, the hair craped and decorated with paste and pearl sprigs. Two or three tier[s] of ruffles on the gown and works, or lace and muslin, long ruffles double or thrible, the hair powder'd white. Then enter the ball room with a graceful air. The manners began then to soften from the rigid rules and forms of aristocracy: we think the manners never were more amiable or pleasant. The minument[10] and rigadoon were danced with graceful air by the Juveniles, and the approving matron smiled sedate. And all was harmony and peace as the tiptoe step was scarcely heard, so lightly did they skim along the floor. No noisy brawl was heard. A soft melodious voice was then most charming to the ear, and men of sense did that approve. The gentlemen's dress at that period was neat and elegant: a white broadcloth coat with the silver basket button [and] silver vellum trimmed button hole on blue cloth with gold vellum, satin waistcoat and small cloths with gold or silver knee bands, a black or white stocking, a long silver buckle or Morocco shoe, the hair craped and powder'd, a gold head cane displayed a handsome worked ruffle around the hand formed a fop complete, but in general, the complete gentleman appeared with pleasing dignity of manners.

[Birthplace of Benjamin Franklin]

After we pass the mill bridge the first thing of note is the blue ball as from the mouth of Franklin. That spot was his birthplace. The blue ball originally designated his father's soap shop; that made the corner. After his father left it and moved, we think to Newbury Street, his Brother lived in Marlboro Street and Benjamin lived with him till he left Boston.

[George Whitefield, under Whose Preaching John Marcy Was Converted]

We now beg leave to notice a worthy black man[11] who had he lived in the present day might have been a deacon in the Africa Church. John Marcy was a wonder in his day. He was a faithful servant of a Mr. John Morey. His master lived in Roxbury.[12] He gave this man a good trade as he put him to a mason. After he learnt the business, his master used to let him come into Boston to work. One day he went with the multitude to hear Mr. Whitefield[13] preach. He was so awakened and impressed by the divine truths as they were delivered by him that he could have no rest till he obtained leave to come into Boston to hear more orthodox preaching than he had been used to hear out of town. The ministers in Boston were then orthodox. His master gave him his freedom, and he came to Boston. Jack was industrious and had as much work as he pleased among the first class. He soon accumulated property enough to build him[self] a small house which he did. He purchased a piece of land at the foot of Essex Street; he used to work for Governor Dummer,[14] who had a very faithful, orthodox Christian black woman. And he made love to her as a young good Christian. Here Jack found an helpmeet. The governour, who was all benevolence after Jack applied to him for leave to marry her, gave her a handsome fitting off, and gave her several hundred dollars to commence life. Jack went the grade of Christian duty. He joined Mr. Morehead's[15] church [and] was a constant attendant. He kept a diary wherein he set down every sermon heard with the text in shorthand, and the preacher's name with the time that it was delivered [and] dated. He was a member of Mr. Morehead's church from 1730 till his death 1774. A few extracts from his Journal as a specimen of the man may amuse the Journal reader of the present day: July 5, 1764 received of my wife a blow on my face. I pray God forgive UM.[16] August 15 received of my wife bail; not to regard what I say to UM. Sept 3 some friends at my house: Mr. Thurber.[17] Same time Thomas Mason, Prince Hall and others.[18] Sept 18 society meet. An argument by Mr. Fisher[19] against drunkenness. January 23, 1766 at four o'clock am an earthquake, two shocks. November first began the New Testament employing the help of God, the Great Jehovah. January 4, 1769 began the Old Testament craving the grace of God, our Lord and Saviour Jesus Christ, to help my infirmity. Poor Jack was an honest, well-meaning man. He left no children, made a will, gave a few legacies to friends. Madam Turell,[20] who was his old mistress, had the settling of his affairs. The British made barracks of his house and left it in 1776 torn to pieces. His journal and day books are now in possession of Mrs. Turell, Brattle Square, opposite the meeting, and the Cannon Ball that struck the house, and scared them all.[21]

[Phillis Wheatley]

Another rara avis[22] of the African tribe may not be amiss to notice in this place, that is Phillis Wheatley, a native of Africa. She was brought to America 1761. She was about seven years of age when Mr. Wheatley purchased her. He bought her to wait on his only daughter. She was a pretty, smart, sprightly child. They grew very fond of her and treated her as well as if their own. Her young Mistress was Miss Mary Wheatley and was afterwards the very amiable wife of D[r] John Lathrop.[23] Phillis was sent to school and educated with Miss Mary. She soon acquired the English language and made some progress in the Latin. She never was looked on as a slave. She could work handsome and read and write well for that day: She wrote a number of pieces of poetry. Some have been printed in a volume. We have several pieces in her own handwriting. Africa may well boast that one of her daughters not twenty one years of age should write poetry so handsome, as many of her pieces are. She married at twenty one a man of notoriety by the name of Peters.[24] He did not treat her well. She soon fell a prey to disappointment, and her keen sensibility proved a sudden decline and she died. We hope to find a better state hereafter in bliss. She died in Boston 1784 only thirty one years old. We will close our account of her with an extract from her poem on imagination. She inscribed it to a daughter of Dᵣ Samuel Mather's.

The following is the extract from the poem:

"On Imagination"[25]

Though winter frowns on fancy's raptured eyes
The field may flourish, and gay scene arise.
The frozen deep may break their iron bands
And bid their waters murmur oe'r the lands.
Flora may now resume her fragrant reign.   5
And with her flowery riches deck the plain.
Sylvanus may diffuse; his honours round.
And all the forest, may, with leaves abound.
Showers may descend, and dew their gems disclose,
And nectar sparkle on the blooming rose.   10

We think the poem is printed in her works.

[Franklin's Visit to Dᵣ Cotton Mather's Study]

The third [newspaper in Boston] was the *Courant* by Franklin, Brother of the Dᵣ,[26] and he lived with him to learn the profession at the time he knocked his head in passing through an entry way from Dᵣ Cotton Mather's study. Having been with a proof sheet for his correction, he stood corrected. Franklin wrote for his Brother's paper many smart pieces that shew his genius.

[Effigy of the Pope]

The parading about the streets with a pope and a number of effigies was an amusement among the lower class of Boys.

Even little ones had their potato popes. The apprentice lads had large ones and paraded the streets with it fixt on a large stage all day; at night had a trial for mastery, gave many blows and then burnt their Popes and supped together in peace and harmony. This folly continued till 1773, then was superseded by the liberty tree which turned the derision from the Pope and powder plot to those who supported the British plans and plots. The tree was hung with a number of effigies of some of the most obnoxious characters who had taken an active part in the drama. Peter Mackintosh, the last Capt. of the Pope, was the first Capt. General of the Liberty Tree.[27] Many persons were compelled to pass the ordeal trial of their faith in political sentiments and faith by taking an oath of allegiance to the true interest of their country.

The flame of liberty spread its influence through every town in the colony. The Stamp Act was declared a cruel imposition on the rights of American subjects; all stamp papers were refused. Town meetings were called, and all citizens very universally agreed that the British government had no right of taxation as the American colonies had no representation in the British parliament. The stamp office was pulled down. The house of Andrew Oliver, the Stamp Master, was assaulted [and] windows broken on August 14, 1765. [On August 26] Judge Story's windows were broken.[28] Capt. Ben Hollowell's house was much damaged, windows broken, his house entered, and the mob drank freely of his good old wine.[29] And in an enraged state they repaired to the house of Judge Hutchinson, Lieutenant Governor, and demanded his person. Not finding him, they destroyed a great part of his house and furniture.[30] His valuable manuscripts, with many valuable ones belonging to his Brother-in-law, Dr Sam Mather, were scattered over the North Square and soaked in his old wine. Many of them drank till they could drink no more. Part of the mob went to Dr Mather's house as the word was given out that he had taken refuge there, which he had on the first appearance of the mob. Dr Mather appeared at his door. The mob demanded Hutchinson. The D^r told them his house was his castle, and he should protect his Brother Hutchinson, though they knew their sentiments did not accord. A few of the ringleaders begged the D^r to give him up or let him escape as they could not answer for damage the mob might do him for protecting the culprits. It was not thought safe for Mr. Hutchinson to continue longer at his sister's house.

The present writer was sent to shew and escort him the pass, a back way through an alley to the house of Mr. Thomas Edes,[31] father of the late Edward Edes, baker, and grandfather of the present Senior Minister in Providence. Mr. Hutchinson continued there till 6 o'clock the next morn. The present writer continued his companion through the night without sleep, then escorted him in safety to his sister's house the same way he retreated. He was calm through the whole scene and partook of Breakfast with the family. After breakfast he went to court in his common dress as his bagwig and robes were destroyed. He opened the court with a very affecting speech. He was then Chief Judge of the Supreme Court. Afterwards he wrote home to the Minister of Great Britain that he could not enforce the laws without a military force. Two regiments were sent over and stationed at fort William. Commissioners were sent over to collect the taxes and duties were laid on every imported article. A military guard was placed at the custom house. Sentries paraded before the door. This was an eyesore and an evil too hard to be tamely born, as free men were determined to be free or die in the cause of freedom.

The case was desperate and the old Roman fire did soon transpire[32] its influence through the whole long room club from the electrick fire of the flint in the Breast of their leader, the late governor Sam Adams,[33] who was in his principles a firm Roman senator. Now we are coming to the point. March 5 1770 a skirmish commenced on King Street. Some rude pope-making Boys began it by pelting the Sentry at the custom house door with snowballs. The contest grew warm. Capt. Preston[34] turned out the main guard and threatened to fire if they did not disperse. The mob increased and at nine o'clock he ordered them to fire, which they did, and several persons were killed and a number wounded. Mr. John Gray,[35] rope maker, was killed on the spot. Others died of their wounds. The town was in great dismay through the whole night. The citizens were determined no troops should be stationed in the town. In the morning a town meeting was called and it was unanimously voted they should be sent to fort William, which was done and the custom house officers took refuge there. In 1768 Bernard[36] was recalled. Hutchinson according to Bernard's prophecy was wheeled into his place for a short time as Gage[37] was appointed in his stead. A number more troops were sent over. The town of Boston was blockaded. The custom house was removed to Salem. No business was done in Boston in 1773. More troops were sent over. In May 1774 Governor Hutchinson sailed for England never more to return to his native country. He died in June 1780 aged sixty nine years; his Brother Foster went to Halifax.[38] There he died and his only son also. Some of his daughters are still living in that place well respected. This ancient and respectable family is now extinct in Boston, after holding in different branches the first offices of distinction for over a century past.

[Boston Tea Party]

Now comes on a new trial for poor Boston. A number of vessels are sent over loaded with tea and more taxes too hard to bear. Town meetings were called, and the citizens voted the tea should not be landed. The ships should be sent back again to tell the tale. The commissioners would not consent to that. It was then determined in the long room club the tea should be destroyed. The plan was laid there to hire some persons from the neighboring towns to come in disguise like Indians and throw the tea overboard. Which took place December 1773. The Indian yell was given to assemble, and all was still till the destruction was over at nine o clock in the evening. In 1774 Gage came over with power to place the town under military government. He began to repair the old fortifications on Boston Neck. He sent a detachment to take possession of the stores in Salem and destroy the arsenal. The powder in the arsenal in Charlestown was seized, [and] the provincial congress then sitting in Watertown meeting declared Gage an inveterate enemy to America. Then Gage issued a proclamation of pardon to all the rebels, except Samuel Adams and John Hancock,[39] and ordered that martial law should take place. He expected to frighten them to a compliance, but he was mistaken in the Americans' character. They were got of firm steady horses: that would not be driven to wrong measures. Liberty of conscience and the right of freeborn Englishmen was their aim. Remonstrances and petitions for redress of grievance were sent to the British parliament, but no redress was granted. America was declared in a state of rebellion. Boston was the seat of war. April 19, 1775 a small detachment of the British troops were sent to take possession of the powder and arms. In Lexington and Concord, the British troops had to dance Yankey[40] Doodle backwards. Yeomanry surrounded the town and Boston became a garrison, and no one was allowed to go out of the town till he delivered up his fire arms. Gage was recalled as not having energy enough to carry on a long war, he embarked in Oct[br]. Howe, Clinton, and Burgoyne arrived just after with other military characters and a long body of troops.[41] Now poor Boston, pent as like Utica,[42] formed but a poor epitome of American freedom. But the truly brave never faint in the day of trial. In fact this was the spirit of the town of Boston. Almost every female in the town became a Roman matron, willing to sacrifice every luxury and submit to any privation for the public interest. Such was the public mind — die, or live free: The town continued in this state of privation and almost starvation from April 19, 1775 till March 17, 1776 when the British left the place in great dismay. Washington was escorted in by the selectmen and inhabitants to the great joy of the remaining few in the town. At the first entrance the town appeared like a deserted village as to the original inhabitants.

[A New Era in Boston]

And now a new era commences as the town is in one grand bustle. What with going out and coming in of new inhabitants from every part of the union, and from that time to the present there has been such an inundation of strangers from every part of the globe that a real Bostonian is a mere rara avis, a rare bird indeed. And I am left almost alone to tell where old and new characters once commenced.[43] Our fathers, where are they? The places that once knew them now know them no more; there is now a generation sprang up that knew not Joseph. But we wish to remind the present generation of the small beginning, but the firm foundation laid by our venerable ancestors for the present generation to renovate, embellish, and renew.

David was not permitted to live long enough after the cruel wars in his day to build the Temple for sacred worship, but he left the order and pattern for his son Solomon with the help of the master mason Hiram to perform the mighty works. Solomon also shewed his wisdom in building a navy in the time of peace, to be ready to meet war with dignity. Tis to be hoped America will learn wisdom by past sufferings and remember a strong navy is a firm bulwark[44] to a commercial Nation. We have brought our reminiscence down to the memory of many of the present generation. Allow us just to say, go thou and do likewise. Preserve, restore and transmit to the rising generation, that they may transmit to future ages; [t]hat they may be led to look to the rock from whence they were hewn; and if only one ship be saved, it may be enkindled by the fire of the flint, when attracting takes place.

Our wish is historical, and antiquarian researches may become as much the Fun as Novels and Music are at the present day. May every branch of science and literature measure and flourish in this improving City, and the present generation and the rising one be heard to say, I would be walking with the wise that wiser I may grow. With this wish, often taking some further notice of a few of our most eminent physicians as a prelude to a few original epitaphs and an appendix will be subjoined of rare and original poetry. Our reminiscences are now respectfully committed to the candour of the benevolent public with all their imperfection as a memento of our respected sires.

By H. M. C.

[Rattlesnake]

In 1790 Sir John Dalton had in Boston, for several months, a very extraordinary rattle snake whose venoum had been extracted that made him very harmless, so much so that the present writer remembers to have had him lay his head in her lap for her to stroke the poor fellow, but he never could beguile her with his fascinating eye or voice. He had nine rattles and made all ring again with the noise. He was ten feet in length when stretched. He continued harmless over two years. Then the venoum began to collect, and he leaped at Sir John several times. He was obliged to have him shot and took his skin home to England for a curiosity.

[D^r. Increase Mather's Dog]

Dr Increase Mather had a very sagacious little Dog, who would go every Saturday evening over to the meeting in Roxbury, would follow Mr. Walter[45] to meeting and sit on the pulpit step till meeting was ended, stay the night at Mr. Walter's and return home on Monday morn. He was so regular that the family would send letters tied round his neck, and he would bring an answer on Monday. D^r M told his Brother Walter he could not account for the little fellow's conduct. Mr. Walter in a very pleasant manner observed the dog was perhaps a judge of good preaching. The dog might be pleased with the harmony of his voice, as he was styled the sweet singing Walter from his melodious voice. The faculty may decide this.

[Origin of Phrase "Cobbler in the Stomach"]

A very hypochondrical man applied to him [Dr. Clark] for assistance in a very critical state of health as he was loaded with the black bile. He had taken it into his head that a little cobbler who lived opposite used to disturb him with singing. The man kindly left off singing to please him. He then took a conceit that the man had got into his stomach. The Dʳ very sagaciously humoured the Whim, assuredly saying he could force him out. He accordingly agreed to come at sunset and not to leave him till he had dislodged the little fellow. The Dʳ stated the case to the honest cobbler, requesting him to follow his direction and hide himself behind the curtain at the head of the bed and as the man puked, as he should give him a smart emetic, he must throw small pieces of bread and water into the Basin, till near the last operation throw an owl in, and finish the farce by throwing himself over the Bed, which he performed by saying, you shall never catch me in your trap again. The man got well as his stomach was cleared of the bile. And in Dʳ Clark's family to the third and fourth generation, it was a common observation [that] if any of them was bilious they had the cobbler in their stomach. This from a descendant of the family. The Dʳ was rich and moved in the first circles. His lady was an heroine of that day 1662 or 3. She was the first Maiden Lady ever ventured on the New England shore, Miss Elizabeth Saltonstall, who accompanied her Brother and family to America, and became the highly respected wife of Dʳ John Clark.[46] He had a number of children; his son and grandson continued in the profession of Physic and Surgery and kept an apothecary's shop on Ann Street till death. His eldest daughter[47] married Mr. Richard Hubbard.[48] After his death she became the greatly respected wife of Dʳ Cotton Mather and was the mother of the late Dʳ Sam Mather, family all gone now to the shades of Copp's hill.

[On Benjamin Franklin Learning to Stoop]

[Increase Mather] lived and died in a large house on Ship Street; his son Dr Cotton Mather was born in the same house and lived there some time after his Father's death. There it was that Franklin learnt to stoop, as he once observed in my hearing, when he was only a printer's Devil. He had been to carry a proof sheet for the D^r to correct. And passing from his study to the door, he struck his head against the staircase as the wall was very low, when the D^r in his way of humour, said, young man, you must learn to stoop. Dr Franklin, in a letter to the late Dr. Sam Mather observes, "It has been of use to me through my whole life."

[Recipe for a Chowder]

Directions for making a chowder.
By a Bostonian.[49]

First lay some onions to keep the pork from burning
Because in Chowder there's no turning.
Then lay some slices very thin.
Thus you with Chowder may begin.
Next lay some fish, cut cross ways very nice.   5
Then season well with pepper, salt, and spice.
Parsley, Sweet Marjoram, Savory, and Thyme,
Then Biscuit next, which must be smoak'd some time.
Thus your foundation laid you will be able
To raise a Chowder high, as Tower of Babel.   10
For by repeating o'er the same again:
You may make chowder for a thousand men.
Last, Bottle of Claret: water enough to smother'em
You'll have a Mess call'd Omnium Gather'em.

[Chimney of Samuel Mather's Home Struck by Lightning]

In the year 1789 the chimneys were struck by lightning in July, the 29. They all went by the run down into the cellar. The family having short notice, lost considerable articles of furniture and glass, crockery, and china. His daughter, who owned the house after him, observed to a friend [that] she though[t] little of the loss sustained when she could look around and view her most precious crockery preserved under the protecting care of a gracious providence. The little circle of Crockers were all safe, the family removed for three months, then returned to the old mansion renovated. Tis now standing in good repair, a monument of the old model of 1676, the year it was built.

[June 24, 1775, Letter to Crocker from Her Parents]

We here give a copy of the letter in answer to the saucy one sent in by General Putnam.[50]

dated June 24, 1775

My dear Girl

We were much concerned about you, not knowing where you were or how you fared, but since we have received your few lines, we are quite easy. Be you calm, quiet, and try to be as amiable, pleasant, and useful as you can while you are absent from your parents, and give yourself no anxiety about us. We are well and comfortable, and being firmly persuaded infinite wisdom governs the world, and that all things will turn out well for us while we love and imitate the universal parent, we give

ourselves no unnecessary concerns about trifling affairs
and occurrences, commending you to the divine regard,
love and protection, while you are away from us, and
when you shall return, and as long as you live.

We are affectionately
Your parents
S and H M.

THE COMMITTEE OF SEQUESTRATION

N. BARBER, JOSEPH RUSSELL, ELIAS PARKMAN,

A COPY.

[Horses and Balaam's Ass]

Governor Hutchinson had great influence over some of the
clergy. Dr Pemberton[51] was a very warm advocate for Hutchinson. He was appointed to pray with the Mandamus Council
in the morning, [so] ordered his carriage out to take him up
to court when, behold, the horses would not stir from the
door, though they had been well broken and never shewed any
pranks before. After the D^r got into the carriage, they stood
erect on the hind legs. The D^r in some consternation got out
of the carriage and turned to a Lady who was standing at her
window in the next house, saying, Madam, what do you think
can be the matter with my horses? The lady adroitly replied,
Balaam's ass rebuked the madness of the prophet. The D^r
turned on his heel, with warmth, saying, then I will walk, and
footed it up to court. But the court was soon stopped, and could
not proceed to business. As we have no faith in witchcraft,
we will unravel the mystery of the D^r's horses, though at the
time it did appear rather marvelous to the bystanders. The
fact was the black man wished his horses to appear equal to

any Mandamus judge on the bench, and to make them hold up their heads he had placed a double curb bridle on them, which, when taken off, ended the farce. And most [of] the absurdities of the superstitions that amuse the idle tale might be removed by searching out the cause.

[Mrs. Cary and the Case of Witchcraft]

About the year 1745 and fifty, poor, innocent Mrs. Cary[52] obtained the character of witch very innocently. Her husband was a skipper of a vessel and followed the trade to Bermudas, used to often bring back a freight of Rosemary, as the plant was much used in case of the asthma. The last voyage he made he brought a large freight, which was stored in an upper loft. The plant was become very scarce. When the old lady heard it would bring a very good price, she sent it forth for sale, and there was much wondering how she could obtain it in so short a time. A very simple tale was told, first for derision, that she went overnight in an eggshell to Bermudas and returned in the morning. As she was a sensible, shrewd woman, she would not satisfy the enquiring gossips where she got the plant. She lived on Fish Street, the house now standing decent. She was buried in the family vault in the North burial ground. The tomb lay open a long while; no heir appeared to take interest in the same, [so] it was closed and filled up when the walk was laid out through the burying place. We have no doubt she was a very innocent, injured good woman as D[r] Sam Mather often asserted her cause. She left several Children. Some of her regular descendants are now living and respectable in and near this City.

[On Physicians Who Require Double Fees]

Quid pro quo
By a Lady

On hearing the Physicians had entered into a combination not to assist any female when ill, till their full fees were paid. A few instances of the D^r leaving the woman in labour actually took place which gave rise to the bitter pill issued from the gall of bitterness.

> Physician: heal thyself,
> Tis ours to save ourselves and pelf.
> We now discharge you one and all
> Will never further on your call.
> As all you do, we plainly see,   5
> Is only done for double Fee.
> Your fees, tho' great, are not so large
> But most poor men could them discharge.
> If you could wait only one day,
> The poor women too might pay.   10
> But in our day was never seen
> A thing so sordid, base, or mean.
> Cruel Physicians, mean and base,
> You do your town and state disgrace.
> For men and beasts in every case   15
> Make all things willing to give place,
> When in distress a female seen.
> Even Brutes are humane, not so mean,
> They run to females, quick and free.
> They neither ask, nor wait for fee.   20
> Ye sons of famed Hippocrates,
> We're willing, to discharge your fees.

And you we willingly discharge,
And tell the public now at large
Your sordid spirit we despise. 25
We'll show ourselves both brave, and wise,
And help ourselves. We do protest
And let you vain physicians rest.
In your profession branch and rood
Live here neglected, die like Brute. 30
With this inscription on your stone,
We never helped your flesh or Bone.
Without double fees, our help denied.
We who saved none, ourselves have died.

Jochebed,
Moses's Mother.[53]
BOSTON 1784

[On Launching the Frigate *Independence*]

Lines by a Lady,

To a gentleman who was much mortify'd that the frigate *Independence* did not go off the first trial of launching her.[54]

1[55]

Where is your independence, say
Fair genius of America.
Pray do not mourn, pray do not weep
She's in her cradle safe asleep.

2

She only waits a federal Band 5
To take her gently by the hand
And lead her forth to public view,
Her constitution firm and true.

3

She from her cradle soon shall rise
And shew the world, to their surprise,   10
That federal measures will prevail
When independence spreads her sail.

4

Our Constitution, firm and strong,
Come brave seamen, join the song.
Let commerce flourish, peace on earth   15
Crown independence at her Birth.

                                                                HMC.

[To a Friend for Sending a Loaf of Bread]

To Mrs L. Howard
On her sending a loaf of bread
Of her own making on hearing
Of my loss of appetite.

Accept, Dear friend, from grateful heart
My gratitude, for the kind part
You take for me by sending Bread
To help to strengthen heart and head.
The sight of it gave me delight   5
And has revived my appetite.
May you and yours be ever fed
With living streams and vital bread.
Could I one moment give delight
For you, my friend, I'd often write.   10
May you through life be fully blest
With bread, and meat, and quiet rest.
May every blessing you attend.

Most fervent wishes, your old friend,
Where time no more on earth is given   15
May you have living bread in heaven.

> Your friend
> HMC.

[Lines to be Read at Opening School]

Lines written by a Lady,
To be read by the assistant at opening school.

Now girls if you would happy be,
Mind all the rules laid down by me.
Tis for your good, I take my part
And seek your welfare from my heart.
By industry and provident care,   5
Learn well your hymns as well as prayers.
Seek wisdom then while you are young,
And safely guard your lips and tongue.
That heaven may hear your early prayer,
And of you take a gracious care.   10
If you in virtuous paths abide,
Your God will be your constant guide.
Pray heaven protect you all your days,
In all your works and childish plays.
Honour your parents, near and dear,   15
And worship God with filial fear.
Love too your neighbour as yourself,
And wrong no one for sake of pelf.
From wicked words restrain your Tongue,
And form good habits now you're young.   20
And you may live good wives to make,
Pray mind, dear children, for my sake.

> HMC.

[A Petition for Pen and Ink]

A Petition
To my aged friend on her telling my granddaughter
to hide my Pen and Ink, my continuing weak
after my having the lung fever, 1821.

Would you of comfort, me deprive,
Tis thinking keeps your friend alive.
I think to live; I live to think.
Pray grant me then my pen and ink.
As I'm just verging from the grave, 5
Your patience, Madam, let me crave,
To hear my story, old but true.
My thoughts are often bent on you.
Your kind attention, tender care,
Demand my constant, fervent prayer. 10
When heaving Lungs and panting Breath
Seem'd certain messengers of death,
At helm calm reason sat sedate,
Resign'd to heaven, my future fate.
Heaven blest the means, my life restor'd, 15
Shall ever bless, and praise the Lord.
If a few years of trial still
Should be appointed by his will,
My heavenly parent still will raise
This heart to celebrate his praise. 20
Shall not then gratitude of soul
My powers of Mind and will control
The few remaining years of life,
Pray heaven preserve from care and strife.
My aged friend, tis all I crave, 25

A quiet life and peaceful grave.
Our days on earth can be but few,
Pray heaven support and comfort you.
Should cares increase, may strength be given[56]
For your support by gracious heaven.   30
At three score years and over ten,
You must allow me ink and pen
To write a line, my friend, to you,
If to the world I've bid adieu:
To say our friendship form'd in youth   35
Has sacredly been held with truth,
And good old age will never part
The little friendship of our heart,
And may that friendship soar above
To realms of bliss where all is love.   40
Then give me paper, pen, and ink
That I may write down as I think.
I often think and pray for you.
Heaven bless my friend, farewell, adieu.

HMC.

[To the Overseer of Ward No. 2 in Boston]

DORCHESTER, AUGUST 30, 1823.

To the overseer of ward No. 2 in Boston.

Well done thou good and faithful, too,
This day with pleasure I did view
Your truly independent spirit
That you from nature do inherit,
Tis the pure spirit of old times.   5
Allow me then in simple rhymes
To bless you, sir, from warmth of heart

For your exertions on the part
Of all the feeble, weak and poor
That you to vigour oft restore.   10
Go on, dear, express the truth,
As you have done from early youth.
You know the duties of your station,
And have the public's approbation.
Fear not, dear sir, the face of Man,   15
Pursue your ancient, well prov'd plan.
In some great tasks we often find
Strong energy of heart and mind.
A Quinsy[57] may attack the poor
That go expelled from door to door   20
To crave a little wood or Bark
As firing; they have not one spark
To keep from Quinsy, cold, and wet.
Poor Mother's freezing; children fret.
To other evils add the Tissick.[58]   25
Though the dispensary will find physic
Your Northern blast may set all right,
Will help the poor, give them delight.
Then may the blessings of the poor
Resound forever at your door.   30
The prayers blessing widow's mite
Attend you will both day and night.
When your declining years require,
That you from public life retire,
May you, sir, hear, this sentence then   35
Well done, thou faithful friend of men.

H M C.

A transferred pauper of ward N. 2

DORCHESTER, 1823

184

[On the Choice of Governor in 1823]

To my friend on her asking my opinion
Of the choice of Governor, 1823.[59]

I was born in the day of wisdom and reason.
I have lived in an age of rebellion and Treason.
I have lived to see wise men at head of the Nation.
I have lived to see folly support dissipation.
I have lately seen wisdom preside over the nation.   5
And now how it grieves me the truth to relate,
The folly of men to place in the chair
A person whose character never stood fair.
For wisdom or virtue, religion or Moral,
Nor can he deliver one sentence by oral.   10
He's form'd with soft manners the lancet to handle[60]
And a Lady on knee can handsomely dandle.
To place such a person at head of the state
Shows Body politic weak and also the pate.
Then blister and bleed every one that you can,[61]   15
And restore to their senses every fool to a man.
Then wisdom and reason will shortly return
And the Nation no longer for wisdom will Mourn.

By H M C.
Prudencia.

[On Reading the Federal Nomination]

On reading the federal nomination for Governor
and Lieutenant Governor, 1821.

By an old disciple of the Washingtonian School.

When wisdom and reason give sanction to choice,
The wise of each party must surely rejoice.[62]
When virtue and goodness with wealth are united,

All parties must be pleas'd and greatly delighted.
The widow and orphan shall sing and rejoice   5
When piety, wisdom and virtue the choice.
When men of staunch virtue are placed in high station,
Tis a blessing indeed to a federal Nation.
When wise men are ruling, the people rejoice.
Then citizens rise to support the wise choice,   10
For purity, goodness, and virtue unite
To give worthy Phillips the suffrage by right.
Then, my good friends, how pleasant it looks,[63]
To view from the fountain our clear purling Brooks[64]
Flowing gently along, so pure and so clear,   15
That his future election does proper appear.
Turn out then, brave Lads, if fair enough weather
To take the strong pull and pull all together.
For divided we fall, by uniting we stand,
If you all hold together, one federal Band.   20
Your Washington calls, tis Washington's choice
That wise men should rule and the Nation rejoice.

Prudencia.

[North Square Creed]

North Square Creed signed 1787.

I believe woman is the ostensible source of man's happiness;
I believe it was not good for man to be alone: and God in
infinite mercy provided him an help meet. I believe a prudent wife is the greatest blessing man can obtain in this life:
I also believe every man that has a prudent [wife] ought to
h[e]arken to his prudent wife:[65] as I firmly believe no good
and prudent woman will ever lead her husband astray: And

I do verily believe every man that has a prudent wife has a blessing from the Lord. Therefore I do believe in all things: as my best friend, my wife, and the other Ladies of this happy circle wish to believe.

In token of approbation we unite,
And hereto affix our names.
I L, T A, I C, W L, P [?], D [?], S H,
I S, T H, I [?], T K J. with others;
Creed drawn *by Prudencia* [italics in original]

[Contest for Best Spinner in 1762 on Boston Common]

After the Highlanders reeled off the common, the next exhibition there was the most interesting to the public view in about the year 1762. North Boston joined their spinning school scholars with the West Boston factory girls to form an exhibition on the common. There were upwards of fifteen hundred spinning wheels in motion at a time, some large and fast wheels. Benches were placed all round by the Mall for the small wheel spinners. The managers gave to the best spinner a premium, and a good repast settled the day. There is one Lady living now who spun on that memorable day, Madam Turell. Since that day, more reeling than spinning has been seen.

[The Mather Chair]

Mr. Richard Mather was born in Lancaster in a small village called Lowton[66] in the year 1596. The family can be traced to John. Thomas was his son, and Richard was son of Thomas. The chair in the antiquarian room belonged to Thomas. Richard sat in it when a child; he was married 1624. His children that were born in Europe sat in the chair before he came to

this country: Samuel, Timothy, Nathaniel, Joseph. The last
named sat in it when he brought the chair to America.[67] Eleazar
and Increase were born in America. They both sat in the same
chair. The chair descended to Increase, and all his children sat
in the same. It came in time to Cotton Mather; his children
all sat in the same. It descended to his son Samuel, and his
children sat in the same chair. His youngest daughter[68] was the
only child that had any children, and she has had ten children
sit in the chair and several grandchildren. As the regular line
of Mathers has run out, she wished the chair to be deposited
in the antiquarian room with the venerable shades, that those
who come after her may look to the rock from whence they
were hewn and find an ancient seat to rest in: a chip of the old
block, as she flatters herself there may some future day a sprig
spring from the root of Jesse and the tribe of Levi may return
to their rest after she is at rest in another world.

[Visit to Plymouth]

Sept 27, 1827.

My friend,

Having just returned from a short tour into the county of
Plymouth, old colony, famous for the rock on which our
ancestors first landed and did not split upon, as they trusted
and in faith had laid their foundation sure even on the
rock of ages: After viewing the rock from whence we were
hewn, as it was general muster through the colony, all was
hilarity and real glee. High military parade: By a retrograde
march we halted at the town of Marshfield, and to keep
alive the old fire of the flint. We sent for the former retreat
of Peregrine White,[69] and was received very hospitably by

the widow Lady who resides on the place. It is really a most obscure and romantic place. The mansion house stands in the middle of a large, open marsh leading quite down to the beach, open sea, not much of the old house standing except the cellar walls and under pinion. To be sure, we had some bars to surmount. You will know old veterans never stick at trifles when on fatigue duty or let any thing impede their march. At last we arrived safe at our destined place of rendezvous and really were paid for all fatigue by viewing the venerable trunk of the first apple tree planted in the town of Marshfield, planted by the first white child born in the colony, Peregrine White. I think the tree has a very singular appearance. Tis a natural monument erected by nature to honour the memory of the venerable man that planted the same. I think the tree is one of the wonders of Nature. I saw D. Webster[70] ingrafted on it. I wished for him or some other genius to take a sketch of the whole trunk. As I struck my eye finding no genius near, with my old pencil took a random sketch, hoping a better one might be taken from it. From this retreat we proceeded to another Lady's house who has in her possession the table chair Peregrine used to sit in and his father brought over with him in the year 1620. I sat in the chair with the enthusiasm of an original antiquarian, and with veneration I ate apple pie and old cheese off the Table. On return home, halted at the mansion of Capt. Daniel Phillips.[71] I there drank to the memory of Peregrine a little good old sherry out of the tumbler he once owned and drank out of. I did not take so much sherry as to prevent my tracing the fine figures on the tumbler with a steady hand. The apples I by leave took from the tree were not of the same nature as the one Mam. Eve partook of, neither did any evil spirit preside at the time.

Respect for our Puritan ancestors inspired my breast. I took the apple pleasant to view but tasted not the fruit. I think the original fruit was the winter pear main. I think mental improvement [here is the end of the entry].

[The Mather Family]

The Mather family are ancient. We trace them to John, the first we hear any thing about. He did some noble feat in chivalry for which a princely coat of arms was given him. Thomas resided in the moated castle in Lancaster for some time till by misfortune he left it. It was standing twenty years since occupied by one of the female line. Richard was born in Lowton in the county of Lancaster in the year 1596. Here commences of Levitical law as he was the first of the tribe of Levi. He had four sons in the ministry: Samuel, Nathaniel, Eleazer and Increase. Born in Dorchester, New England, Increase was the son of Richard, Cotton was the son of Increase, Samuel was the son of Cotton. I am the only little limb and the only grandchild of Cotton.

Dr Byles' Mother was sister to Cotton, daughter to Increase. He has two maiden daughters living in this city well on to 80, myself to 76. That the race must soon be run out in the line of Increase, from the line of Eleazer numbers are now in Connecticut and North Hampton respectable as ministers and physicians. I am myself a wonder to many that with a very slender frame I still have my small power of mind hold out to my advanced age, my hearing good, my sight holds out without the aid of glasses, and I flatter myself I shall see clear the rest of my few days. What I do I must do quickly. Sir Richard Hawkins was the first of my family on the maternal line. He had a patent right of a space of land at then North Boston.

He formed some settlement there. He came to this country in company with Billingham,[72] 1634. He had several children. One son had some taste for poetry, wrote pretty for the day of wags. He had several daughters. Hannah was married to Col. John Foster, an opulent merchant. Col. Foster had two daughters[,] Hannah, and Lydia. Thomas Hutchinson, Father of the late governor, was my Grandfather. My mother was own sister to the governor. Edward Hutchinson was Grandfather to the present Judge H. Robbins[73]: his Father was an honest, worthy, upright man, minister in the town of Milton a number of years till his death. Never great but good.

Notes

Introduction

1. Hutchinson further aroused public sentiment against him by not taking swift action to expel all British troops from Boston after the Boston Massacre on March 5, 1770. As Bernard Bailyn notes in *The Ordeal of Thomas Hutchinson* (Cambridge: Belknap Press of Harvard University Press, 1974), acting governor "Hutchinson believed that a decisive turning point had been reached. What was a stake in retaining these troops was nothing less than the British government maintaining its authority in America" (160). Although Hutchinson eventually allowed the troops to be removed, his extreme reluctance to do so unleashed a torrent of criticism. John Adams, adopting the persona of Crispus Attucks, a man of African and Native American ancestry believed to be the first person killed in the massacre, wrote, "Hutchinson was chargeable before God and man with our blood" (quoted in Bailyn, 163). The final straw came three years later. Hutchinson's role in events that provoked the Boston Tea Party in 1773 led to his removal from office as governor of Massachusetts Bay. In 1774 he was replaced by a military governor, Gen. Thomas Gage, and banished to England, where he served as an advisor to King George III. Hutchinson died in 1780.

2. Hannah Mather Crocker, "Reminiscences and Traditions of Boston, Being an Account of the Original Proprietors of That Town, the Manners and Customs of Its People," ca. 1829, R. Stanton Avery Special Collections Department, New England Historic Genealogical Society, Boston, 157 (hereafter referred to as "Reminiscences"). Instead of August 26, Crocker dates the destruction of Hutchinson's home as August 14, apparently confusing it with the destruction of Oliver's home, which did take place on that date.

3. For a discussion of the incidents of August 14–15 and August 26, see Bailyn, *The Ordeal*, 35–38; Robert Middlekauff, *The Glorious Cause:*

The American Revolution, 1763–1789 (New York: Oxford University Press, 1982), 89–93.

4. Crocker, "Reminiscences," 166–67. Hutchinson lost far more than his bagwig and his papers; returning later to his home to assess the damage he found that it had been stripped down to the brick-work and that the cost of repairs would be about 2,500 pounds. The wine-soaked manuscripts and other papers he rescued as best he could (Thomas Hutchinson, *History of the Colony and Province of Massachusetts Bay* [New York: Kraus Reprint, 1970], 124).

5. Anne Hutchinson (1591–1643) was excommunicated by a church synod in Boston for holding the Antinomian view that Christians are under grace and therefore not bound by the legal system of the Old Testament. Although Hutchinson drew support from Governor Henry Vane and her brother-in-law John Wheelwright (as well as her minister John Cotton initially), the ire she provoked among the ministers by charging that almost all of them were preaching a covenant of works and not a covenant of grace, a hallmark of Reformation theology embraced by Puritans, sealed her fate. The Hutchinson family moved to Rhode Island in 1638 and five years later to New York, where all were killed by Indians except for one daughter.

6. Of ten children born to Hannah and Joseph Crocker, three died in infancy: Joseph Allen, their fourth child; Maria Stevens, their sixth; and James Bowdoin, their ninth. Two children died before the age of seven: William Shaw, their seventh child, and another, Maria Stevens, their eighth. Five lived to adulthood: Hannah Mather, Samuel Mather, and Rebecca Allen, their first three children; another, Joseph Allen, their fifth; and Eliza Clark, their last. See Francis S. Drake, *Memorials of the Society of the Cincinnati of Massachusetts* (Boston, 1873), 231.

7. [H. Mather Crocker], *Observations on the Real Rights of Women, with Their Appropriate Duties, Agreeable to Scripture, Reason and Common Sense* (Boston, 1818), 86.

8. A commonplace book (from the Latin phrase *locus commenis*, a common place or passage, as in a book) may be a collection of quotations on a given topic, a collection in a given genre (e.g., aphorisms or poetry), or a collection in mixed genres (aphorisms, poetry, prose passages, recipes,

letters). Although Crocker's "Reminiscences" appears to qualify as a commonplace book, whether *Observations on the Real Rights of Women* ought to be so regarded is a matter of debate.

9. The term is used by Susan Phinney Conrad in *Perish the Thought: Intellectual Women in Romantic America, 1830–1860* (New York: Oxford University Press, 1976), 12, to describe intellectual women in America between 1830 and 1860, but it can also be applied to early women writers such as Crocker.

10. As Mary Kelley notes in *Learning to Stand and Speak: Women, Education, and Public Life in America's Republic* (Chapel Hill: University of North Carolina Press, 2006), 16, female academies and seminaries constituted "the grounds for women's entry into public life," the subtitle of the first chapter of her book.

11. See Robert A. Ferguson, *The American Enlightenment, 1750–1820* (Cambridge: Harvard University Press, 1997) for a nuanced discussion of the many ways American views of the Enlightenment converged and diverged from those of Europeans, especially chapter 2, 22–43. Ferguson's observation that "the Scottish Enlightenment, in turn, furnishes a secular vocabulary that nevertheless keeps Providence safely in mind" (30) is especially helpful for an understanding of Crocker's desire to base her defense of women's rights on the interlocking triad of scripture, reason, and common sense.

12. Mather Family Papers, Box 12, loose paper, Folder 10, American Antiquarian Society. Hereafter "Mather Family Papers" will be abbreviated as MFP and "American Antiquarian Society" as AAS.

13. MFP, Box 12, Folder 10, AAS.

14. Steven C. Bullock, *Revolutionary Brotherhood: Freemasonry and the Transformation of the American Social Order, 1730–1740* (Chapel Hill: University of North Carolina Press, 1996), 360n67.

15. MFP, Box 12, loose paper, Folder 10, AAS.

16. The practice was common among woman writers of this era, for example, Judith Sargent Murray's use of the male persona "Mr. Vigilius" in *The Gleaner*, no. 12, *Massachusetts Magazine* (March 1793), 137–38. Choosing a pseudonym of the opposite gender was not restricted to women, however, as male writers might use a female pseudonym, for example,

Benjamin Franklin's adoption of the persona of Mrs. Silence Dogood in the "Silence Dogood Letters," fourteen letters published from April 2 to October 8, 1722, in the *New-England Courant*, the newspaper started by Franklin's older brother, James. Sometimes more than one writer adopted the same name, which, as David S. Shields notes, is exactly what happened to Sarah Wentworth Morton, who used the name "Constantia" (*Civil Tongues and Polite Letters in British America* [Chapel Hill: University of North Carolina Press, 1997], 264n65). Although Shields does not identify the woman Morton found to be using the cognomen "Constantia," this name was used by Judith Sargent Murray in several of her essays, including her first, "On the Equality of the Sexes," in the March/April 1790 issue of *Massachusetts Magazine*.

17. Major symbols and beliefs of Freemasonry appear directly or indirectly in much of what Crocker wrote and furnish many of her most important tropes (e.g., the cornerstone). Her apparent enthusiasm for the group was so great that she recommended the formation of St. Ann's Lodge as a women's counterpart for the male-only organization. See *A Series of Letters on Free Masonry* (Boston, 1815), 43–45.

18. As Leonard W. Levy points out in *The Establishment Clause: Religion and the First Amendment* (Chapel Hill: University of North Carolina Press, 1994), 123, declaring fast days seemed totally out of character for Madison, who "believed that military chaplains or a fast day constituted a national religion."

19. See, for example, Cotton Mather's *Days of Humiliation: Times of Affliction and Disaster: Nine Sermons for Restoring Favor with an Angry God (1696–1727)*, introduction by George Harrison Orians (Gainesville FL: Scholars' Facsimiles and Reprints, 1970).

20. P. 14. See MFP, Box 12, Folder 8, n.p., AAS.

21. P. 24. See MFP, Box 12, Folder 3, n.p., AAS.

22. P. 32. See MFP, Box 12, Folder 5, n.p.; also Folders 4 and 6, n.p., AAS.

23. Thomas Maurice, *Indian Antiquities*, 7 vols. (London, 1793–1800); Claudius Buchanan, *The Works of the Rev. Claudius Buchanan, LL.D.* (New Brunswick NJ, 1812). The interest in comparative religion during this period is evident in the work of a contemporary of Crocker's, Hannah Adams's *An Alphabetical Compendium of the Various Sects Which Have Appeared in*

*the World, from the Beginning of the Christian Era to the Present Day. With
an Appendix, Containing a Brief Account of the Different Schemes of Religion
Now Embraced among Mankind* (Boston, 1784). The book went through
many printings and many changes in the title.

24. Stephen C. Bullock, noting the dramatic decrease in lodge activity
as a result of the anti-Masonic movement during the late 1820s, states, "By
the middle of the 1830s, northern Freemasonry virtually ceased to exist"
(*Revolutionary Brotherhood*, 282).

25. Crocker, *A Series of Letters on Free Masonry*, "Boston, Sept. 7,
1810," 46.

26. On the subject of companionate marriage, see Lawrence Stone,
The Family, Sex, and Marriage in England 1500–1800 (New York: Harper
and Row, 1977), 392.

27. Crocker's link of the study of languages with intellectual achievement
has its roots in the requirement that Puritan ministers in New England
study Hebrew in addition to Latin and Greek. Besides these languages, her
grandfather Cotton Mather attained proficiency in an additional four.

28. Benjamin Franklin, *The Autobiography of Benjamin Franklin*, ed.
Leonard W. Labaree et al., 2nd ed. (New Haven: Yale University Press,
2003), 116–17. Members of the Junto helped Franklin form an academy that
later became the University of Pennsylvania (192–96, especially 196n7).

29. MFP, Box 12, loose paper, Folder 10, AAS.

30. The phrase, attributed by Crocker to Benjamin Franklin, also appears at the end of her 1819 unpublished play, *The Midnight Beau*, as does
the character Philanthropus, who provides the six lines with which Crocker
ends her humorous piece.

31. Although Crocker is quick to warn against the "too free use of ardent
spirit" in this essay (7), she does not take the position that there should be
no use whatsoever, unlike L. M. Sargent in *Mr. Sargent's Address before the
Massachusetts Society for the Suppression of Intemperance* (Boston, 1833). In
the address, given on May 27, 1833, Sargent expresses outrage at the willingness of the state legislature to grant licenses to sellers of ardent spirits,
in effect making them dispensers of poison (34). Sargent, who notes that
there were a thousand temperance societies in Massachusetts at the time
of his address, considers the decline in the number of gallons of imported

spirits to the United States from 5,285,000 in 1824 to 4,090,000 in 1830 as a sign that the temperance societies are meeting with some measure of success in their attempts to suppress the vice of drinking (11). The absolutist line against alcohol consumption taken by many of these societies was also adopted by the Women's Christian Temperance Union, which was formed in Cleveland in 1874.

32. Judith Sargent Murray's *The Gleaner* appeared in 1798 in a compilation of pieces. See [Constantia, pseud.], *The Gleaner*, 3 vols., introduction by Nina Baym (Schenectady NY: Union College Press, 1992).

33. The frontispiece of Moira Ferguson's *First Feminists: British Women Writers, 1578–1799* (Bloomington: Indiana University Press, 1985) is a reproduction of Richard Samuel's 1799 painting, *Nine Living Muses*, which depicts Hannah More, Elizabeth Montague, Elizabeth Griffith, Catherine Macaulay, Elizabeth Carter, Anna Letitia Barbauld, Angelica Kauffman, Elizabeth Linley, and Charlotte Lenox. Of the nine women only two are included in Ferguson's anthology. More is not one of the two.

34. For a discussion of the popularity of catalogs of women, see Constance J. Post, "Making the A-List: Reformation and Revolution in Crocker's *Observations on the Real Rights of Women*," *Resources for American Literary Study* 29 (2005): 67–88.

35. A notable exception is Thomas Fuller's 1642 *The Holy State and the Profane State* (London, 1840). Books by her contemporaries include the following: Mary Wollstonecraft, *A Vindication of the Rights of Woman*, 3rd ed. (London, 1796); Hannah More, *Strictures on the Modern System of Female Education* (1799; Oxford: Woodstock Books, 1995); Samuel Johnson, *The Rambler*, in *The Works of Samuel Johnson, LL.D., with an Essay on His Life and Genius by Arthur Murphy, Esq.*, 12 vols. (London, 1823) and "An Account of the Life and Writings of the Earl of Rochester," in Gilbert Burnet, *Some Passages in the Life and Death of John, Earl of Rochester, D.D.* (London, 1787); Mercy Otis Warren, *History of the Rise, Progress and Termination of the American Revolution*, ed. Lestern H. Cohen (1805; Indianapolis: Liberty Classics, 1988); Thomas Coke, *A Commentary on the Holy Bible*, 6 vols. (London, 1801–7); Lucy Aikin, *Epistles on Women, Exemplifying Their Character and Condition in Various Ages and Nations, with Miscellaneous Poems* (London, 1810); Isaac Watts, *Horae Lyricae and*

Divine Songs by Isaac Watts, with a Memoir, by Robert Southey (Boston, 1854); L. M. Stretch, *Beauties of History; Or, Pictures of Virtue and Vice, Drawn from Real Life; Designed for the Instruction and Entertainment of Youth* (1770; London, 1808); Henry Kett, *Elements of General Knowledge*, 2 vols. (Baltimore, 1812); William Alexander, *The History of Women from the Earliest Antiquity, to the Present Time; Giving Some Account of Almost Every Interesting Particular concerning That Sex, among all Nations, Ancient and Modern*, 2 vols. (Dublin, 1799); Henry Hunter, *Sacred Biography: or, The History of the Patriarchs: To which is added, the History of Deborah, Ruth, and Hannah*, 6 vols. in 3 (Boston, 1794–95); [William] Russell, *Essay on the Character, Manners, and Genius of Women in Different Ages*, by [Antoine Leonard] Thomas, *Enlarged from the French of M. Thomas by Mr. Russell*, 2 vols. (Philadelphia, 1774); Boudier de Villemert, *The Friend of Women*, trans. Alexander Morrice (Philadelphia, 1803).

36. L. W. Koengeter, "Crocker, Hannah Mather," in *American Women Writers: A Critical Reference Guide*, vol. 1, *From Colonial Times to the Present*, ed. Lina Mainero (Detroit: St. James Press, 1979), 421.

37. In "'Drawing the Line of Equality': Hannah Mather Crocker on Women's Rights," *American Political Science Review* 100, no. 2 (May 2006): 265, Eileen Hunt Botting and Sarah L. Houser make the claim that "Crocker was the leading American political theorist between 1800 and 1820 to engage the controversial question of sex equality" and praise her as a "subtle rhetorician."

38. Rosemarie Zagarri, *Revolutionary Backlash: Women and Politics in the Early Republic* (Philadelphia: University of Pennsylvania Press, 2007), 176. For an excellent analysis of how the political meaning of virtue in this period is intertwined with the history of male and female symbolism, see Ruth H. Bloch, "The Gendered Meanings of Virtue in Revolutionary America," *Signs* 13, no. 1 (1987): 37–58.

39. Quoted in Gordon S. Wood, *The Creation of the American Republic* (Chapel Hill: University of North Carolina Press, 1969), 418.

40. Gordon S. Wood, *The Radicalism of the American Revolution* (New York: Knopf, 1992), 68. Wood argues that this virtue "became less the harsh self-sacrifice of antiquity and more the willingness to get along with others for the sake of peace and prosperity" (216).

41. An American edition appeared the following year, 1799, and another five years later.

42. For a discussion of the fallout from the publication of Godwin's *Memoirs* and the charged meaning of Wollstonecraftism, see Cathy N. Davidson, *Revolution and the Word: The Rise of the Novel in America* (New York: Oxford University Press, 1986), 132–33.

43. Although Zagarri claims that Crocker's *Observations on the Real Rights of Women* is a refutation of Wollstonecraft's *A Vindication of the Rights of Woman* (*Revolutionary Backlash*, 42), I believe a strong case can also be made that Crocker wants to refute the view about women expressed by More, who, referring to herself in the third person, stated, "It is her zeal for their true *interests* which leads her to oppose their imaginary *rights*" (*Strictures*, 2:24, italics in original). More may refute Wollstonecraft, but Crocker's choice of "real rights" over "imaginary rights" suggests her willingness to part company with More on this issue.

44. In *The Family, Sex, and Marriage in England*, Lawrence Stone argues that a major shift toward affective individualism in the relationship between husband and wife as well as parent and children occurred between 1500 and 1700 (164–72). The growing emphasis on loving personal relationships, which Stone attributes in large part to the influence of Puritanism, gave greater prominence to matrimonial choice based on love.

45. In *Uncommon Women: Gender and Representation in Nineteenth-Century U.S. Women's Writing* (Columbus: Ohio State University Press, 2009), Laura Laffrado identifies Crocker's comment about Sarah Knight in *Observations* as "the earliest published reference to Knight herself" (25, 33; cf. 38).

46. Barbara Welter, "The Cult of True Womanhood: 1820–1860," *American Quarterly* 18 (1966): 151–74. Recent challenges to this notion suggest that the fluidity of women's roles in the early part of the nineteenth century in the United States may not have hardened into separate spheres as Welter suggests.

47. Warren, *History*, 2:237–38.

48. Crocker does not supply the source for this anecdote. The reference to Mrs. Jackson may be to the wife of Maj. William Jackson (1752–1822), who served as an aide-de-camp to General Washington in the Revolutionary War.

49. In *Liberty's Daughters: The Revolutionary Experience of American Women, 1750–1800* (Boston: Little, Brown, 1980), Mary Beth Norton tackles the difficulty of assessing the outcome of that experience: "Republican womanhood eventually became Victorian womanhood, but at the same time the egalitarian rhetoric of the Revolution provided the women's rights movement with its earliest vocabulary, and the republican academies produced its first leaders. Few historical events can ever be assessed in absolute terms. With respect to its impact on woman, the American Revolution is no exception" (299).

50. Mather quoted in Kenneth Silverman, *A Cultural History of the American Revolution* (New York: Thomas Y. Crowell, 1976), 66.

51. For the treatment of theatrical metaphors in Cotton Mather, see Jeffrey H. Richards, *Theatre Enough: American Culture and the Metaphor of the World Stage, 1607–1789* (Durham: Duke University Press, 1991), 165–73.

52. On the Panic of 1819, see Jennifer J. Baker, *Securing the Commonwealth: Debt, Speculation, and Writing in the Making of Early America* (Baltimore: Johns Hopkins University Press, 2005), especially chapter 6, for a discussion of the insights Crocker's contemporary Judith Sargent Murray brought to an understanding of the interconnections between the marriage market and the commercial market.

53. Crocker is omitted entirely from Barbara Berg's *The Remembered Gate: Origins of American Feminism* (New York: Oxford University Press, 1978). Although publication of Crocker's *Observations* falls just outside the period that Conrad focuses on in *Perish the Thought*, her omission from Conrad's overview of feminist foremothers in chapter 1 is curious, given Conrad's inclusion of Mary Wollstonecraft, for example, but not her contemporary Hannah More. No mention, moreover, is made of Crocker in Linda K. Kerber, *Toward an Intellectual History of Women* (Chapel Hill: University of North Carolina Press, 1997); Karen L. Kilcup, ed., *Nineteenth-Century American Women Writers: A Critical Reader* (Malden MA: Blackwell, 1998); or Bruce Dorsey, *Reforming Men and Women: Gender in the Antebellum City* (Ithaca NY: Cornell University Press, 2002). Notable exceptions include Robert E. Riegel's *American Feminism* (Lawrence: University of Kansas Press, 1963), in which he acknowledges that Crocker wrote the first "feministic" book in America (8); Keith E. Melden, *Beginnings of Sisterhood: The*

American Woman's Rights Movement, 1800–1850 (New York: Schocken Books, 1977), 9; and Janet Wilson James, *Changing Ideas about Women in the United States, 1776–1825* (New York: Garland, 1981), which refers to Crocker's *Observations* as "a homely tract" that was "written in the Yankee vernacular" (290–91). For recent scholarship that takes Crocker into account, see Gay Gibson Cima, *Early American Women Critics: Performance, Religion, Race* (Cambridge: Cambridge University Press, 2006); Laffrado, *Uncommon Women*; and especially Zagarri, *Revolutionary Backlash*.

54. Other than the three texts printed during her lifetime, only Crocker's *Observations on the Real Rights of Women* has appeared since and usually as a short selection. See, for example, Aileen S. Kraditor, ed., "Selection from *Observations on the Real Rights of Women*," in *Up from the Pedestal: Selected Writings in the History of American Feminism* (Chicago: Quadrangle Books, 1968), 40–44; Sharon Harris, ed., "Selection from *Observations on the Real Rights of Women*," in *Women's Early American Historical Narratives* (New York: Penguin, 2003), 229–49; Marion Ann Taylor and Heather E. Weir, eds., "Selection from *Observations on the Real Rights of Women*," in *Let Her Speak for Herself: Nineteenth-Century Women Writings on the Women of Genesis* (Waco: Baylor University Press, 2006), 25–29. A facsimile of the entire text of *Observations* was reprinted in Leon Stein and Annette K. Baxter, advisory eds., *Sex and Equality*, series on Women in America from Colonial Times to the 20th Century (New York: Arno Press, 1974).

Fast Sermon

"Aug. 20—1812, Fast Sermon" appears on the first page of the manuscript but is omitted here. "Fast Sermon," which is in the MFP, Box 12, Folder 7, AAS, evokes the practice of many Puritan ministers who called for a day of fasting and prayer by their congregation when the community was beset with political disruption, unusual weather disturbances, Indian attacks, and more. Although the observance of this practice diminished in the eighteenth century it was occasionally used by political figures as well. On July 9, 1812, President James Madison, for example, called for a day of fasting and prayer to be observed "the third Thursday in August next," August 20, the date Crocker assigned to her own fast sermon.

The date in the title was originally placed after the author.

In adopting the pseudonym "Increase Mather Jun. of the inner Temple," Crocker links the name of her paternal great-grandfather with herself as a sort of "Junior" Mather, albeit one writing about public matters apparently for her private meditation, as the phrase "inner Temple" suggests. The allusion to the Temple also recalls Crocker's interest in Freemasonry, which traces its beginnings to Solomon's building of the temple in Jerusalem. See introduction.

1. In *James Madison* (New York: Times Books, 2002), 155–56, Gary Wills notes that Madison, unlike John Adams, used nondenominational language in making religious proclamations. Madison's later reversal of his position on religious proclamations in his "Detached Memoranda," including five reasons for not recommending them at all, are examined by Rodney A. Grunes in "James Madison and Religious Freedom," in *James Madison: Philosopher, Founder, and Statesman*, ed. John R. Vile, William D. Pederson, and Frank J. Williams (Athens: Ohio University Press, 2008), 120–21. For Madison's "Detached Memoranda," see *William and Mary Quarterly*, 3rd ser. (October 1946): 554–60.

2. Spelled "Cannaday" in the text.

3. Crocker's use of the phrase "howling wilderness" resonates because of its frequent use by early New England historians. See, for example, Cotton Mather's description of the settlement of Massachusetts Bay in *Magnalia Christi Americana*, 2 vols. (1702; Hartford CT, 1853): "Never was any plantation brought unto such a considerableness, in a space of time so inconsiderable! an *howling wilderness* in a few years became a *pleasant land*, accommodated with the *necessaries*—yea, and the *conveniences* of humane life" (1:80).

4. From Ps. 119:2.

5. Gal. 5:1.

6. From Ps. 122:7.

7. From James 5:16.

8. Quoted almost verbatim from Mic. 6:8.

9. From Psa. 144:15.

10. From Gen. 18:22. See Gen. 18:23–33 for the complete story of Abram's bargaining with God to save the destruction of Sodom and Gomorrah.

11. From Mic. 6:8.

12. Ps. 37:25.

Thanksgiving Sermon

"Aug. 24—1813, Thanksgiving Sermon" appears on the first page of the manuscript but is omitted here. Crocker's "Thanksgiving Sermon" is in the MFP, Box 12, Folder 8, AAS. Days of Thanksgiving, like days of fasting and prayer, were used by Puritan ministers to thank God for military victories, deliverance from pestilence, and so on. Although President James Madison declared on November 16, 1814, that a day of Thanksgiving for peace should be observed on January 12, 1815, Crocker does not follow suit as she did in her "Fast Sermon"; instead she designates the third Thursday in November, November 24, 1813, as her day of Thanksgiving. A second day of Thanksgiving was declared by President Madison on March 4, 1815, to be observed on the second Thursday in April of that year. See the unnumbered note to "Fast Sermon" for a discussion of Madison's stance about religious proclamations.

For Crocker's use of "Increase Mather Jun. of the inner Temple," see the unnumbered note to "Fast Sermon."

1. The first thanksgiving is described by Edward Winslow in William Bradford and Edward Winslow, *Mourt's Relation, or, Journal of the Plantation at Plymouth*, ed. Henry Martyn Dexter (1622; Boston, 1845), 133. Dexter adds, "Here began that peculiar New England festival,—the annual autumnal *Thanksgiving*" (133n417).

2. See "Fast Sermon," 6.

3. Possibly "vigour."

4. From Phil. 4:4.

5. From Phil. 4:8.

6. From Phil. 4:9.

7. From Phil. 4:7.

8. Originally "deploy."

9. For an understanding of the role of Christian eschatology in the development of Anglo-American radicalism, see Ruth Bloch, *Visionary Republic: Millennial Themes in American Thought, 1756–1800* (Cambridge: Cambridge University Press, 1985), especially chapter 1. According to Bloch,

"Historians of American revolutionary thought now generally trace the origins of eighteenth-century Anglo-American radicalism to the civil republican tradition imported from the English radical whigs." It is her contention, however, that "this ideology grew out of the experience of the English Revolution and the Commonwealth of the 1640's and 1650's." These years "were also years of millennial expectation. Millennial and civic republicanism gained ascendancy together in revolutionary England, and together they gave rise to American revolutionary ideology during the next century" (3).

10. This early expression of Crocker's confidence in the ameliorative power of institutions also appears in *A Series of Letters on Free Masonry*, 49, and *Observations on the Real Rights of Women*, 86–87.

11. The phrase recalls the title of one of the many books by Crocker's grandfather Cotton Mather, *The Good Old Way* (Boston, 1706). For a succinct explanation of how the Puritans imaginatively appropriated what they believed to be the history of salvation and made it their own by inserting themselves into it, see Sacvan Bercovitch, ed., *The American Puritan Imagination: Essays in Revaluation* (London: Cambridge University Press, 1974), 6–14. His extended treatment of this aspect of the Puritan imagination appears in "The Ends of Puritan Rhetoric," in *The Rites of Assent: Transformations in the Symbolic Construction of America* (New York: Routledge, 1993), 68–89.

12. See, for example, Deut. 24.

13. From Mic. 6:8.

An Humble Address

In the original title "reason" is not capitalized, and there is a comma after it.

1. Crocker spells "earthen" as "earthern," as does her contemporary Thaddeus Mason Harris in *Treasure of the Gospel in Earthern Vessels* (Salem MA, 1804).

2. According to Crocker, Paul's statement "We have this treasure in earthern vessels" (2 Cor. 4:7) bears a striking resemblance to the parable of Jesus in which the kingdom of God is likened to a rich man "who, when he had found one pearl of great price, went and sold all that he had, and

bought it" (Mt. 13:46). To support her claim, Crocker states that the English translation of the original Hebrew obscures the fact that "earthern vessel" ought to be rendered as "oyster shell," which is problematic since both of Paul's letters to the Corinthians were originally written in Greek, not Hebrew.

3. From 1 Kings 3:7.

4. From 1 Kings 10:22.

5. From 1 Kings 10:23.

6. From 1 Kings 10:1.

7. From 1 Kings 10:7.

8. From 1 Kings 10:10.

9. From 1 Kings 10.11.

10. A victorious navy seemed a dim prospect in 1812, when a bill introduced by Langdon Cheves to construct twelve ships of the line and twenty frigates "was defeated by a vote of 62 to 59." See Harry L. Coles, *The War of 1812*, ed. Daniel J. Boorstin (Chicago: University of Chicago Press, 1966), 21. The prospect brightened, says Gordon S. Wood, when "Congress finally agreed that the country needed a navy and in January 1813 voted to construct six additional frigates and four ships of the line" (*Empire of Liberty: A History of the Early Republic, 1789–1815* [New York: Oxford University Press, 2009], 683). Jonathan R. Dull points out that "between the 1650s and the 1850s, naval warfare was ruled by the ship of the line and the line of battle after which it was named. These huge, wooden-masted ships were some 120 to 210 feet long with a beam (width) of 30 to 60 feet. They carried between 40 and 130 cannon mounted along two, three, or . . . four decks." According to Dull, "The line of battle—a string of warships following each other bow to stern—was the best way to bring its power to bear, as each ship could give support to neighboring ships" (*The Age of the Ship of the Line: The British and French Navies, 1650–1815* [Lincoln: University of Nebraska Press, 2009], 1).

11. Spelled "grainary" in the text.

12. Crocker's concern about mutual needs, a major theme in her writings, is focused here on northerners and southerners, already a long-standing division between two regions of the country that she acknowledges may hold different views. The truly different view she seems at a loss to understand

is why timber and agricultural interests of both regions favor a Republican stand on trade even though it is at odds with their economic interests. In short, the difference, as she describes it here, is not so much regional as rural versus urban. A Federalist, Crocker tended to view trade as foreign rather than domestic, and for that reason was confounded by support for the embargo. For a discussion of the shift in recognizing the importance of Continental trade, see Wood, *Empire of Liberty*, chapter 19.

13. Crocker applies a well-known line from Thomas Paine's *The American Crisis*, no. 1, dated December 19, 1776, to the War of 1812. The essay, which was read to Washington's troops as they retreated across the Delaware to Trenton, begins with the following lines: "These are the times that try men's souls: The summer soldier and the sunshine patriot will, in this crisis, shrink from the service of his country; but he that stands it NOW, deserves the love and thanks of man and woman" (*Collected Writings of Thomas Paine*, ed. Eric Foner [New York: Library of America, 1995], 91–99).

Antiquarian Researches

The first page of the manuscript has a short title page on which "Antiquarian researches" appears. Information on the full title page appears flush left. Crocker's preference for "researches" rather than "research" has been retained throughout the essay; however, the title, "Antiquarian researches, Pleasant and easy, By an original Antiquarian," has been rendered with capitals for each of the key words. This essay is in MFP, Box 12, Folder 5, AAS. For other versions, see Folders 4 and 6, the latter of which contains a version with the following inscription: "This little work is now humbly dedicated by the author to the respected Memory of her friend Thomas Pemberton[,] Esqr. as the first proposer of an historical society" (n.p.). The voluminous papers of Thomas Pemberton (1728–1807) at the Massachusetts Historical Society cover a broad range of topics, such as the American Revolution, American biographies, Boston colonial history, and a chronology of Massachusetts history (1700–1800) and include his diaries from 1800 to 1805.

1. Gamaliel the Elder (fl. first half of the first century AD), a member of the Sanhedrin, was a teacher of the Apostle Paul, according to Paul's

statement in Acts 22:3: "I am verily a man which am a Jew, born in Tarsus, a city in Cilicia, yet brought up in this city at the feet of Gamaliel, and taught according to the perfect manner of the law of the fathers, and was zealous toward God, as ye all are this day."

2. Quoted almost verbatim from the last line of "False Greatness," a poem by Isaac Watts in *Horae Lyricae*, first published in 1706: "The mind's the standard of a man" (154).

3. This appears to be a paraphrase of material in an appendix in Hannah Adams, *The History of the Jews from the destruction of Jerusalem to the nineteenth century* (1812; London, 1818), 556–61. After noting that Menasses Ben Israel, author of *The Hope of Israel*, believed that American Indians are descended from the ten tribes of Israel, Adams provides a summary of the main points in support of this claim by James Adair, author of *The History of the American Indians*.

4. For a list of the women praised by Jerome, see Crocker's *Observations on the Real Rights of Women*, 98.

5. Crocker's reference to Moses and "the grand secret" is one of many ways she renders Jewish history through the filter of Freemasonry. See also the many references in this text to the wisdom of Solomon and his role in the building of the temple.

6. Most of the images in this passage are associated with Freemasonry: "the magnetic power of attraction," which links Freemasonry with the occult; "fire . . . extracted from the flint," which Freemasonry traces back to Moses striking the rock; and the compass, a major symbol of Freemasonry but which here refers to a tool of navigation. According to Albert G. Mackey, Cagliostro developed what he called Egyptian Masonry in the 1770s. Although Mackey regarded Cagliostro as a charlatan and did not believe that Magnetic Masonry would ever gain official status among Freemasons, Mackey nevertheless defended the right of a Mason "to search everywhere for the means of moral, intellectual, and religious perfection," noting, "If he can find anything in magnetism which would aid him in that search, it is his duty and wisest policy to avail himself of it" (*An Encyclopaedia of Freemasonry and Its Kindred Sciences* [Philadelphia, 1879], 482).

7. See Exod. 28:4–30, especially 28:21.

8. Spelled "Lemiel" in the text.

9. See Prov. 31:1–31, especially 31:19: "She layeth her hands to the spindle, and her hands hold the distaff."

10. Crocker's use of the word suggests "necessities," in this instance the recovery of historical material that she deems to be of such significance that it may usher in the millennium. Compare her earlier assertion in this passage that "even a matron" may play an important role in saving a nation.

11. From Amos 5:24.

12. From Matt. 10:29.

13. "It is," which precedes "one," has been deleted.

14. This statement appears elsewhere in Crocker's writings: "Thanksgiving Sermon," 16; *A Series of Letters on Free Masonry*, 49.

15. From Eccl. 1:14.

16. Elsewhere Crocker spells this word "relick."

17. See 1 Kings 19:19.

18. Contraction of "revered."

19. These four lines appear horizontally at the start of a new page. For Timothy Dwight's "Columbia," see *American Poems*, ed. Elihu Hubbard Smith (1794), facsimile reproduction ed. William K. Bottorff (Gainesville FL: Scholars' Facsimiles and Reprints, 1966), 62–64.

A Series of Letters on Free Masonry

On the title page above "Lady of Boston" is the inscription, "By Mrs[.] Hannah Crocker[,] daughter of Rev. Sam Mather."

1. An abbreviation for "Most Worshipful."

2. Thaddeus Mason Harris (1768–1842) not only held a number of official titles in Boston lodges, as the dedication by Crocker reveals, but also served as minister of the First Church of Dorchester, where her great great-grandfather Richard Mather was one of its earliest ministers. Harris wrote widely on topics ranging from Freemasonry to natural theology, the history of Dorchester, and biography in addition to numerous sermons, some of which were delivered as eulogies for fellow Masons. He is also the author of *The Journal into the Territory Northwest of the Alleghany [sic] Mountains, Made in the Spring of the year 1803, With a Geographical and Historical Account of the State of Ohio* (Boston, 1805).

3. As Crocker notes, Thomas Maurice, author of *Indian Antiquities*, references the work of Jacques Basnage, *The History of the Jews*, trans. Tho[mas] Taylor (London, 1708), in support of his claim in volume 4 about the Hebrew trinity and the Oriental triads of deity.

4. Maurice, *Indian Antiquities*, 4:188.

5. Brackets in original text.

6. Quoted almost verbatim from Maurice, *Indian Antiquities*, 4:187. Crocker, however, renders several names of the Sephiroths differently from Maurice: "Gedular" for "Gedulah," "Thipherath" for "Tipheroth," "Jehod" for "Jesod," "Melcuth" for "Malcuth"; "Gebutah," "Hod," and "Nersah" are spelled the same by Crocker and Maurice.

7. Crocker quotes Maurice almost verbatim in the first half of the sentence: "This is the order in which they are arranged in the circular table engraved in the work of M. Basnage of which I have presented the reader with a copy" (*Indian Antiquities*, 4:187; the copy of the engraving appears opposite page 185). Below the engraving Basnage writes, "Of these Sephiroths, or Celestial Splendors, the three Superiour denote the Three Hypostases in the Divine Essence; and afford indubvitable evidence that the ancient Hebrews had these notions of a Trinity, which are denied, or forgotten, by their descendants."

8. Quoted almost verbatim from Maurice, *Indian Antiquities*, 4:187.

9. Spelled "thus" in original text.

10. "Tis" is preceded by an apostrophe in the original text.

11. See Thaddeus Mason Harris, *Discourses, Delivered on Public Occasions, Illustrating the Principles, Displaying the Tendency, and Vindicating the Design, of Freemasonry* (Charlestown MA, 5801 [1805]), 256.

12. "[Bending] the knee within due square" appears to be a reference to the ceremonial practice of Freemasons in which the adept assumed the following form in imitation of the carpenter's square, which was oblong: "He first steps off with the left foot and brings up the heel of the right into the hollow thereof, the heel of the right foot against the ancle [*sic*] of the left, will of course form the right angle of an oblong square; the candidate then kneels on his left knee, and places his right foot so as to form a square with the left, he turns his foot round until the ancle bone is as much in front of him as the toes on the left foot." R. S. (By a gentleman belonging

to the Jerusalem Lodge), *Jachin and Boaz; or, An Authentic key to the door of Free-Masonry, both ancient and modern* (Suffield CT, 1799), 13. Bending the knee to form a square with the other knee was performed, moreover, within an oblong square, the shape of a Masonic hall. In *A Manual of the Lodge* (New York, 1865), Albert G. Mackey notes Dr. (George) Oliver's description of the tabernacle built by Solomon as the type of a Mason's lodge: "an oblong square, and, with its courts and appendages, it represented the whole habitable globe" (54). The square also symbolizes morality in Freemasonry, hence the link with "a virtuous life" that Crocker invokes at the end of the sentence.

13. Although Crocker's lodge had less visibility than the African Lodge founded by Prince Hall, Bullock notes that both mounted a challenge to traditional ways of thinking about their groups (*Revolutionary Brotherhood*, 161).

14. Elsewhere this appears as "Dʳ."

15. Crocker does not reveal the identity of "Dr. M.," but it may be her father, Samuel Mather, D.D., whom she often describes as "a great scholar," which she does here.

16. According to Nancy Cott, "Women's prayer groups, charitable institutions, missionary and education societies, Sabbath School organizations, and moral reform and maternal associations all multiplied phenomenally after 1800, and all of these had religious motives." Although Cott notes that "women thus exercised as fully as men the American penchant for voluntary association noted by Tocqueville in the 1830s," Crocker's female lodge suggests that there may be exceptions to Cott's claim that "women's associations before 1835 were *all* allied with the church, whereas men's also expressed a variety of secular, civic, political, and vocational concerns" (*The Bonds of Womanhood* [New Haven: Yale University Press, 1977], 132–33, italics in original). For a discussion of the rise of benevolent societies in Philadelphia in the same period, see Dorsey, *Reforming Men and Women*, 52–56.

17. Lodge, plumb, and square are just a few of the many Masonic symbols that appear in this text and elsewhere in her writings. In *The Symbolism of Freemasonry* (New York, 1869), Albert G. Mackey notes "that peculiar mode of masonic symbolism by which the speculative mason is supposed

to be engaged in the construction of a spiritual temple, in imitation of, or, rather, in reference to, that material one which was erected by his operative predecessors at Jerusalem" (161). Hence the lodge is important as "a symbol of the world, or universe" (344); the plumb as "a symbol of rectitude of conduct" (353); and the square as "a symbol of morality, or the strict performance of every duty" (357).

18. Although Crocker signs the dedication "P. Americana," she uses "A. P. Americana" for each of her three letters in *A Series*. For a possible meaning of "A. P.," see the narrative at the end of *Observations* about Aurelius and Prudencia, a couple she does not identify as her parents although she provides unmistakable clues. By combining "A." with "P." before "Americana," Crocker succinctly ties together several themes that appear throughout her work: the appropriation of Roman names to signify the embrace of Enlightenment ideals in the early republic and the mutual importance she ascribes to men and women. Note, however, Crocker's use of "Amilia Prudencia" as the name of the matron in *The Midnight Beau*.

19. Brackets in original text.

20. See Acts 26:28: "Then Agrippa said unto Paul, Almost thou persuadest me to be a Christian."

21. Although Crocker herself enjoyed a cheerful glass (see narrative of her visit to the home of Peregrine White, "Reminiscences," 189), she chiefly valued the associations to which she belonged for the chance they gave her to pursue her intellectual interests.

22. The phrase also appears in "Thanksgiving Sermon" (16) and *Observations* (87).

23. Crocker's defense of Freemasonry as an example of a benevolent institution reflects an awareness of long-standing criticisms leveled against the society. According to Thaddeus Mason Harris, these include the charges that Freemasonry sought "to destroy the religion of Christ, to subvert every established government upon earth, and to overthrow every system of civil society" ("Discourse X," in *Discourses*, 180–81). See also "Discourse IX" and "Discourse XI" for Harris's rebuttal of these charges.

24. The argument that Crocker advances here is entwined with the argument that women should not be isolated in their home, as the address

of Charlotte Perkins Stetson before the National-American Convention
of 1896 makes clear:

> Everything came out of the home; but because you began in a cradle
> is no reason why you should always stay there. Because charity begins
> at home is no reason why it should stop there, and because woman's
> first place is at home is no reason why her last and only place should
> be there. Civilization has been held back because so many men have
> inherited the limitations of the female sex. You can not raise public-
> spirited men from private-spirited mothers, but only from mothers
> who have been citizens in spite of their disfranchisement. In holding
> back the mothers of the race, you are keeping back the race. (Quoted
> in Susan B. Anthony and Ida Husted Harper, *The History of Woman
> Suffrage*, 4 vols. [Rochester NY, 1883–1900], 4:259)

25. Albert G. Mackey acknowledges that Freemasonry is indebted to
Judaism for its elaborate system of types, and especially to Moses, who,
"skilled in all the learning of Egypt, brought with him, from that cradle
of the sciences, a perfect knowledge of the science of symbolism, as it was
taught by the priests of Osiris and Isis." According to Mackey, one of the
richest sources of symbolism for Freemasonry is the Temple of Solomon,
which furnished many types and figures (*The Symbolism of Freemasonry*,
79, 85).

26. Although Freemasonry subscribed to the ideal of the Brotherhood of
Man and hence respected all religions, its ties to Christianity were especially
close. As Thaddeus Mason Harris notes, "Inasmuch as Masonry is professed
in those nations which have not yet been converted to the Christian faith,
and as it enkindles benevolence and excites virtue so accordant with the
genius of the Gospel, it may eventually have no inconsiderable tendency
towards introducing and propagating among them the most glorious system of revealed truth; at least by humanizing the disposition, softening the
manners, and removing the prejudices, may prepare the way for that most
desirable event." When Harris confidently asserts that no one can attain
the sublime grades of Freemasonry except by acknowledging Christianity,
he not only staves off the criticism that Freemasonry is anti-Christian, but
also stakes a claim that Freemasonry's special contribution to the spread

of Christianity is preparatory, much as John the Baptist, said to have been the first Christian Freemason, announced that he was preparing the way of the Lord (*Discourses*, 33–34). Mackey, however, did not view the Christianizing impulse of Freemasonry in England and America as a positive development (*An Encyclopaedia of Freemasonry*, 162–63).

27. From 2 Tim. 2:15: "Study to shew thyself approved unto God, a workman that needeth not to be ashamed, rightly dividing the word of truth."

28. See Bullock, *Revolutionary Brotherhood*, 360n67 for the correct date of this poem in the *Columbian Centinel*. Here the editor, Benjamin Russell, is referred to as "Brother Russell."

29. Original brackets. Note the use of "W. S. B.," which designates a brother Mason by the last initial rather than the first, as in "B. William Shattuck." Shattuck gained admission to the Lodge of Saint Andrews in 1777, according to *The Lodge of Saint Andrews* (Boston, 1870), 235.

30. The 1778 date appears to be in error as the *Centinel* was first published as the *Massachusetts Centinel and the Republican Journal*, Mar. 24–Oct. 13, 1784; later as the *Massachusetts Centinel*, Oct. 16, 1784–June 1, 1790; and finally as the *Columbian Centinel*, the name of the newspaper through 1800. Although Crocker dates the poem as 1784 in "Reminiscences" (362), the poem has not been found in the issues of the *MC&RJ* or the *MC* for that year.

31. Spelled "Biglow" in the text. For the address by Timothy Bigelow (1767–1821), see *An eulogy on the life, character and services of Brother George Washington* (Boston, 1800). Crocker's poem about this event was published in the *Columbian Centinel*, March 12, 1800 (4).

32. Jachin and Boaz (spelled "Boas" in the text) are names of free-standing pillars at the entrance to Solomon's Temple (1 Kings 7:21; 2 Chron. 3:17).

33. Original brackets.

The School of Reform

The title page of the AAS copy of this text bears the inscription: "Presented to the American Antiquarian Society by the Author. Aug. 1816. Clark."

1. Crocker's choice of Columbus as the pilot of the ship heading to

the Cape of Good Hope identifies her concern for reform as distinctively American. Here as elsewhere in her writings private and public well-being are inextricably intertwined.

2. See Acts 27:14: "But not long after there arose against it a tempestuous wind, called Euroclydon." This is the wind out of the Adriatic Gulf believed to have caused the shipwreck of Paul of Tarsus off of the coast of Malta.

3. Crocker does not identify the source of the quotation she attributes to Benjamin Franklin.

4. A reference to Luke 23:34: "Then said Jesus, Father, forgive them; for they know not what they do."

5. From Col. 3:9–10: "Lie not one to another, seeing that ye have put off the old man with his deeds; and have put on the new *man*, which is renewed in knowledge after the image of him that created him."

6. See Phil. 2:12–13: "Wherefore, my beloved, as you have always obeyed, not as in my presence only, but now much more in my absence, work out your own salvation with fear and trembling, for it is God which worketh in you both to will and to do of *his* good pleasure."

7. The specific phrase, a man with "a withered hand," appears in Mark 3:1. Cf. Matt. 12:10 and Luke 6:6.

8. Rom. 12:1: "I beseech you therefore, brethren, by the mercies of God, that ye present your bodies a living sacrifice, holy, acceptable unto God, *which is* your reasonable service."

9. In an appendix added by Hannah Adams to the fourth edition of *A Dictionary of All Religions and Religious Denominations, Jewish, Heathen, Mahometan, and Christian, Ancient and Modern* (Boston, 1817), she concludes, "Why providence has suffered the Christian religion to be hitherto confined to so small a portion of the globe is also a mystery which we cannot fathom. But we are encouraged by many prophecies in the sacred scriptures to expect a period when the gospel shall be universally extended, and received with unanimity; when all superstition shall be abolished; the Jews and Gentiles unitedly become the subjects of Christ's universal empire, *and the knowledge of the Lord fill the earth, as the waters cover the sea*" (376, italics in original).

10. For an account of the range of such societies in Europe and America,

see T. Williams, "A Brief Sketch of the State of Religion throughout the World," in Adams, *A Dictionary of All Religions and Religious Denominations*, 325–65.

11. The phrase is part of Matt. 5:16: "Let your light so shine before men, that they may see your good works, and glorify your Father which is in heaven."

12. See Eph. 2:20: "And are built upon the foundation of the apostles and prophets, Jesus Christ HIMSELF being the chief cornerstone."

13. From Matt. 16:18: "And I say also unto thee, That thou art Peter, and upon this rock I will build my church; and the gates of hell shall not prevail against it."

14. The phrase appears in a different context in Cotton Mather's *Magnalia Christi Americana*, 1:560. For a discussion of the gap Mather perceived between Indian culture and that of the New England settlers, see Constance J. Post, "Old World Order in the New: John Eliot and 'Praying Indians' in Cotton Mather's *Magnalia Christi Americana*," *New England Quarterly* 66 (September 1993): 416–33.

15. The suggestion is that the crimes are committed by men whose wives can corroborate the conditions under which they were committed. Given the law of *feme couvert* [*sic*], a woman could hardly take legal action in the matter. For a discussion of the extent of the law of *feme couvert* in the early republic, see Davidson, *Revolution*, 117–22.

16. See "Reminiscences," 185.

17. In *Mr. Sargent's Address*, delivered on May 27, 1833, Sargent reports that five hundred ships had stopped carrying grog (19), a far sterner measure than Crocker's suggestion to sailors that they avoid "drinking hard." In a later passage he invokes an analogy with tea, asking, "[If] our forefathers and mothers willingly gave up tea for liberty—why not ardent spirits to avoid enslavement?" (23).

Observations on the Real Rights of Women

1. Hannah More (1745–1833), who began her career as a writer of plays before turning to poems and essays, is best known for *Strictures on the Modern System of Female Education*.

2. More, *Strictures*, vol. 2, chap. 13.

3. The foundation stone and other key concepts in Freemasonry often appear in Crocker's writings.

4. Lord Coke. [Author's note.]

5. Coke, *A Commentary on the Holy Bible*, 1:11. Crocker identifies the "able commentator" as Lord Coke, which is misleading since that is the correct title for the British jurist Edward Coke (1552–1634) but not for Thomas Coke (1747–1814), who is referred to here. Thomas Coke was called "Bishop" in Methodist circles even though that was not his official title.

6. Possibly from the French *parler*.

7. Gen. 3:12.

8. Coke, *A Commentary on the Holy Bible*, 1:14. Coke's reference is to Jacques Saurin (1677–1730), who fled with his family to Geneva after the Revocation of the Edict of Nantes and became the most well-known French Protestant minister of the period. A prolific writer, Saurin served the French Protestant community at The Hague for twenty-five years. Although he embraced the Enlightenment, he was not uncritical of it, as his observation about the limits of reason in the matter of the temptation of Eve indicates.

9. Gen. 3:16.

10. The reference is to *Epistles on Women*, a four-part poem by Lucy Aikin (1781–1864), spelled "Akin" in the text. The full title is *Epistles on Women, Exemplifying Their Character and Condition in Various Ages and Nations, with Miscellaneous Poems*. Here Crocker quotes from 1, 11:116–29, but with 11:120–21 and 126–27 omitted. I have retained the quotation marks because this is one of very few instances in which Croker uses them.

11. "Torpid" in Aikin's text.

12. "Stature" in Aikin's text.

13. A reference to light raying out from the godhead, similar to the halo or nimbus.

14. Crocker's use of nautical metaphors in this passage recalls her pamphlet *The School of Reform, or Seaman's Safe Pilot to the Cape of Good Hope* (Boston, 1816).

15. Cf. Judith Sargent Murray, "On the Equality of the Sexes," in *Se-*

lected Writings of Judith Sargent Murray, ed. Sharon M. Harris (New York: Oxford University Press, 1995), 3–14.

16. See Psa. 128:3. Cf. Cotton Mather's use of the metaphor in *Bonifacius: An Essay upon the Good* (1710; Cambridge: Harvard University Press, 1966), 3.

17. Crocker here invokes the link between "cymical" and the art of alchemy.

18. Cf. Cotton Mather's *Successive Generations* (Boston, 1715).

19. See also "Thanksgiving Sermon," 16, and *A Series of Letters on Free Masonry*, 49.

20. Getting Roland Nightramble to prefer domestic bliss is the focus of Crocker's unpublished farce, *The Midnight Beau*.

21. Spelled "Sadduces" in the text. The Sadducees were rivals of the Pharisees. Although both parties held strict views about the law and temple observances, the Sadducees favored a literal interpretation of the law (e.g., "An eye for an eye, and a tooth for a tooth").

22. Crocker chiefly refers to Isaac Watts (1674–1748) as a poet and hymnist. The founder of English hymnody, he also wrote widely on other topics, including education and Christian doctrine.

23. From Isaac Watts's poem "The Indian Philosopher" (dated September 3, 1701) in *Horae Lyricae*, 211–12. In a note to Henry Bendish dated August 24, 1705, Watts explains that the poem was occasioned by Bendish's disappointment in love. Watts notes, however, that in the intervening years Bendish found his soul mate (210). Sir Henry Bendish married Catherine Gosling at St. Paul's Cathedral in London in 1706.

24. Alexander, *The History of Women*, 2:68. See chapter 19 for his extended treatment of the topic of witches.

25. The starting point of Crocker's genealogy of witchcraft is Moses. Deuteronomy, the last of the five books of Moses, issues an edict against witchcraft: "Let no one be found among you who sacrifices his son or daughter in the fire, who practices divination or sorcery, interprets omens, engages in witchcraft" (18:10).

26. From Alexander, *The History of Women*, 2:79. This idea accords with the view of many modern historians, including Carol F. Karlsen. In *The*

Devil in the Shape of a Woman: Witchcraft in Colonial New England (New York: Norton, 1987), she notes that women of any age in New England might be accused of witchcraft, but only a few of the accused under forty were ever brought to trial. Of those under forty who faced trial proceedings, about half *"were* related to (older) female witches" (66, italics in original). According to Karlsen, the debate among historians about the age of women against whom the charge of witchcraft was more likely to result in a trial has chiefly focused on two age groups: those forty to fifty-nine and those sixty and older. As the original settlers aged the number of those over sixty increased, as did the perception of older women as a problem in the community. Karlsen, who points out "that the heightened vulnerability of old women as targets of witchcraft fear was not limited to the Salem episode" (69), identifies marital status as an important aspect of their vulnerability. In the matter of witchcraft accusations, to be a woman put you at risk, to be an old woman put you at greater risk, and to be an old woman alone put you at greatest risk (75).

27. From Alexander, *The History of Women*, 2:57.

28. From Alexander, *The History of Women*, 2:58.

29. Spelled "Montague" in the text, which is the way the name appears in Alexander's *History of Women*, Crocker's source for the quotation from Lady Mary Wortley Montagu (1689–1762).

30. See Alexander, *The History of Women*, 2:58, for the passage in Montagu's letter 25, which she wrote to the abbot from Constantinople on May 29, 1718: "Our vulgar notion, that they don't own women to have any souls, is a mistake. 'Tis true, they say, they are not of so elevated a kind, and therefore must not hope to be admitted into the paradise appointed for the men, who are to be entertained by celestial beauties. But there is a place of happiness destined."

31. More's comparative view of the sexes is part of chapter 13, which is the first chapter in volume 2 of *Strictures* (volume 2 has new pagination but not a new numbering of chapters).

32. Crocker omits quotation marks around the phrases "rich nor poor" and "bond nor free," which More includes to indicate that she is quoting even though she does not provide the source. The source for the second pair in More is Gal. 3:28: "There is neither Jew nor Greek, there is nei-

ther bond nor free, there is neither male nor female: for ye are all one in Christ Jesus."

33. From More, *Strictures*, 2:31–33, beginning with "whatever characteristical distinctions may exist." By omitting ellipses Crocker appears to be quoting More verbatim when she is skipping entire pages. After the phrase "superior advantage," Crocker goes from page 33 to page 40 before resuming her lengthy quotation.

34. Spelled "past" in the text, even though More spells it "passed" in *Strictures*.

35. From More, *Strictures*, 2:40–42, beginning with "though it be one main object."

36. Occasionally the name of the author appears in italics in the text when the title is not cited.

37. Even before Crocker refers to Villamont, she quotes almost verbatim from the text she attributes to him but that was written by Boudier de Villemert, *The Friend of Women*. Here Villemert gives advice to women through the voice of Particeps (92).

38. The title of this is rendered as "friend to women" without capitalization or italics. By substituting "to" for "of" Crocker slightly alters the title of Villemert's book, *The Friend of Women*.

39. From Villemert, *The Friend of Women*, 185.

40. This passage, beginning "As well as us with a soul," is from Villemert, *The Friend of Women*, 187.

41. This passage, beginning with "A woman of real good sense," is from Villemert, *The Friend of Women*, 189.

42. From Villemert, *The Friend of Women*, 103.

43. From Alexander, *The History of Women*, 1:31.

44. From Alexander, *The History of Women*, 1:36–37, starting with "Moses" in the first sentence of this paragraph.

45. Here "superior" is spelled without a second "u," whereas on page 24 in Crocker's text it has a second "u."

46. From Alexander, *The History of Women*, 1:65.

47. From Luke 17:35.

48. From Alexander, *The History of Women*, 1:69–70, beginning with "Even two women" in the previous sentence.

49. Alexander, *The History of Women*, 1:324.

50. This appears to be Crocker's own opinion about women. In contrast, Alexander minimizes the difference between women permitted to be in the company of men and those who are not, noting that even nuns "are not altogether excluded from the company of men" (Alexander, *The History of Women*, 2:325).

51. The source for Crocker's quotation about Isaac Newton (1642–1727) is Alexander, *The History of Women*, 1:339.

52. From the last line of "False Greatness," a poem by Isaac Watts in *Horae Lyricae*: "The mind's the standard of a man" (154). Cf. "Antiquarian Researches," 28.

53. Spelled "Biogrophy" in the text. The reference is to Henry Hunter (1741–1802), author of *Sacred Biography*.

54. This lengthy passage, beginning with "And whither are our eyes," is from Hunter, *Sacred Biography*, 6: Lecture 2, 36–38.

55. From Hunter, *Sacred Biography*, 6: Lecture 3, 53, beginning with "In her" in the last sentence of the previous paragraph.

56. From Hunter, *Sacred Biography*, 6: Lecture 6, 86, starting with "To her life" in the second sentence of this paragraph.

57. From Hunter, *Sacred Biography*, 6: Lecture 6, 86.

58. The reference to Naomi as Ruth's mother is rendered in Hunter as Ruth's mother-in-law. The passage is from Hunter, *Sacred Biography*, 6: Lecture 6, 87.

59. Quoted verbatim from Hunter, *Sacred Biography*, 6: Lecture 7, 97, bottom of the page.

60. From Hunter, *Sacred Biography*, 6: Lecture 7, 97, top of the page.

61. From Hunter, *Sacred Biography*, 6: Lecture 8, 112.

62. From Hunter, *Sacred Biography*, 6: Lecture 15, 196.

63. From Hunter, *Sacred Biography*, 6: Lecture 16, 200.

64. From Hunter, *Sacred Biography*, 6: Lecture 17, 216.

65. From Hunter, *Sacred Biography*, 6: Lecture 18, 226.

66. The reference to "Russel" is to William Russell, who translated into English and expanded the book by Antoine Leonard Thomas, *Essay on the Character, Manners, and Genius of Women in Different Ages, Enlarged from the French of M. Thomas by Mr. [William] Russell*. This source appears in

the bibliography under "Russell" since Crocker always refers to this volume by the name of Russell rather than Thomas.

67. Capitalizing "The" after "Russel says," suggests that a quotation is to follow. Although quotation marks are omitted here, Crocker does use them for lengthy passages of poetry and occasionally for long passages of prose. The passage, starting with "The courage," is quoted almost verbatim from Russell, *Essay*, 1:59.

68. From Russell, *Essay*, 1:59–61, on St. Jerome. The lengthy passage is a paraphrase of Russell without benefit of any indication from Crocker that changes have been made. Jerome (ca. 342–420) translated the Bible into Latin in the version known as the Vulgate.

69. Spelled "woman" in the text.

70. Arius (256–336), who disputed the deity of Christ, insisted that in Christianity there is only one God, God the Father. Beginning with "But he who speaks of them with most zeal," this lengthy passage is quoted almost verbatim with an occasional paraphrase from Russell, *Essay*, 1:59–63.

71. From Russell, *Essay*, 1:104.

72. From Russell, *Essay*, 1:105.

73. This passage, beginning with "If the women" in the concluding sentence of the preceding paragraph, is quoted almost verbatim from the start of section 3 in Russell, *Essay*, 1:106.

74. The Greek orator Demosthenes (384–322 BC) reputedly overcame a speech impediment by placing pebbles in his mouth as he recited verses by the sea.

75. This passage, beginning with "Greece was governed" and ending with "day," is from Russell, *Essay*, 1:28–29.

76. The spelling of the Palmyran Queen Zenobia is "Zenomia" in the text.

77. Not only did Longinus (third century BC) serve as a tutor and counselor to Zenobia, but he is also believed to be the author of "On the Sublime," an early major text of literary criticism.

78. From Russell, *Essay*, 1:51.

79. This appears to be material added by Crocker between the preceding and the following quotations, almost verbatim, from Russell.

80. From Russell, *Essay*, 1:51.

81. Jane of Flanders (ca. 1300–1374), Countess of Montfort.

82. According to D. R. Woolf in *Reading History in Early Modern England* (New York: Cambridge University Press, 2000), the most popular history of England in the first third of the eighteenth century was that of Paul Rapin de Thoyras (1661–1725), whose 1724 *Histoire d'Angleterre* was translated into English by Nicholas Tindal and appeared in serial form (279).

83. English spelling is "Brittany."

84. This lengthy passage, beginning with "When John was taken prisoner," appears in L. M. Stretch, *Beauties of History*, 1:120–21. Crocker does not indicate whether she is quoting from this book, which first appeared in 1770, or the version by William Dodd, which was first published in 1773. Page numbers for Crocker's references to this title, which she usually shortens to *Beauties*, are to Stretch's book.

85. This appears as "has" in the text.

86. *The Generous Woman*, published in Paris in 1643, is not identified in Russell, *Essay*, except to note that the female writer "shews that her Sex is more noble, more patriotic, more brave, more learned, more virtuous, and more oeconomical than that of man" (1:123).

87. Although Pierre de Bourdeille, Abbé de Brantôme, wrote *Illustrious Dames*, the book is identified in Russell, *Essay*, with the following information: "In 1665, another lady published at Paris [this title]" (1:123). For the English translation by Katharine Prescott Wormeley, see *The Book of the Ladies* (London, 1899).

88. See François de Poullain de La Barre, *The Equality of the Sexes*, trans. Desmond M. Clark (1673; Manchester: Manchester University Press, 1990).

89. Here Crocker quotes from Russell, *Essay*, 1:123, with little alteration.

90. Marie Le Jars de Gournay (1565–1645). The sentence from Russell that Crocker quotes almost verbatim omits his comment that Gornay "deserved to be adopted by Montagne [*sic*]" (Russell, *Essay*, 1:122).

91. Anna Maria van Schurman (1607–78). The source of Crocker's comments about Schurman is Russell, who spells the name "Shurman."

92. The sentence about Schurman's many talents is quoted verbatim by Crocker from Russell, *Essay*, 1:122, although the reference on that page

to "Cologn" as Schurman's birthplace has been changed in Crocker's text to "Colona."

93. Elizabeth I (1533–1603), daughter of Henry VIII and Anne Boleyn, was the last Tudor monarch in England.

94. Crocker does not supply the source for the extract of the letter from Roger Ascham (1515–68) to the humanist Johannes Sturmius (Jakob Sturm, 1489–1553), whose name she spells "Sturminus."

95. This sentence is from Hannah More, *Hints towards Forming the Character of a Young Princess*, 2 vols. (London, 1805), 1:11.

96. From Russell, *Essay*, 2:80–81.

97. The reign of Queen Anne (1665–1714), daughter of James II of England and VII of Scotland, preceded that of William III of England and II of Scotland.

98. The historian whom Crocker quotes here almost verbatim is Russell, *Essay*, 2:101.

99. Spelled "Gray" in the text. Lady Jane Grey (1536/37–54) is variously referred to as the Nine-day Queen or the Thirteen-day Queen, depending on the date used for the start of her reign.

100. Thomas Fuller (1608–61), who served as a chaplain to Charles II after the Restoration, wrote several histories as well as many other books, including *Good Thoughts in Bad Times*, with two sequels, *Good Thoughts in Worse Times* and *Mixt Contemplations in Better Times*. His vast compendium, *Anglorum Speculum, or The Worthies of England*, provides a full description of the counties of England together with brief biographies of many inhabitants in a wide variety of occupations for each of the counties.

101. Fuller, *The Holy State and the Profane State*, 250.

102. Sir Thomas More (1478–1535), author of *Utopia*, was lord chancellor of England under Henry VIII. He was beheaded at the Tower of London on charges of treason.

103. As Pamela Joseph Benson notes, this Latin epigram "was the only description of More's female ideal available to the public in his lifetime in published form." See *The Invention of the Renaissance Woman: The Challenge of Female Independence in the Literature and Thought of Italy and England* (University Park: Pennsylvania State University Press, 1992), 159.

104. Beginning with the phrase "as neither his religion," this passage

is quoted almost verbatim from Russell, *Essay*. Between the end of this sentence and the start of the next, Crocker omits the following passage that Russell renders in English from More's Latin poem:

> You will find in her an even, cheerful, good-humoured friend, and an agreeable companion for life. She will infuse knowledge into your children with their milk, and from their infancy train them up to wisdom. Whatever company you are engaged in, you will long to be at home; and will retire with delight from the society of men, into the bosom of a woman who is so dear, so knowing, and so amiable. If she touches her lute, and more particularly if she sings to it any of her own compositions, it will sooth[e] your solitude, and her voice will sound sweeter in your ear than the song of the nightingale. You will spend whole days and nights with pleasure in her company. (2:77–78)

105. The passage beginning with "She will be your friend" four sentences earlier and ending here is from Russell, *Essay*, 2:78.

106. Cornelia was married to Publius Scipio Africanus the Elder.

107. As tribunes in the second century BC, Cornelia's two sons instituted many reforms. Tiberius, who sought to redistribute land from patricians to plebeians, was assassinated. His brother Caius, who went even further in reform measures, commanded his servant to stab him to death when he was confronted with an angry mob. See Plutarch, "Tiberius and Caius," in *Plutarch's Lives*, trans. Bernadotte Perrin, Loeb Classical Library (London: William Heinemann, 1921), 10:145–241.

108. The entire paragraph, beginning with "Cornelia, the illustrious mother," is from Stretch, *Beauties of History*, 1:15–16.

109. The reference to Valerius Maximus is to his widely popular *Memorable Deeds and Sayings*. Crocker appears to be quoting Maximus indirectly almost verbatim from Stretch, *Beauties of History*, 1:30.

110. Not to be confused with the famous Xantippe, wife of Socrates.

111. This appears as *"Plin. Hist."* in the text. Crocker, however, is not quoting Pliny directly but indirectly from Stretch, *Beauties of History*, 1:30.

112. From Stretch, *Beauties of History*, 1:62.

113. Françoise d'Aubigné Scarron, Marquise de Maintenon (1635–

1719), second wife of King Louise XIV of France, wrote frequently to her brother. Marie de Rabutin-Chantal, Marquise de Sévigné (1626–96), spelled "Severns," corresponded with her daughter. Hester Mulso Chapone (1727–1801), whose name Crocker spells "Chapon," originally wrote *Letters on the Improvement of the Mind* for her niece.

114. The reference is to Mary Wollstonecraft (1759–97), whose last name is spelled with a single "l" by Crocker.

115. This appears as "are wrote" in Crocker but "are written" in Wollstonecraft.

116. From Wollstonecraft, *A Vindication*, 234–35.

117. Catherine Macaulay (1731–91), whose name appears in the text as "Macauly," was a strong supporter of the American Revolution. In addition to an eight-volume *History of England*, she also wrote essays about politics, philosophy, and education.

118. From Wollstonecraft, *A Vindication*, 235.

119. From Wollstonecraft, *A Vindication*, 235.

120. Crocker refers to Wollstonecraft's *A Vindication of the Rights of Woman* as *Rights of Women*.

121. Wollstonecraft's assessment of Madame Chapone is borrowed in part by Crocker for her own comments about Wollstonecraft. Of Hester Chapone, Wollstonecraft wrote, "I cannot, it is true, always coincide in opinion with her; but I always respect her" (*A Vindication*, 235).

122. From Wollstonecraft, *A Vindication*, 273.

123. The English poet John Milton (1608–74) was best known in America for his 1667 epic poem, *Paradise Lost*.

124. Although Milton's (1638?) poem "Ad Patrem" has been cited as the source for Wollstonecraft's observation about Milton's confidence that he would achieve something of great magnitude, what Milton initially thought his achievement might be remains in dispute. See D. L. Macdonald and Kathleen Scherf, *The Vindications: The Rights of Men and The Rights of Women* (Peterborough, Canada: Broadview Press, 1997), 252; John T. Shawcross, *The Self and the World* (Lexington: University of Kentucky Press, 1993), 66–70, 95–99.

125. George Washington (1732–99) became commander in chief of the Continental Army in June 1775.

126. From Wollstonecraft, *A Vindication*, 274.

127. The reference to Wollstonecraft's *Vindication* appears in italics except for the page number: *Vol. II. p. 314*.

128. Crocker substitutes "old gypsies" for Wollstonecraft's "lurking leeches" (*A Vindication*, 415).

129. From Wollstonecraft, *A Vindication*, 416–17, starting with the question, "Do you believe that there is but one God."

130. Wollstonecraft, *A Vindication*, 417. This appears as "*Wolstonecraft's Observation*" in the text, although Crocker may be confusing the title with her own.

131. Samuel Wallis commanded the *Dolphin* on its second voyage to the Pacific, from 1766 to 1768.

132. Spelled Oberach in the text. The anecdote about Obereah appears in Alexander, *The History of Women*, 2:44.

133. "Staal" is the spelling in the text of Madame de Staël (1766–1817), a French-Swiss woman of letters whose writings were deeply influential, especially her book on Germany, *De l'Allemagne*, and her novel *Corrine, or Italy*. For a discussion of Madame de Staël as a woman of genius who created Corrine in a similar mold, see Ellen Moers, "Performing Heroinism: The Myth of Corrine," in *Literary Women* (New York: Doubleday, 1977), 263–319. Madame de Staël, who had a salon in Paris and later in Coppet, maintained a voluminous correspondence, eight volumes of which had already appeared in print by 1807.

134. The text by Madame de Staël, *The Influence of Literature upon Society* (Boston, 1813) is slightly altered by Crocker as *The Influence of Literature on Society*.

135. See the earlier reference to Lucy Aikin, 80.

136. See excerpt from Aikin, *Epistles*, 1, ll.116–29 (80–81).

137. Aikin, *Epistles*, 4, ll.476–94.

138. Prov. 31:29.

139. Cf. Thomas Jefferson (1743–1826), query 6 in *Notes on the State of Virginia* (1785; New York: Penguin Books, 1999), 70, in which he states, "America, though but a child of yesterday, has already given hopeful proofs of genius," citing as examples George Washington, Benjamin Franklin, and William Rittenhouse.

140. The American poet Sarah Wentworth Morton (1759–1846) adopted the pseudonym "Philenia, a Lady of Boston" in *Ouâbi; or, The Virtues of Nature* and *Beacon Hill: A Local Poem, Historic and Descriptive* as well as in many of her occasional poems. *My Mind and Its Thoughts* was published under her own name.

141. Mercy Otis Warren (1728–1814) wrote in a variety of genres, ranging from political satires about Loyalists during the American Revolution in *The Adulateur* and *The Group* to verse tragedies in *Poems Dramatic and Miscellaneous*. Her *History of the Rise, Progress and Termination of the American Revolution* remains an important contemporary account of the period.

142. Hannah Adams (1755–1831), regarded as the first woman in the United States to be a professional author, wrote *An Alphabetical Compendium of the Various Sects Which Have Appeared in the World, from the Beginning of the Christian Era to the Present Day*, which underwent several revisions and was later given the title *A Dictionary of all Religions and Religious Denominations*. She also wrote *A Summary History of New England, The Truth and Excellence of the Christian Religion Exhibited*, and *The History of the Jews from the Destruction of Jerusalem to the Present Time*.

143. Crocker's text truncates the title of Warren's *History of the Rise, Progress and Termination of the American Revolution, interspersed with Biographical, Political and Moral Observations* (1:iv). The specific reference here is to Warren's "Address to the Inhabitants of the United States," which Crocker notes as on page 4 rather than page iv. For a modern edition based on the 1805 text, see Warren, *History*, 1:xli–xliv, edited by Lester H. Cohen. Subsequent references to Warren's *History* are to Cohen's 1988 edition.

144. Neither the first name of Mrs. Ackland nor that of her husband is mentioned in Warren's 1805 edition; see Warren, *History*, 1:236–38.

145. The source for this anecdote is not identified by Crocker. It is possible that the reference is to the wife of Michael Jackson, colonel of the Eighth Massachusetts regiment and later promoted to brigadier general. General Jackson, who fought at Lexington and Bunker Hill as well as the city of New York, had four sons who fought in the Revolutionary War. See Edward Hagaman Hall, ed., *The Sons of the American Revolution: New York State Society, 1893–1894* (New York, 1894), 159. Crocker, however, mentions a Mrs. Jackson who brought six sons to the battlefront. Although

two recent studies on women and the Revolutionary War do not mention Mrs. Jackson and her many sons, they are important sources about the contribution women made at the battlefront: Holly A. Mayer, *Belonging to the Army: Camp Followers and Community during the American Revolution* (Columbia: University of South Carolina Press, 1996); Nancy K. Loane, *Following the Drum: Women at the Valley Forge Encampment* (Washington DC: Potomac Books, 2009).

146. This passage, beginning with "Having personally known her," is a paraphrase of Warren, *History*, 2:638.

147. A paraphrase of Villemert, *The Friend of Women*, 46.

148. A footnote in Villemert provides the basis for Crocker's comments about Pandora's box. According to Villemert, Epimetheus opened the box, letting loose everything in it except hope, and this in turn brought about the Iron Age (*The Friend of Women*, 2).

149. Throughout *Observations* Crocker refers to this book as *The Friend to Women* and to its author as "De Villamont" instead of Villemert and spells the name of the translator "Maurice" instead of "Morrice." It is possible she confused Morrice with Thomas Maurice, author of *Indian Antiquities*, a book to which she refers in several of her writings.

150. The passage beginning with "every one speaks of women" in the previous paragraph is from Villemert, *The Friend of Women*, 2–3.

151. From Villemert, *The Friend of Women*, 15.

152. From Villemert, *The Friend of Women*, 32–33, beginning at the start of this long sentence, "Let women then."

153. The passage beginning "Happily for us" in the previous paragraph is quoted almost verbatim from Villemert, *The Friend of Women*, 34–35, although Crocker omits an intervening sentence.

154. From Villemert, *The Friend of Women*, 57, beginning with "If any thing can add" in the previous paragraph.

155. See n. 111.

156. Beginning with "I shall here give you Pliny's receipt" in the previous paragraph Crocker is not quoting directly from *Natural History* by Pliny the Elder (23–79) but indirectly by way of Villemert almost verbatim (*The Friend of Women*, 59).

157. From Villemert, *The Friend of Women*, 92.

158. From Villemert, *The Friend of Women*, 93.

159. From Villemert, *The Friend of Women*, 99.

160. From Villemert, *The Friend of Women*, 156–57, beginning with "as soon as a woman wishes to raise herself."

161. From Villemert, *The Friend of Women*, 163–64.

162. "*So says Villamont*" is another instance in which Crocker italicizes an entire reference to an author, in this case, Villemert.

163. This did not deter Crocker from presiding over St. Anne's, a female Masonic lodge in Boston. See Crocker's first letter and her poem "A Song," in *A Series of Letters on Free Masonry*, 42–43, 57–58.

164. The passage beginning with "love is the life and soul" in the previous paragraph is quoted almost verbatim from Stretch, *Beauties of History*, 1:204.

165. The passage beginning with the phrase "without which life" is quoted almost verbatim from Stretch, *Beauties of History*, 1:228.

166. Josh. 24:15.

167. See 217n15, especially the poem at the start of Murray's essay, "On the Equality of the Sexes."

168. The reference is to black bile, one of the four humors identified by Hippocrates in ancient Greece and further elaborated in Robert Burton's 1621 *Anatomy of Melancholy*. The other three are blood, phlegm, and yellow bile. Each of the four is associated with a specific temperament: blood, sanguine; yellow bile, choleric; phlegm, phlegmatic; black bile, melancholic. In the twentieth century this typology was developed further by Hans J. Eysenck, *The Biological Basis of Personality* (1967; New Brunswick NJ: Rutgers University Press, 2006), 34–36, who acknowledges the widespread use of Kant's description of the four temperaments but notes that it was Wilhelm Wundt and other researchers in the nineteenth century who determined that the four are not mutually exclusive.

169. Crocker expressed a similar concern in "Jephthah Vow, explained," an unpublished essay "By Increase Mather Jun. of the inner Temple" to which "Mrs[.] Hannah Crocker, grand-daughter of Rev. Cotton Mather" has been added, MFP, Box 12, Folder 2, AAS.

170. From Stretch, *Beauties of History*, 1:219.

171. Crocker uses material from Stretch, *Beauties of History*, 1:230, three

times in this passage: first, a sentence from the bottom of the page, beginning with "Nothing ought to be concealed"; second, a sentence from the middle that starts with "The necessary advantages of friendship"; and third, a part of another sentence farther down on the same page, beginning with "no hazard in trusting to a well chosen friend."

172. The lengthy passage beginning with "This idea leads us" in the previous paragraph is from Russell, *Essay*, 2:10–12.

173. From Russell, *Essay*, 2:20, beginning with "It seems in consequence." Between the first and second of these two sentences, Crocker omits a sentence from Russell.

174. From Russell, *Essay*, 2:46.

175. This appears as *"Russel's Hist. of Women"* in the text.

176. Euclid (ca. 325–ca. 270 BC) was the father of geometry.

177. Spelled "As" in the text, even though all of the other chapters begin with each letter of the first word capitalized.

178. Spelled "Knights" in the text. According to Crocker, Benjamin Franklin and her father, Samuel Mather, were pupils of Sarah Kemble Knight (1666–1727), whose account of a trip she made from Boston to New York appears in the selections from Crocker's "Reminiscences and Traditions of Boston" in this volume (159–60). Why Crocker uses "Knights" here instead of "Knight" is unclear; however, in "Reminiscences" she includes four lines of verse attributed to Knight in which "frights" rhymes with "Knights."

179. For the use of the phrase "American Israel" by a contemporary of Crocker, see Ezra Stiles, "The United States Elevated to Glory and Honour," in *God's New Israel: Religious Interpretations of American Destiny*, ed. Conrad Cherry (Chapel Hill: University of North Carolina Press, 1971), 83. Stiles, president of Yale College, preached the sermon before Governor Jonathan Trumbull and the General Assembly of the State of Connecticut at Hartford on the occasion of the Anniversary Election, May 8, 1783.

180. An extra space in the text suggests that the omission of the comma may be a printer's error.

181. A major doctrine of Calvinism. Cf. Jean Calvin, *Institutes of the Christian Religion*, 2 vols., ed. John T. McNeill, trans. Ford Lewis Battles, Library of Christian Classics (1559; Philadelphia: Westminster Press, 1960): "But he [the Lord] shows that the emotion of love, which out of natural

depravity commonly resides within ourselves, must now be extended to another, that we may be ready to benefit our neighbor with no less eagerness, ardor, and care than ourselves" (1:418).

182. Crocker uses a variant of this phrase in the subtitle of *The School of Reform, or Seaman's Safe Pilot to the Cape of Good Hope.*

183. From Luke 22:42.

184. The influence of Samuel Johnson (1709–84), poet, biographer, literary critic, and lexicographer, was so great that the second half of the period in English literature known as the Long Eighteenth Century is also called the Age of Johnson (1740–1810).

185. Johnson, *The Rambler*, no. 72, November 24, 1750, in *The Works*, 3:7–8.

186. Crocker, who identifies the lodge as an ancient Jewish practice in *A Series of Letters on Free Masonry* (42), uses "lodge" here as a synonym for "heavenly home."

187. See the earlier reference to twin soul in Watts, 89.

188. Acts 10:34.

189. Obsolete for "showed."

190. A reference to the book of Acts 8:27–39.

191. John Wilmot, second earl of Rochester (1648–80).

192. Gilbert Burnet (1643–1715), historian, theologian, and church prelate, wrote *The History of the Reformation of the Church of England and History of His Own Time* in addition to books on church polity and other matters.

193. This appears in the text as "Some passages of the life and death of John, Earl of Rochester" rather than *in the life*. Burnet's full title is *Some Passages in the Life and Death of John, Earl of Rochester, Written by Gilbert Burnet, D.D., Bishop of Salisbury, with a Sermon, Preached at the Funeral of the said Earl, by the Rev. Robert Parsons, A.M., to this Edition is Prefixed An Account of the Life and Writings of the Earl of Rochester, by Dr. Samuel Johnson* (London, 1787).

194. All italics in the original. The passage beginning with "To him Lord Rochester" is from Johnson in Burnet, *Some Passages*, 6.

195. The historian Flavius Josephus (AD 37–ca. 95), born Joseph ben Mattathias, wrote *Antiquities of the Jews* and *Wars of the Jews* in addition to other works, including his autobiography.

196. The title of Josephus's *Wars of the Jews*, which has been variously rendered in translation, appears without italics in the text. Cornelius Tacitus (AD 55–ca. 117) and Dio Cassius (AD ca. 155–163/164) wrote voluminous histories of Rome. Flavius Philostrates (AD 170–245), a philosopher, is the author of *The Life of Apollonius of Tyana*.

197. The lengthy passage beginning with "Christians can appeal" at the start of this paragraph is from Kett, *Elements*, 1:23.

198. From Kett, *Elements*, 1:38, beginning with "if the Infidel" in Crocker's preceding sentence.

199. Francis Bacon (1561–1626), philosopher and statesman, wrote *Essays*, *The Advancement of Learning*, *Novum Organum*, *New Atlantis*, and numerous other works on a wide range of topics, including history and the law. The philosopher and political theorist John Locke (1632–1704), whose surname is spelled without a final "e" in the text, is chiefly known for his *Essay concerning Human Understanding*, *two Treatises of Government* although he also wrote about other matters, including education, toleration, monetary policy, and religion. Of the many contributions to modern science made by Sir Isaac Newton (1642–1727), mathematician, physicist, and natural philosopher, *Philosophiae Naturalis Principia Mathematica* remains his most deeply influential work. On Milton, see n. 123. The work of the jurist Sir William Jones (1746–94) in comparative philology includes a version of the Arabic *Moallakat*, the translation of Persian texts, and a study of Hindu law.

200. Kett's designation of the following writers as atheists accords with the prevailing opinion about the religious ideas of these men in their lifetime. Voltaire (1694–1778), perhaps best known for his satiric novella, *Candide*, was also a prolific Enlightenment writer on a variety of subjects and a strong advocate of toleration. David Hume (1711–76) was a philosopher, political theorist, and historian and a key figure in the Scottish Enlightenment, whose *Enquiry concerning Human Understanding*, *Political Discourses*, and *History of Great Britain* number among his many works. The English historian Edward Gibbon (1737–94), whose surname is spelled with a final "s" by Crocker, wrote *The Decline and Fall of the Roman Empire*. William Godwin (1756–1836), a writer of fiction, history, and political theory and the husband of Mary Wollstonecraft, is the author of *An En-*

quiry Concerning Political Justice, for which he is regarded as the founder of philosophical anarchism. Thomas Paine (1737–1809), the author of the *Rights of Man,* became an ardent supporter of the American Revolution upon his arrival in Philadelphia; in addition to *Common Sense, The Crisis,* and other pamphlets, he also wrote *The Age of Reason.*

201. From Kett, *Elements,* 1:33–34, beginning with "Where can we find" in the second sentence of this paragraph.

202. *"See Kett's Elements"* appears in italics in the text.

203. See earlier reference to Pliny, 112.

204. The passage beginning with "Pliny" is quoted almost verbatim from Stretch, *Beauties of History,* 1:7.

205. From Stretch, *Beauties of History,* 1:7.

206. The entire citation, *"See Beauties of H. Ist. vol.,"* is placed in italics in the text. The passage beginning with "accept therefore our united thanks" is from Stretch, *Beauties of History,* 1:8.

207. Marcus Tullus Cicero (106–43 BC), philosopher, statesman, and orator, was also noted for his voluminous correspondence, especially to his friend Atticus.

208. From Stretch, *Beauties of History,* 1:9, beginning with "Cicero was in all respects" at the start of this paragraph.

209. Crocker says of Cicero what she says earlier about Pliny: you can judge a man by how he treats a woman.

210. The lengthy passage beginning with "it gives pleasure" in the previous paragraph is from Stretch, *Beauties of History,* 1:10–11.

211. From Stretch, *Beauties of History,* 1:11, although the passage does not identify the poet.

212. This entire paragraph is from Stretch, *Beauties of History,* 1:11–12.

213. The passage beginning with "She openeth her mouth" is from Prov. 31:26–28.

214. The long paragraph on the good wife is from Stretch, *Beauties of History,* 1:12. The quotation in the final sentence is from Prov. 31:30.

215. The passage on a good father is from Stretch, *Beauties of History,* 1:19, although ten lines between "reluctance" and "he is prudent" are omitted.

216. From Stretch, *Beauties of History*, 1:13, beginning with "Parents repeat their lives in their offspring."

217. See Crocker's earlier references to Jerome, 97–99 and 137.

218. Jean Calvin (1509–64), a French theologian and leader of the Protestant Reformation, wrote *The Institutes*. Martin Luther (1483–1546), a leader of the Reformation in Germany, translated the Bible into German, a translation referred to as the Lutheran Bible. Melancthon (Philip Schwartzerd, 1497–1560), a professor of Greek at Wittenberg University, was a staunch supporter of the Reformation.

219. Richard Baxter (1615–91), a Presbyterian minister who served as a military chaplain for the Puritans during the English Civil War, wrote numerous books, including *The Saint's Everlasting Rest*, *Call to the Unconverted*, and a lengthy autobiography titled *Reliquiae Baxterianae*. John Howe (1630–1705), also a chaplain to Cromwell during the English Civil War, wrote *The Blessedness of the Righteous* and *The Living Temple*. John Owen (1616–83) wrote numerous books, including *Display of Arminianism* and *On Temptation*. *The Saints Treasury* and *The Rare Jewel of Christian Contentment* are two of the many collections of published sermons by Jeremiah Burroughs (1599–1646), an Anglican who served as a teacher in the English Church at Rotterdam.

220. To the previous list of four English ministers, Crocker appears to be adding two from Scotland: likely possibilities are Ebenezer Erskine (1680–1754), a leader in the secessionist movement from the Church of Scotland and the author of many published sermons as well as a lengthy diary; and John Ogilvie (1733–1814), a minister and the author of *Rona*, *Providence*, and many other poems as well as essays such as *An Inquiry into the Causes of the Infidelity and Scepticism of the Times*. Given her description of the two as men "in our own time," she may have another Erskine in mind, as the lives of Ebenezer Erskine and Crocker overlap by only two years.

221. See the earlier reference to Watts, 88–89, 94.

222. Crocker omits the final "e" in the spelling of the surname of Anne Steele (1716–78), an English hymn writer who enjoyed popularity in the United States. A hymnal published by Episcopalian Trinity Church in Boston included 59 of Steele's hymns out of 152 songs, more than a third of the total, notes Amos Wells in *A Treasury of Hymns* (Boston: United

Society of Christian Endeavor, 1914), 353. The choice seems unusual for an Episcopal church, given that Steele was a Baptist.

223. Although the Whig statesman William Pitt, first Earl of Chatham (1708–75), did not support independence for the American colonies, he was firmly opposed to the severe measures taken against them. Edmund Burke (1729–97), critical of the way the British were conducting the war in America, delivered the speech titled "On Conciliation with the American Colonies" to the British Parliament in March 1775. The speech had thirteen resolutions, as many as the number of American colonies at the start of the War of Independence. The jurist Lord Thomas Erskine (1750–1823), celebrated for his oratory, was given the title of baron and made lord chancellor of Great Britain in 1793 after serving as the king's counsel. The English poet John Dryden (1631–1700) was also a playwright, essayist, and translator. Alexander Pope (1688–1744) wrote *The Dunciad, An Essay on Man, The Rape of the Lock*, and many other poems as well as verse translations of *The Odyssey* and *The Iliad* by Homer. Matthew Prior (1664–1721), celebrated for his epigrammatic style, wrote occasional poems, longer poems such as *Henry and Emma, Upon the Model of the Nut-Brown Maid*, and *Alma or the Progress of the Mind*, and essays (e.g., *Four Dialogues of the Dead*). Joseph Addison (1672–1719), a poet and playwright, collaborated with Richard Steele in producing *The Spectator*; his most successful play was the tragedy *Cato*, originally performed in 1713.

224. Sir Edward Coke (1552–1634) was an attorney general and scholar of English common law. Francis Bacon (1561–1626), who trained for the law and served as a member of Parliament, wrote papers on public affairs as well as literary and philosophical essays (see n. 199). Sir Matthew Hale (1609–76), lord chief justice, was the author of *History of the Common Law of England*.

225. See n. 139 on Jefferson.

226. For an understanding of the trajectory Crocker traces from Columbus (ca. 1451–1506) to the founding of America, see her imitation of Timothy Dwight's poem "Columbia" ("Antiquarian Researches," 35–36).

227. The phrase, which appears in Deut. 32:10, "He found him in a desert land, and in the waste howling wilderness," was applied to New

England by writers as diverse as Cotton Mather and Daniel Boone. See Mather, *Magnalia Christi Americana*, 1:276; Daniel Boon[e], *The Life and Adventures of Colonel Daniel Boon[e]* (Brooklyn, 1823), 13.

228. William Bradford (1590–1657), who arrived with the Puritan Separatists on the *Mayflower* in 1620, was elected governor of Plymouth Colony many times. He is best known as the author of the "History of Plimmoth," first published in its entirety in 1856 as the *History of Plymouth Plantation*, printed from the original manuscript for the Massachusetts Historical Society (Boston). Cambridge-educated John Winthrop (1588–1649), the author of "A Modell of Christian Charity," established the Massachusetts Bay Colony in 1630. He often served the colony as governor or deputy governor. Simon Bradstreet (1630–97), the husband of the poet Anne Bradstreet, had a variety of administrative posts, including that of governor of the Massachusetts Bay Colony. Included in a roll call of early settlers, the Allen reference is likely to John Allen (1596–1671), a clergyman who became the first minister of Dedham, Massachusetts, shortly after his arrival in New England in 1639. William Brewster (ca. 1566–1644), who arrived on the *Mayflower* in 1620, served the church in the Plymouth Colony as a ruling elder. Myles Standish (ca. 1584–1656), recruited by those embarking on the *Mayflower* for his military experience in the Low Countries, is credited with several achievements, including the building of the first port, which may be a reason why Crocker refers to him as "the enterprizing Standish."

229. Thomas Hooker (1586–1647) came with fellow ministers John Cotton and Samuel Stone from England to Massachusetts Bay in 1633, although Hooker left after three years to found the Connecticut Colony. Many of his sermons were published during his lifetime; *A Survey of the Summe of Church-discipline* (1648), a succinct statement of the main tenets of Congregationalism, appeared in print the year after his death. Ralph Partridge (1579–1658), who arrived in Massachusetts Bay in 1636, was the first minister of Duxbury and a framer of the model of church government for the synod of 1648 at Cambridge, Massachusetts. John Eliot (1604–90) came to Massachusetts Bay in 1631, where he preached to the Indians in their own language and established more than a dozen "Praying Indian" towns. Known as the "Apostle to the Indians," Eliot completed the first

translation of the Bible printed in the English colonies. The New Testament was published in 1651 and the Old Testament in 1653. The Puritan minister John Cotton (1584–1652) served as dean of Emmanuel College, Cambridge, before leaving for Boston, where initially he was a firm supporter of Anne Hutchinson in the Antinomian controversy that began in 1636. He wrote voluminously on a variety of topics, including New England Congregationalism and practical piety. His catechism *Milk for Babes* was a staple of Puritan early childhood education. On the Mather line, see the introduction, xv. Most of the names Crocker cites in this passage are those of early New England figures, so the reference to Chauncy here is likely to Charles Chauncy (1592–1672), who taught Greek at Trinity College, Cambridge, before leaving England in 1638 for America, where he became president of Harvard College in 1654.

230. Sewall is probably Joseph Sewall (1688–1769), minister of the Old South Church. He was the son of Samuel Sewall, one of the judges during the Salem witchcraft trials in 1692 but the only judge to confess later that he had been in error. Thomas Prince (1687–1758), a minister at Old South Church in Boston, wrote widely about theology and revised the psalter. An early collector of Americana, including the Mather papers, he also wrote *A Chronological History of New England in the Form of Annals.* Benjamin Colman (1673–1747), minister of the Brattle Street Church in Boston, was a leader among Congregationalist clergy. His daughter Jane (1708–35) married Ebenezer Turrell, who included several of her poems in his memoirs about her in *Reliquiae Turellae, et lachrymae paternae. The father's tears over his daughter's remains, Two sermons preach'd at Medford, April 6[,] 1735. By Benjamin Colman, D.D., The Lord's Day after the funeral of his beloved daughter Mrs. Jane Turell. To which are added, some large memoirs of her life and death, by her consort, the Reverend Mr. Ebenezer Turell, M.A., Pastor of the church in Medford [Four lines from Psalms].* Crocker notes that the Coopers were the predecessors of Peter Thacher at Brattle Street Church in Boston. William Cooper (1694/95–1743) was a minister at Battle Street from 1716 to 1743, and his son Samuel Cooper (1725–83) was a minister there from 1746 to 1783. Crocker's designation of Thacher as "our respected friend" suggests that he may be a contemporary of hers, in which case the reference is to Peter Thacher (1752–1802), a Congregational minister at Malden and later

at Brattle Street in Boston. As a founder of the Massachusetts Historical Society he shared Crocker's interest in the history of New England.
Thacher's great-grandfather Peter Thacher (1651–1727) was a Congregational
minister in Milton, and his son Samuel Cooper Thacher (1785–1818) was
the Unitarian minister of New South Church, Boston. Samuel Stillman
(1737–1807), minister of the First Baptist Church in Boston, served as one
of the original trustees of what is now Brown University.

231. Although many Pembertons and Lathrops were ministers in early
New England, Crocker appears to have in mind Ebenezer Pemberton
(1704–79), minister of New Brick Church in Boston, and John Lathrop
(1740–1816), who succeeded him.

232. Here Crocker suggests that Benjamin Franklin's achievements in
science are worthy of comparison with those of the English mathematician
and physicist Isaac Newton (1642–1727). See earlier reference to Paine in
Observations, 133. The 1776 publication of *Common Sense* catapulted Paine
to fame among those who supported independence from England. He also
wrote sixteen pamphlets for *The American Crisis* (December 1776–April
1783). No. 1, dated December 19, 1776, was read to Washington's troops as
they retreated across the Delaware to Trenton. The opening line, "These
are the times that try men's souls," is invoked by Crocker in "An Humble
Address," 25. Theophilus Parsons (1750–1813), a framer of the Constitution of Massachusetts and a member of the state convention that ratified
the U.S. Constitution, served as chief justice of Massachusetts. Jeremy
Belknap (1744–98), a Congregational minister and founding member of
the Massachusetts Historical Society, wrote a multivolume *History of New
Hampshire and American Biography*. George Minot (1758–1802) wrote *The
History of the Insurrection in Massachusetts in the Year 1786*, a critical treatment
of the rebellion organized by farmers and led by Revolutionary War veteran
Daniel Shay, hence the name Shay's Rebellion. Minot also contributed two
volumes to the *History of Massachusetts Bay* started by Thomas Hutchinson.
John Adams (1735–1826) was a delegate to the first Continental Congress,
a member of the committee that drafted the Declaration of Independence,
a negotiator of the Paris Peace Treaty of 1783, the first vice president of the
United States, and the second president of the United States (1797–1801).
James Bowdoin (1727–90) was elected president of the Council of Mas-

sachusetts in 1775 and later president of the convention that wrote the state constitution, which was adopted in 1780. He was also a governor of Massachusetts. Fisher Ames (1758–1808), a congressman from Massachusetts, was a staunch Federalist and strong advocate of a meritocracy of talent. Samuel Dexter (1761–1816), a congressman from Massachusetts and later a senator, also served as secretary of war and secretary of the treasury during the presidency of John Adams.

233. The reference to Chatham appears to be to William Pitt, the first Earl of Chatham (see n. 223). For the reference to Erskine, see n. 223.

234. Crocker refers to herself as "a real Washingtonian" in the complete manuscript of "Reminiscences" (220, Crocker's pagination).

235. Warren is likely James Warren (1726–1808), the husband of the writer Mercy Otis Warren, cited by Crocker, 109. James Warren, who served as a Massachusetts legislator and was a supporter of Shay's Rebellion in 1786, insisted that the U.S. Constitution include a bill of rights before he would lend support to its ratification. Levi Lincoln (1749–1820), a Massachusetts legislator and lawyer, made an early contribution to the antislavery struggle by arguing in three legal cases against the right to hold a Negro in slavery, claims that were later upheld by the Supreme Court. Although this may be a reference to Alexander Hamilton, it is much more likely a reference to Paul Hamilton (1762–1816), a revolutionary soldier who served as a governor of South Carolina. He later became secretary of the navy (1809–12), leading the department at a time when it was denied funding by Congress. Support for the U.S. Navy was a matter of great concern to Crocker. Henry Knox (1750–1806), colonel of artillery during the Revolutionary War, was a close advisor to George Washington.

236. An abbreviated reference, which appears without italics in the text, to the history by Crocker's grandfather, Cotton Mather, titled *Magnalia Christi Americana*.

237. The "A" in the title of Adams's history is not capitalized in the text, nor is the rest of the title placed in italics. Crocker, who refers to *The History of the Jews* by Hannah Adams as *A Compendious History of the Jews*, notes her use of the following authors: Josephus (see n. 195); Basnage, a reference to Jacques Basnage de Beauval (1653–1723), *The History of the Jews*; a

work on Turkish history that she does not identify; and *Magnalia Christi Americana*, the history of New England by her grandfather Cotton Mather.

238. A duodecimo, a sheet folded over twelve times to create twelve leaves or twenty-four pages, is the size of a commercial paperback. It was often used for popular abridgements of works printed initially in octavo or folio.

239. Spelled "Quintillian" in the text. The Roman rhetorician Quintilian (ca. 35–ca. 100) wrote *Institutio Oratoria*, a handbook on the education of an orator.

240. Crocker is quoting Quintilian from Stretch, *Beauties of History*, 1:179.

241. Boyle's Law, one of the three basic laws of gases, is named for Robert Boyle (1627–91), a founding member of the Royal Society and the author of *The Sceptical Chymst.*

242. This entire phrase, "*See Life of Boyle*," appears in italics in the text. Crocker is quoting the author of the *Life of Boyle* from Stretch, *Beauties of History*, 1:66.

243. Marcus Aurelius (121–180), Roman emperor from 161 to 175 and a proponent of Stoicism, is the author of *Meditations.* The first English translation, by Meric Casaubon, *Marcus Aurelius Antoninus, His Meditations concerning himselfe* (1634), was followed by two more versions before the highly praised translation by James Moor and Francis Hutcheson appeared in 1742. Crocker is quoting Marcus Aurelius almost verbatim from Stretch, *Beauties of History*, 1:68.

244. This appears to be a reference to Marcus Porcius Cato (234–149 BC), known as Cato the Elder. The austerity of Cato the Elder, consul and censor of Rome, was legendary. From Stretch, *Beauties of History*, 1:68.

245. The passage beginning "There is more satisfaction" appears as two paragraphs in Stretch, *Beauties of History*, 1:58.

246. The statement in the previous sentence beginning "We ought to consult the worth of the person" is from Stretch, *Beauties of History*, 1:58; the statement in this sentence beginning "Let a benefit" is from 1:59.

247. Setting the name of the author in italics appears to be Crocker's shortened reference to the text by that author. Here Crocker quotes al-

most verbatim from Samuel Johnson's *The Rambler*, no. 17, May 15, 1750, in *The Works*, 2:115.

248. From Johnson, *The Rambler*, no. 20, May 26, 1750, in *The Works*, 2:133.

249. From Johnson, *The Rambler*, no. 145, August 6, 1751, in *The Works*, 4:32–33.

250. Crocker's comment on the Roman writer Seneca the Younger (BC ca. 4–65 AD) is from Johnson, *The Rambler*, no. 150, August 24, 1751, in *The Works*, 4:58.

251. From *The Rambler*, no. 152, August 31, 1751, in *The Works*, 4:69. Johnson, however, uses quotation marks for Seneca's words.

252. From Johnson, *The Rambler*, no. 152, August 31, 1751, in *The Works*, 4:69.

253. From Johnson, *The Rambler*, no. 154, September 7, 1751, in *The Works*, 4:86.

254. From Stretch, *Beauties of History*, 1:99, but without attribution to Seneca the Younger. See Seneca's *Morals of a Happy Life, Benefits, Anger and Clemency*, trans. Sir Roger L'Estrange (Chicago, 1882), 235.

255. From Stretch, *Beauties of History*, 1:99.

256. The line from Shakespeare's *Titus Andronicus*, I.1.390, appears in Stretch, *Beauties of History*, 1:99.

257. Following the practice during the early republic period of assigning Roman names to figures who exemplify republican values, Crocker uses "Aurelius" to refer to her father, Samuel Mather, and "Prudencia" for her mother, Hannah Hutchinson Mather. Crocker says the couple was married for fifty years, which makes the identity of this pair certain: Crocker's parents were married in 1731, and her mother died in 1781.

258. Samuel Mather was born on October 30, 1706, graduated from Harvard College in 1723, and is the last minister in the "fourfold line of Mathers," the phrase employed by Crocker for the four generations of ministers on her father's side of the family: Richard, Increase, Cotton, and Samuel. Samuel's father, Cotton Mather, is the "eminent clergyman" to whom Crocker refers here.

259. Hannah Hutchinson, the daughter of Thomas Hutchinson, whom

Crocker describes as an "opulent merchant," was born on August 23, 1713. She was the sister of Governor Thomas Hutchinson.

260. Acts 17:26.

261. Samuel and Hannah Mather had five daughters and three sons: the eldest, Samuel, born in 1736, followed by Thomas; Elizabeth; Increase; Sarah; Abigail; and the youngest, Hannah, born in 1752.

262. Extra space in the text indicates that the omission of a period may be a printer's error.

263. This is one of the instances in which "honorable" is spelled in this text without a "u."

264. Hannah Hutchinson Mather died at the age of sixty-eight in 1781; her husband, Samuel, died four years later at age seventy-nine in 1785.

265. The quotation mark appears outside the semicolon in the text, which refers here to Luke 2:29.

266. Matt. 25:23.

267. These seem to be lines by Crocker.

The Midnight Beau

Formatting has been regularized, stage directions have been set in italics, and acts and scenes are rendered as numbers.

1. Spelled "Persona" in the text.

2. Although Crocker spells "Phylanthropus" with a "y" here, she spells it with an "i" more frequently in the play than any other variant, including "Phailanthropus."

3. Spelled "Anglelica" in the text. Other variants include "Anglica" and "Anglicia."

4. Crocker uses "Hony" as a variant of "honey" and both "honys" and "honies" to form the plural.

5. Crocker puts an apostrophe in several words in the play that she does not use elsewhere: "ha'" and "Ar'ra" or "Ar'ry."

6. An abbreviation of "Oh Glee." Occasionally Crocker shortens the names of other characters in the play: "Philan." for "Philanthropus," "Rant" for "Rantapole," "Ramble" for "Nightramble," and "Strip" for "Stripling." She also abbreviates Franklin as "Fran." on the last page of the text. Omit-

ted parts of the name of a character appear in brackets. The use of D^r not followed by a proper name has been silently changed to "Doctor."

7. Spelled "No" in the text.

8. A reference to the Embargo Act of 1807, passed by Congress at the request of President Thomas Jefferson, who used it as a major foreign policy initiative. Passed during Jefferson's second term, the Embargo Act was followed by the Non-Intercourse Act of 1809 and the Non-Intercourse Act of 1811. The second of these angered Federalists because of Madison's insistence that the French had removed their restrictions, although John Quincy Adams and others were not convinced that Napoleon was willing to do so. Eager to use France's lifting of restrictions as leverage to get Great Britain to remove its own, Madison cast a letter from France's foreign minister, the duc de Cadore, in the best possible light, choosing to believe that France had dropped the restrictions. When Madison finally declared war on Great Britain on June 18, 1812, the ostensible reasons were British impressment of American sailors and its violation of America's neutral rights. See Wood, *Empire of Liberty*, chap. 17, especially 645–58, 666–67.

9. A sinking fund is a fund into which the issuer of notes or bonds for private or public debt makes periodic payments to ensure that the debt is gradually paid off before the note or bond matures. The money in the fund is invested, but there is no guarantee that it will yield a profitable rate of return for the holder of the note. Many investors lost significant sums in the Panic of 1819, and the precariousness of investing is derided throughout this passage. A sinking fund in the United States was first proposed by Alexander Hamilton in 1790 as a way to retire Revolutionary War debt. Adam Smith, as Wood notes in *Empire of Liberty*, warned that such a fund may "sink" old debt but also give rise to new" (96). Adam Smith, however, endorsed "multiplicative banking" as a way to "free up metal languishing as 'dead stock' in the vaults" so that it "could do double duty in circulation," according to Jennifer J. Baker, who notes that Smith favored a one-to-four or one-to-five ratio "between reserves and circulating banknotes" (*Securing the Commonwealth*, 13–14).

10. Blank spaces, ellipses, or a period used by Crocker to indicate a missing letter or letters in a word (e.g., "D . . m'd," "D m," and "d m"; "G." and "G'd" for "God"; "H ll" for "Hell") have been replaced with hyphens.

Exception: "G." has been replaced with a hyphen and "d" as "G-d" to avoid confusion. In conversation with Philanthropus, Stripling uses "damn" several times within earshot of Stripling's mother, Prudencia, who calls Stripling a "reprobate" but refrains from criticizing his language. Crocker's willingness to have Stripling and other male characters use such language may be an attempt to create authentic dialogue.

11. Crocker did not number the first stanza but did number stanzas 2–4, so the first stanza has been designated 1. The beginning of the second stanza, however, was marked by Crocker as "2" before the fourth line of the first stanza even though each stanza has four lines. Stanza 2 is now marked as beginning at the fifth line.

12. Variant of "Botheration."

13. Possibly "take'd" in the text.

14. A related phrase appears in the *Oxford English Dictionary* as "*To give leg bail* (jocular): to be beholden to one's own legs for escape, to run away." Crocker's variant, "to take leg bail," places the emphasis on the action of the men in seizing the opportunity to flee from the watchmen.

15. Since Crocker uses both "quaters" and "quarters" for stage directions and dialogue with no apparent distinction for how the characters use it, I have regularized the spelling of this word in the play as "quarters."

16. The use of the phrase "Grand Master" suggests that the group may be young Freemasons. See Crocker's *A Series of Letters on Free Masonry* for a discussion of the boisterous conduct of some lodge members.

17. In this text Crocker uses "sh" to spell the following words: "condishions" for "conditions," "manshion" for "mansion," and "compashion" for "compassion."

18. "Rare bird" (Latin). Crocker drops the initial "r" for this phrase here and elsewhere, rendering it "ara avis."

19. In two instances I replaced Crocker's use of an apostrophe at the end of "Oh" with a comma. Elsewhere in the text Crocker uses the word without an apostrophe.

20. This appears to be a reference to St. Anthony, whose name Crocker may be deliberately misspelling in order to suggest the slurred speech of an intoxicated Oh Glee.

21. Spelled "Mical" in the text.

22. Elsewhere Crocker spells this name "Jesus," so it is possible that the variant spelling here is her attempt to represent an Irish accent.

23. Spelled "emcombent" in the text.

24. Crocker does not identify the source of this quotation in Franklin's writings. For an early version of this quotation, see George Herbert (1593–1633), "The Church Porch," preface to *The Temple*, 2nd ed. (London, 1633), 1: "A verse may finde him, who a sermon flies."

"Reminiscences and Traditions"

Crocker's miscellany is roughly divided into three sections. The first, "Reminiscences and Traditions of Boston," roughly half of the manuscript, bears the place and date of Boston, 1827; the second, "Interesting Memoirs and original anecdotes," comprises a fourth of the manuscript, as does the third section, which bears the same title as the second. Miscellaneous papers have been pasted onto the back pages of the manuscript. Although the manuscript has two titles, "Reminiscences" is the title used to refer to selections from the three parts of this manuscript. For each selection I have added a heading for each entry, which appears in brackets. The New England Historic Genealogical Society, the repository of the manuscript, lists the date for the text in its entirety as ca. 1829. Crocker includes more than one version of several entries in her "Reminiscences."

1. Thomas Kemble (1621–88/89), at the behest of Oliver Cromwell, disposed of the Scottish prisoners taken at the battle of Dunbar in 1650 who were sent to New England. There they were sold as indentured servants for periods of six to eight years, according to W. R. Dean's notes on "Journey of Madam Knight from Boston to New York in 1704," *The Living Age*, no. 735 (June 26, 1858), in *Littell's Living Age*, ed. Eliakim Littell, 3rd series (Boston, 1858), 1:964.

2. Spelled "Scarlete's Wharf" in the text.

3. The journey made by Sarah Kemble Knight (1666–1727) is recorded in Sarah Knight and Thomas Buckingham, *The Journals of Madam Knight, and Rev. Mr. Buckingham, From the Original Manuscripts Written in 1704 & 1710*, ed. Theodore Dwight Jr. (New York: Wilder and Campbell, 1825). For a modern edition, see Sarah Knight, *The Journal of Madame Knight*, ed. Sargent Bush Jr., in *Journeys in New Worlds: Early American Women's*

Narratives, ed. William J. Andrews (Madison: University of Wisconsin Press, 1990).

4. Hannah Mather Crocker's father.

5. See 231n178.

6. Line added by Hannah Mather Crocker.

7. Spelled "Papillian" in the text. The *New-England Courant*, no. 45, June 4–11, 1722, reported that Capt. Peter Papillion had been selected by the Massachusetts government to lead an effort to capture pirates off the New England coast (2).

8. Spelled "Wolcut" in the text. This is likely a reference to the Hon. John Wolcutt (1701–47), owner of Scarlet's Wharf at Salem and husband of Elizabeth Papillon (m. 1730).

9. In "A Modell of Christian Charity," John Winthrop used the image of the community as a city on a hill in his lay sermon aboard the *Arabella* in 1630. For the text of the entire sermon, see *America: A Narrative Anthology*, ed. Alan Heimert and Andrew Delbanco (Cambridge: Harvard University Press, 1985), 81–92. The "city sett upon a hill" is an allusion to Matt. 5:14: "Ye are the light of the world. A city that is set on an hill cannot be hid."

10. Variation of "minuet."

11. Crocker refers to Marcy as "Black Jack" elsewhere in "Reminiscences."

12. John Morey had a farm in Roxbury.

13. George Whitefield (1714–70), an English itinerant minister who preached in many of the early colonies starting in 1739, appealed to colonists rich and poor, slave and free, rural and urban, northern and southern.

14. William Dummer (1677–1761) was the acting provincial governor of Massachusetts from 1722 to 1728.

15. Spelled "Morhead" in the text and "Moorhead" or "Moorehead" in some historical records. John Morehead (1729–73) became the minister of the first Presbyterian church in Boston around 1727 and served in that capacity until his death. According to Caleb Hopkins Snow, the church "was originally constituted by a number of Presbyterian families from the North of Ireland, the descendants of immigrants to Ireland from Scotland in the reign of James I" (*A History of Boston: The metropolis of Massachusetts from Its origin to the present period* [Carlisle MA, 1825], 221–22). Snow notes

that the "Church of Presbyterian strangers," officially organized in 1729, adopted the congregational order shortly after Morehead's successor, the Rev. David Annan, left the church in 1786. The church met in the "Long-Lane meeting-house," later changed to the "Federal-Street Church" to honor its role as the site where the Massachusetts state convention ratified the U.S. Constitution on February 8, 1788 (Justin Winsor, ed., *The Memorial History of Boston, including Suffolk County, Massachusetts, 1630–1880*, vol. 2, *The Provincial Period* [Boston: James R. Osgood, 1881], 514).

16. "UM" is not identified.

17. The reference is likely to John Thurber, who is listed in *A Report of the Record Commissioners, City of Boston, Containing the Selectmen's Minutes from 1754 through 1763* (Boston: Rockwell and Churchill, 1887). In "City Doc No. 147," which gives the number of years "Free Negroes" had been free and the number of days they were required to do work for the town, a "John Thurbur" is recorded as having been free for twenty-three years and ordered to work two days (195). The same document provides a list of the names of Free Negroes in Boston, including a man named "John Thurber," who owed four days to the town (240).

18. Thomas Mason remains unidentified. Unlike John Thurber, he is not listed as a "Free Negro" in *A Report of the Record Commissioners*. Prince Hall (ca. 1735–1807) organized Africa Lodge No. 1, the first lodge of black Freemasons, on July 3, 1755, and served as its grand master. The lodge, however, did not receive its official charter until 1784.

19. Unidentified.

20. The reference to Madam Turell, Crocker's friend, is to Mary Morey Turell, who married Joseph Turell in 1768.

21. The shot fired into the church was extracted by Mr. Turell, a parishioner of the Brattle Street Church, according to its pastor, Samuel Kirkland Lothrop, in his *History of the Church in Brattle Street, Boston* (Boston, 1851), 107–8. The Turells lived in Brattle Square.

22. Originally in text as "ara avis." See *The Midnight Beau*, 245n18.

23. "Mistress" is abbreviated as "Mrs" in the text.

24. John Peters and Phillis Wheatley were married in 1778. A free black, Peters worked as a grocer but fell on hard times. In 1784 he was imprisoned for debt.

25. Crocker does not quote the stanza from Wheatley's "On Imagination" exactly. See "On Imagination" in *Poems on Various Subjects, Religious and Moral*, in *The Poems of Phillis Wheatley*, ed. Julian D. Mason Jr. (1773; Chapel Hill: University of North Carolina Press, 1989), 78–80.

26. Crocker often uses the abbreviation "Dr" for a doctor to whom she may have referred earlier by title and surname.

27. This is likely Ebenezer Macintosh (?–1812) rather than Peter. Bernard Bailyn identifies Ebenezer Macintosh as "an expert in hanging and burning effigies and pulling down houses" (*The Ordeal*, 72). Robert Middlekauff likewise links Ebenezer Macintosh, a shoe cobbler, to the Stamp Act riots, noting his role in the destruction of Andrew Oliver's home on August 14 and Thomas Hutchinson's on August 26, 1765 (*The Glorious Cause*, 89–90), as does Howard Zinn, who credits Ebenezer Macintosh as a leader of the mob on both of those occasions (*A People's History of the United States: 1492–Present* [New York: HarperCollins, 2003], 61). No mention is made of a Peter Macintosh by any of these historians in connection with the Stamp Act riots.

28. The office of William Story, deputy registrar of the Vice Admiralty Court at Boston, was ransacked and his papers destroyed, according to William A. Warden, *The Ancestors, Kin and Descendants of John Warden and Narcissa (Davis) Warden, His Wife, Together with Records of some other Branches of Warden Family in America* (Worcester MA: Maynard-Gough, 1901), 84.

29. Capt. Benjamin Hallowell (1725–?) was comptroller of customs at the time of the Stamp Act riots. "The beauty of Hallowell's house may have provided a special inducement to do a thorough job," notes Middlekauff (*The Glorious Cause*, 92). As comptroller Hallowell was ordered by the commissioners to seize John Hancock's sloop *Liberty* in 1768 (166–67), which may account in part for why he "was exempted from pardon by the provincial Congress, June 16, 1775," according to Justin Winsor, *The Memorial History of Boston, including Suffolk County, Massachusetts, 1630–1680* (Boston, 1882), 2:343–44.

30. See the introduction, 193n3.

31. Spelled "Edy" in the text. Thomas Edes, a ship joiner who married Sarah Larrabee in 1738, was the father of Edward Edes (1745–1803), a ship baker.

32. Spelled "stranspire" in the text.

33. Samuel Adams (1722–1803), an early supporter of the American Revolution, was a delegate from Massachusetts to the Continental Congress from 1774 to 1781 and the fourth governor of Massachusetts, from 1793 to 1797.

34. Capt. Thomas Preston (ca. 1722–ca. 1798) commanded British troops the night of the Boston Massacre, March 5, 1770, when five men were killed and six wounded. At his trial Preston, defended by John Adams, was declared innocent by the court. See Middlekauff, *The Glorious Cause*, 204–6.

35. Crocker is confusing John Gray, whose rope works were the site of the Boston Massacre, with the rope maker Samuel Gray, who was killed instantly. Two other men died immediately: James Caldwell and Crispus Attucks.

36. The reference is to Sir Francis Bernard (1712–79), briefly governor of New Jersey before his appointment as governor of Massachusetts, an office he held for ten years. He was replaced by Thomas Hutchinson in 1769.

37. Gen. Thomas Gage (ca. 1719–87) replaced Thomas Hutchinson as governor of Massachusetts on April 2, 1774, and served as commander of the British forces at the start of the Revolutionary War.

38. Foster Hutchinson, Thomas Hutchinson's younger brother, served as associate justice of the superior court and fled to Halifax after the evacuation in 1776. He died in Nova Scotia in 1799. An older brother by the same name died in 1721. See Bailyn, *The Ordeal*, 183; James H. Stark, *The Loyalists of Massachusetts and The Other Side of the American Revolution* (Boston: James H. Stark, 1910), 177–78.

39. John Hancock (1737–93), one of the signers of the Declaration of Independence, was elected to the Continental Congress in 1774 and became its president in 1795. He later served as the first and third governor of the Commonwealth of Massachusetts, from 1780 to 1785 and 1787 to 1793.

40. Variation of "Yankee."

41. Spelled "How" in the text, Gen. William Howe succeeded General Gage as the commander of the British forces during the Revolutionary War. Spelled "Cliton" in the text, Gen. Henry Clinton (ca. 1738–95) fought on the side of the British at the Battle of Bunker Hill and was later appointed second in command to General Howe. For his part in the Battle

of Long Island, he received a knighthood. Spelled "Burgoyn" in the text, Gen. John Burgoyne (1722–92) led the British forces in their capture of Fort Ticonderoga on July 6, 1777.

42. Ancient city in North Africa led by Cato, who urged the inhabitants to negotiate with Caesar after Caesar conquered Scipio at Thapsus in 46 BC.

43. See Job 1:15: "And I only am escaped alone to tell thee."

44. The original reads, "a strong Navy is a firm and firm Bulwark," with the first "firm" crossed out.

45. Nehemiah Walter (1663–1750), minister of the church in Roxbury, married Sarah Mather, daughter of Increase Mather.

46. John Clark (1598?–1664) married Elizabeth Saltonstall, sister of Sir Richard Saltonstall, who came to New England in 1630 but returned to England in 1631.

47. Elizabeth (d. 1713), daughter of the physician Dr. John Clark and widow of Richard Hubbard, became the second wife of Cotton Mather in 1703 and the mother of six of his children. (He had nine children by his first wife, Abigail Phillips, and none by his last wife, Lydia George.) Samuel, the son of Elizabeth and Cotton Mather, married Hannah Hutchinson and was the father of Hannah Mather Crocker.

48. Spelled "Hubard" in the text.

49. Printed in the *Boston Evening Post*, September 23, 1751.

50. A likely reference to Israel Putnam (1718–90), "Old Put," who fought at the battle of Lexington and afterward was made major general, second in command only to George Washington; or to Gen. Rufus Putnam (1738–1824), who was made brigadier in 1783 and brigadier general in 1791. Cf. Middlekauff, *The Glorious Cause*, 282–84, 309.

51. This is an apparent reference to Ebenezer Pemberton, D.D. (1704–79), grandson of James Pemberton, a founder of the Old South Church in Boston and the son of Ebenezer Pemberton, also a minister. *Heaven, the Residence of the Saints*, Dr. Pemberton's sermon on the death of George Whitefield, includes an elegy by Phillis Wheatley.

52. Spelled "Carry" in the text. Given Crocker's date of "1745 to fifty" for the incident, the reference appears to be to Samuel Cary (1713–69) and Margaret Greaves Cary (1719–62), who were married in 1741. Whether his

wife went by the name of "Mary" is unknown. His father, Samuel Cary (1683–1740), also called Captain, married Mary Foster, who died in 1718, and Mary Martyn, who died in 1740 or 1741. Cf. William Richard Cutter and William Frederick Adams, eds., *Genealogical and Personal Memoirs Relating to the Families of the State of Massachusetts* (New York: Lewis Historical Publishing Co., 1910), 4:2191.

53. Although Crocker uses many pseudonyms, they are rarely biblical as is her choice of Jochebed, wife of Amram and mother of Miriam, Aaron, and Moses. Three months after the birth of Moses, Jochebed hid him in the bulrushes where he was found by the Pharaoh's daughter when she came to wash in the river. Standing nearby, Miriam volunteered to find a nurse for the baby and quickly summoned Jochebed in whose care Moses was placed (Exod. 2:1–9).

54. To the right of "Lines by a Lady" and slightly above it, Crocker notes "not printed." The frigate *Independence*, launched in Boston on June 22, 1814, was the first ship of the line commissioned in the U.S. Navy. According to Jonathan R. Dull, "Between the 1650s and the 1850s, naval warfare was ruled by the ship of the line of battle after which it was named. These huge, three-masted wooden ships were some 120 to 210 feet long with a beam (width) of 30 to 60 feet" (*The Age of the Ship of the Line*, 1).

55. Crocker marks stanzas 2–4 but not the first, which is now designated in the same manner.

56. Having reached the end of a page, Crocker writes, "turn over."

57. An inflammation of the throat.

58. A reference to a condition as mild as a cough or as severe as tuberculosis, also known as phthisis or consumption.

59. John Brooks (1752–1825), governor of Massachusetts from 1816 to 1823, was replaced in 1823 by William Eustis (1753–1825), after three attempts. Eustis died in office two years later.

60. Both John Brooks and William Eustis were doctors and fought in the Revolutionary War. Brooks, however, was a Federalist; Eustis, a Democrat-Republican. As a staunch Federalist, Crocker's jibes about the doctor handling a lancet and dandling a Lady may perhaps be attributed to her political affiliation. In the preceding line she also criticizes the candidate's poor speaking ability.

61. The practice of bloodletting and blistering became controversial in the United States in Crocker's lifetime, as the treatment of George Washington attests. Drs. James Craik and Elisha Dick in "A Statement on Washington's Death," which appeared in the December 31, 1799, *Virginia Herald* (Fredericksburg), note that twelve to fourteen ounces of Washington's blood were let on December 13, followed by an additional two bloodlettings plus a final bleeding, when about thirty-two ounces of his blood were removed and several blisters applied before he died on Saturday. In the January 13, 1800, issue of *Porcupine's Gazette* (Philadelphia), William Cobbett, who opposed bloodletting, complained in an address "To the Subscribers of this Gazette" that Washington had been subjected to four bloodlettings in twenty hours or less. Cobbett, who estimates that nine pounds of blood (a gallon plus a pint) were taken from Washington in these bloodlettings, notes that a man in his prime would have a maximum of only fifteen pounds of blood and a man past his prime far less. In his opinion the bloodlettings hastened Washington's death. See Patricia L. Dooley, *The Early Republic: Primary Documents on Events from 1799 to 1820* (Westport CT: Greenwood Press, 2004), 8–9.

62. Crocker was pleased that John Brooks, governor of the Commonwealth of Massachusetts, ran for reelection in 1821 with William Phillips Jr. (1750–1827) again as his running mate for lieutenant governor. Both had held office since 1816. Phillips earlier served as lieutenant governor with Caleb Strong, governor, also a Federalist, from 1812 to 1816.

63. "Gover" (go over, meaning "turn the page") appears at the end of the line.

64. Crocker's pun on "purling Brooks" highlights the contrast between him and William Eustis, who replaced Governor Brooks in 1823. Crocker describes Eustis as rhetorically challenged in her poem "To my friend on her asking my opinion, Of the choice of Governor, 1823." Although she does not mention his name in the poem, he is clearly the target of her barb "Nor can he deliver one sentence by oral."

65. The word "her" has been crossed out in the manuscript, but the next word, "of," has not. It has been removed in this edition to render the phrase as "ought to h[e]arken to his prudent wife." Since "prudent wife" occurs earlier in the sentence, Crocker's first choice "ought to h[e]arken to her" would have avoided the repetition of "prudent wife."

66. Spelled "Lawton" here and elsewhere in the text.

67. It was Richard Mather who brought the chair to America.

68. Crocker is referring to herself.

69. The first child born in the New World to passengers on the *Mayflower* was Peregrine White (1620–1704). His parents, Susanna and William White, began the trip in Leiden. Peregrine, from "peregrinate," meaning "to travel from place to place," was born aboard the *Mayflower* in Provincetown Harbor (Bradford and Winslow, *Mourt's Relation*, 31). Another *Mayflower* passenger, Elizabeth Hopkins, wife of Stephen Hopkins, holds the distinction of having given birth to a son, Oceanus, during the voyage of the *Mayflower* (Bradford, *History of Plimouth Plantation*, 442).

70. Possibly a reference to the statesman Daniel Webster (1782–1852), who moved to Marshfield, Massachusetts, in 1828. Webster staunchly opposed the War of 1812 because of its impact on New England shipping interests, a position that would have endeared him to Crocker.

71. Crocker may be referring to the son of Benjamin and Hannah Phillips, Daniel B. Phillips (1756–?), who fought during the Revolutionary War. Although she refers to him as a captain, he was a private, as were eight other soldiers from Massachusetts bearing the name Daniel Phillips. See *Massachusetts Soldiers and Sailors of the Revolutionary War: A Compilation from the Archives, Prepared and Published by the Secretary of the Commonwealth in accordance with Chapter 100, Resolves of 1891* (Boston: Wright and Potter, State Printers, 1904), 312–13. Benjamin Phillips, the father of Daniel B. Phillips, did hold the title of captain.

72. Richard Bellingham (1592–1672), who emigrated to Massachusetts Bay during the Great Migration of the 1630s, served the colony as deputy governor (thirteen times) or governor (ten times) beginning in 1635. Terms of service, however, were not always consecutive.

73. Spelled "Robins" in the text. Judge Edward Hutchinson Robbins (1758–1837) served as lieutenant governor of Massachusetts from 1802 to 1806. His grandfather and Hannah Crocker's maternal grandfather, Thomas Hutchinson, governor of Massachusetts, were brothers.

Bibliography

Primary Sources by Hannah Mather Crocker

Miscellaneous Papers. Mather Family Papers, Box 12, Folder 10. Unpublished papers. American Antiquarian Society, Worcester MA.

"Reminiscences and Traditions of Boston, Being an Account of the Original Proprietors of That Town, the Manners and Customs of Its People." ca. 1829. R. Stanton Avery Special Collections Department. New England Historic Genealogical Society, Boston.

[Candidus Maximus Originalis.] "The United Trinity or consistant [*sic*] Catholic Christian." 1814. Mather Family Papers, Box 12, Folder 1. American Antiquarian Society, Worcester MA.

[H. Mather Crocker.] *Observations on the Real Rights of Women, with Their Appropriate Duties, Agreeable to Scripture, Reason and Common Sense.* Boston, 1818.

[Increase Mather Jun. of the inner Temple.] "Fast Sermon." 1814. Mather Family Papers, Box 12, Folder 7. American Antiquarian Society, Worcester MA.

[Increase Mather Jun. of the inner Temple.] "An Humble Address to the reason, and Wisdom of the American Nation." 1814. Mather Family Papers, Box 12, Folder 3. American Antiquarian Society, Worcester MA.

[Increase Mather Jun. of the inner Temple.] "Jephthah Vow, explained." 1814. Mather Family Papers, Box 12, Folder 2. American Antiquarian Society, Worcester MA.

[Increase Mather Jun. of the inner Temple.] "Thanksgiving Sermon." 1814. Mather Family Papers, Box 12, Folder 8. American Antiquarian Society, Worcester MA.

[A Lady of Boston.] *A Series of Letters on Free Masonry.* Boston, 1815.

[No author.] *The Midnight Beau: A Farce in 2 Acts.* 1819. Mather Family

Papers, Box 12, Folder 9. American Antiquarian Society, Worcester
MA.

[An Original Antiquarian.] "Antiquarian researches, Pleasant and easy."
1814. Mather Family Papers, Box 12, Folders 4–6. American Antiquarian Society, Worcester MA.

[The Seaman's Friend, H. M. Crocker.] *The School of Reform, or Seaman's
Safe Pilot to the Cape of Good Hope.* Boston, 1816.

Recent Editions of Crocker's *Observations*
Complete Text of *Observations*

Stein, Leon, and Annette K. Baxter, advisory eds. *Observations on the Real
Rights of Women.* Facsimile reprinted in *Sex and Equality.* Series on
Women in America from Colonial Times to the 20th Century. New
York: Arno Press, 1974.

Selections from *Observations*

Harris, Sharon M., ed. "Selection from *Observations on the Real Rights of
Women*." In *Women's Early American Historical Narratives.* New York:
Penguin, 2003.

Kraditor, Aileen S., ed. "Selection from *Observations on the Real Rights
of Women*." In *Up from the Pedestal: Selected Writings in the History of
American Feminism.* Chicago: Quadrangle Books, 1968.

Taylor, Marion Ann, and Heather E. Weir, eds. "Selection from *Obser-
vations on the Real Rights of Women*." In *Let Her Speak for Herself:
Nineteenth-Century Women Writing on the Women of Genesis.* Waco
TX: Baylor University Press, 2006.

Other Primary Sources

Adams, Hannah. *An Alphabetical Compendium of the Various Sects Which
Have Appeared in the World, from the Beginning of the Christian Era to
the Present Day. With an Appendix, Containing a Brief Account of the
Different Schemes of Religion Now Embraced among Mankind.* Boston,
1784.

———. *A Dictionary of All Religions and Religious Denominations, Jewish,*

Heathen, Mahometan, and Christian, Ancient and Modern, with an Appendix Containing a Sketch of the Present State of the World, as to Population, Relation, Religion, Toleration, Missions, Etc., and the Articles in Which All Christian Denominations Agree. 4th ed. Boston, 1817.

———. *The History of the Jews from the destruction of Jerusalem to the nineteenth century.* 1812. London, 1818.

Aikin, Lucy. *Epistles on Women, Exemplifying Their Character and Condition in Various Ages and Nations, with Miscellaneous Poems.* London, 1810.

———. *Memoirs of the Court of Queen Elizabeth.* 2nd ed. 2 vols. London, 1818.

Alexander, William. *The History of Women from the Earliest Antiquity, to the Present Time; Giving Some Account of Almost Every Interesting Particular concerning That Sex, among all Nations, Ancient and Modern.* 2 vols. Dublin, 1799.

Anthony, Susan B., and Ida Husted Harper. *The History of Woman Suffrage.* 4 vols. Rochester NY, 1883–1900.

Basnage de Beauval, Jacques. *The History of the Jews, From Jesus Christ to the Present Time: Containing Their Antiquities, Their Religion, Their Rites, the Dispersion of the Ten Tribes in the East, and The Persecutions This Nation Has Suffer'd in the West. Being a Supplement and Continuation of the History of Josephus.* 1706. Translated by Tho[mas] Taylor. London, 1708.

Bigelow, Timothy. *An eulogy on the life, character and services of Brother George Washington, deceased: Pronounced before the fraternity of Free and Accepted Masons, by request of the Grand Lodge, at the Old South Meeting-House, Boston, on Tuesday, Feb. 11, 1800.* Boston, 1800.

Boon[e], Daniel. *The Life and Adventures of Colonel Daniel Boon[e].* Brooklyn, 1823.

Bradford, William. *History of Plymouth Plantation.* Printed from the original manuscript for the Massachusetts Historical Society. Boston, 1856.

———. *Of Plymouth Plantation, 1620–1647.* Edited by Samuel Eliot Morison. New York: Knopf, 1959.

Bradford, William, and Edward Winslow. *Mourt's Relation, or, Journal of the Plantation at Plymouth.* 1622. Edited by Henry Martyn Dexter. Boston, 1845.

Brantôme, Pierre de Bourdeille, Seigneur de. *Illustrious Dames.* 1665. Translated by Katharine Prescott Wormeley as *The Book of the Ladies.* London, 1899.

Buchanan, Claudius. *The Works of the Rev. Claudius Buchanan, LL.D., Comprising his Christian Researches in Asia, with Notice of the Translation of the Scriptures into the Oriental Languages, His Memoir of the Expediency of an Ecclesiastical Establishment for British India, and his Star in the East, with Three New Sermons. To Which Is Added, Dr. Kerr's Curious and Interesting Report, Concerning the state of the Christians in Cochin and Travancore, made at the request of the Governor of Madras. And To this edition is added, for the first time, The Healing Waters of Bethesda, A Sermon By Dr. Buchanan. And his Speech before the London Society for promoting Christianity among the Jews.* New Brunswick NJ, 1812.

Burnet, Gilbert. *Some Passages in the Life and Death of John, Earl of Rochester, Written by Gilbert Burnet, D.D., Bishop of Salisbury, with a Sermon, Preached at the Funeral of the said Earl, by the Rev. Robert Parsons, A.M., to this Edition is Prefixed An Account of the Life and Writings of the Earl of Rochester, by Dr. Samuel Johnson.* London, 1787.

Burton, Robert. *Anatomy of Melancholy.* Oxford, 1621.

Calvin, Jean. *Institutes of the Christian Religion.* 2 vols. 1559. Edited by John T. McNeill. Translated by Ford Lewis Battles. The Library of Christian Classics. Vols. 20–21. Philadelphia: Westminster Press, 1960.

Cobbett, William. "To the Subscribers of this Gazette." *Porcupine's Gazette,* January 13, 1800. In Dooley.

Coke, Thomas. *A Commentary on the Holy Bible.* 6 vols. London, 1801–7.

Craik, James, and Elisha Dick. "A Statement on Washington's Death." *Virginia Herald* (Fredericksburg), December 31, 1799. In Dooley.

Cutter, William Richard, and William Frederick Adams, eds. *Genealogical and Personal Memoirs Relating to the Families of the State of Massachusetts.* Vol. 4. New York: Lewis Historical Publishing Co., 1910.

Dean, W. R. Notes on "Journey of Madam Knight from Boston to New York in 1704." *The Living Age,* no. 735 (June 26, 1858). In *Littell's Living Age,* edited by Eliakim Littell. 3rd series, vol. 1 (April–June). Boston, 1858.

Dooley, Patricia L. *The Early Republic: Primary Documents on Events from 1799 to 1820.* Westport CT: Greenwood Press, 2004.

Drake, Francis S. *Memorials of the Society of the Cincinnati of Massachusetts.* Boston, 1873.

Dwight, Timothy. "Columbia." In *American Poems,* edited by Elihu Hubbard Smith. 1794. Facsimile reproduction edited by William K. Bottorff. Gainesville FL: Scholars' Facsimiles and Reprints, 1966.

Franklin, Benjamin. *The Autobiography of Benjamin Franklin.* Edited by Leonard W. Labaree et al. 2nd ed. New Haven: Yale University Press, 2003.

———. [Silence Dogood.] Letters addressed "To the Author of the *New-England Courant.*" Nos. 1–14. *New-England Courant,* April 2–October 8, 1722.

Fuller, Thomas. *The Holy State and the Profane State.* 1642. London, 1840.

Godwin, William. *Memoirs of the Author of A Vindication of the Rights of Woman.* London, 1798.

Hall, Edward Hagaman, ed. *The Sons of the American Revolution: New York State Society, 1893–1894.* New York, 1894.

Harris, Thaddeus Mason. *Discourses, Delivered on Public Occasions, Illustrating the Principles, Displaying the Tendency, and Vindicating the Design, of Freemasonry.* Charlestown MA, 5801 [1805].

———. *Treasure of the Gospel in Earthern Vessels.* Salem MA, 1804.

Herbert, George. "The Church Porch." Preface to *The Temple.* 2nd ed. London, 1633.

Hunter, Henry. *Sacred Biography: or, The History of the Patriarchs: To which is added, the History of Deborah, Ruth, and Hannah.* Being a course of lectures delivered at the Scots Church. First American edition. 6 vols. in 3. Boston, 1794–95.

Hutchinson, Thomas. *History of the Colony and Province of Massachusetts Bay.* Edited from the author's own copies of vols. 1 and 2 and his manuscript of vol. 3, with a memoir and additional notes by Lawrence Shaw Mayo. New York: Kraus Reprint, 1970.

Jefferson, Thomas. *Notes on the State of Virginia.* 1785. New York: Penguin, 1999.

Johnson, Samuel. "An Account of the Life and Writings of the Earl of Rochester." In Burnet.

———. *The Rambler*. In *The Works of Samuel Johnson, LL.D., with an Essay on His Life and Genius by Arthur Murphy, Esq.* 12 vols. London, 1823.

Kett, Henry. *Elements of General Knowledge.* 2 vols. Baltimore, 1812.

Knight, Sarah. *The Journal of Madame Knight.* Edited by Sargent Bush Jr. In *Journeys in New Worlds: Early American Women's Narratives,* edited by William J. Andrews. Madison: University of Wisconsin Press, 1990.

Knight, Sarah, and Thomas Buckingham. *The Journals of Madam Knight, and Rev. Mr. Buckingham, From the Original Manuscripts Written in 1704 & 1710.* Edited by Theodore Dwight Jr. New York: Wilder and Campbell, 1825.

The Lodge of Saint Andrews, and the Massachusetts Grand Lodge. Boston, 1870.

Lothrop, Samuel Kirkland. *History of the Church in Brattle Street, Boston.* Boston, 1851.

Mackey, Albert G. *An Encyclopaedia of Freemasonry and Its Kindred Sciences: Comprising the Whole Range of Arts, Sciences and Literature as Connected with the Institution.* Philadelphia, 1879.

———. *The Symbolism of Freemasonry: Illustrating and Explaining Its Science and Philosophy, its Legends, Myths and Symbols.* New York, 1869.

Madison, James. "Detached Memoranda." *William and Mary Quarterly,* 3rd series (October 1946): 554–60.

Massachusetts Soldiers and Sailors of the Revolutionary War. A Compilation from the Archives, Prepared and Published by the Secretary of the Commonwealth, In Accordance with Chapter 100, Resolves of 1891. Boston: Wright and Potter, State Printers, 1904.

Mather, Cotton. *Bonifacius: An Essay upon the Good.* 1710. Cambridge: Harvard University Press, 1966.

———. *Days of Humiliation: Times of Affliction and Disaster: Nine Sermons for Restoring Favor with an Angry God (1697–1727).* Introduction by George Harrison Orians. Gainesville FL: Scholars' Facsimiles and Reprints, 1970.

———. *The Good Old Way.* Boston, 1706.

———. *Magnalia Christi Americana*. 2 vols. 1702. Hartford CT, 1853.

———. *Successive Generations*. Boston, 1715.

Mather Family Papers. Box 12, Folders 1–10. American Antiquarian Society, Worcester MA.

Maurice, Thomas. *Indian Antiquities: Or, Dissertations, Relative to the Ancient Geographical Divisions, the Pure System of Primeval Theology, the Grand Code of Civil Laws, the Original Form of Government, the Widely-Extended Commerce, and the Various and Profound Literature, of Hindostan, Compared, throughout, with the Religion, Laws, Government, and Literature, of Persia, Egypt, and Greece, the Whole Intended As Introductory to the History of Hindostan, upon a Comprehensive Scale*. 7 vols. London, 1793–1800.

More, Hannah. *Strictures on the Modern System of Female Education*. 2 vols. 1799. Oxford: Woodstock Books, 1995.

[More, Hannah.] *Hints towards Forming the Character of a Young Princess*. 3rd ed. 2 vols. London, 1805.

Morton, Sarah Wentworth. [Philenia, pseud.] *Ouâbi; or, The virtues of nature; an Indian tale in four cantos*. Boston, 1790.

Murray, Judith Sargent. "On the Equality of the Sexes." *Massachusetts Magazine*, March–April 1790. In *Selected Writings of Judith Sargent Murray*, edited by Sharon M. Harris. New York: Oxford University Press, 1995.

———. [Constantia, pseud.] *The Gleaner*. 3 vols. 1798. Introduction by Nina Baym. Schenectady NY: Union College Press, 1992.

Paine, Thomas. *"The American Crisis*, No. 1." In *Collected Writings of Thomas Paine*, edited by Eric Foner. New York: Library of America, 1995.

Pemberton, Ebenezer. *Heaven, the Residence of the Saints*. Boston, 1771.

Pemberton, Thomas. The Papers of Thomas Pemberton. Massachusetts Historical Society, Boston.

Plutarch. "Tiberius and Caius." In *Plutarch's Lives*, translated by Bernadotte Perrin. Loeb Classical Library. Vol. 10. London: William Heinemann, 1921.

Poullain de La Barre, François de. *The Equality of the Sexes*. 1673. Translated by Desmond M. Clark. Manchester, UK: Manchester University Press, 1990.

A Report of the Record Commissioners, City of Boston, Containing the Selectmen's Minutes from 1754 through 1763. Boston: Rockwell and Churchill, 1887.

Russell, [William]. *Essay on the Character, Manners, and Genius of Women in Different Ages. By [Antoine Leonard] Thomas. Enlarged from the French of M. Thomas by Mr. Russell.* 2 vols. Philadelphia, 1774.

S., R. (By a gentleman belonging to the Jerusalem Lodge). *Jachin and Boaz; or, An authentic key to the door of Free-Masonry, both ancient and modern: Calculated not only for the instruction of every new-made Mason; but also for the information of all who intend to become brethren.* Suffield CT, 1799.

Sargent, L. M. *Mr. Sargent's Address before the Massachusetts Society for the Suppression of Intemperance.* Boston, 1833.

Snow, Caleb Hopkins. *A History of Boston: The metropolis of Boston from Its origin to the present period.* Carlisle MA, 1825.

Staël, Madame de (Anne-Louise-Germaine). *The Influence of Literature upon Society.* Translated from the French of Madame de Staël-Holstein, To which is prefixed, a memoir of the life and writings of the author by D. Bolieu. 2 vols. Boston, 1813.

Stiles, Ezra. "The United States Elevated to Glory and Honour." A sermon preached before Governor Jonathan Trumbull and the General Assembly of the State of Connecticut at Hartford on the occasion of the Anniversary Election, May 8th, 1783. Reprinted in *God's New Israel: Religious Interpretations of American Destiny*, edited by Conrad Cherry. Chapel Hill: University of North Carolina Press, 1971.

Stretch, L. M. *Beauties of History; Or, Pictures of Virtue and Vice, Drawn from Real Life; Designed for the Instruction and Entertainment of Youth.* 1770. London, 1808.

Thinks-I-to-Myself, Who? [Edward Nares.] *Thinks-I-to-Myself: A Serio-Ludicro, Tragico-Comico Tale.* Brattleborough VT, 1814.

Villemert, [Pierre-Joseph] Boudier de. *The Friend of Women.* Translated by Alexander Morrice. Philadelphia, 1803.

Warden, William A. *The Ancestors, Kin and Descendants of John Warden and Narcissa (Davis) Warden, His Wife, Together with Records of some other Branches of Warden Family in America.* Worcester MA: Maynard-Gough, 1901.

Warren, Mercy Otis. *The Adulateur.* 1773. In *The Plays and Poems of Mercy Otis Warren,* edited by Benjamin Franklin V. Delmar NY: Scholars' Facsimiles and Reprints, 1980.

———. *History of the Rise, Progress and Termination of the American Revolution, interspersed with Biographical, Political and Moral Observations.* 3 vols. 1805. Edited by Lester H. Cohen. 2 vols. Indianapolis: Liberty Classics, 1988.

Watts, Isaac. *Horae Lyricae and Divine Songs by Isaac Watts, with a Memoir, by Robert Southey.* Boston, 1854.

Wheatley, Phillis. *Poems on Various Subjects, Religious and Moral.* 1773. In *The Poems of Phillis Wheatley,* edited by Julian D. Mason Jr. Chapel Hill: University of North Carolina Press, 1989.

Winsor, Justin, ed. *The Memorial History of Boston, including Suffolk County, Massachusetts, 1630–1680.* 4 vols. Boston, 1882.

Winthrop, John. "A Modell of Christian Charity." In *America: A Narrative Anthology,* edited by Alan Heimert and Andrew Delbanco. Cambridge: Harvard University Press, 1985.

Wollstonecraft, Mary. *A Vindication of the Rights of Woman.* 3rd ed. London, 1796.

Secondary Sources

Bailyn, Bernard. *The Ordeal of Thomas Hutchinson.* Cambridge: Belknap Press of Harvard University Press, 1974.

Baker, Jennifer J. *Securing the Commonwealth: Debt, Speculation, and Writing in the Making of Early America.* Baltimore: Johns Hopkins University Press, 2005.

Benson, Pamela Joseph. *The Invention of the Renaissance Woman: The Challenge of Female Independence in the Literature and Thought of Italy and England.* University Park: Pennsylvania State University Press, 1992.

Bercovitch, Sacvan, ed. *The American Puritan Imagination: Essays in Revaluation.* London: Cambridge University Press, 1974.

———. *The Rites of Assent: Transformations in the Symbolic Construction of America.* New York: Routledge, 1993.

Berg, Barbara. *The Remembered Gate: Origins of American Feminism.* New York: Oxford University Press, 1978.

Bloch, Ruth. "The Gendered Meanings of Virtue in Revolutionary America." *Signs* 13, no. 1 (1987): 37–58.

———. *Visionary Republic: Millennial Themes in American Thought, 1756–1800.* Cambridge: Cambridge University Press, 1985.

Botting, Eileen Hunt, and Sarah L. Houser. "'Drawing the Line of Equality': Hannah Mather Crocker on Women's Rights." *American Political Science Review* 100, no. 2 (May 2006): 265–78.

Bullock, Steven C. *Revolutionary Brotherhood: Freemasonry and the Transformation of the American Social Order, 1730–1740.* Chapel Hill: University of North Carolina Press, 1996.

Cima, Gay Gibson. *Early American Women Critics: Performance, Religion, Race.* Cambridge: Cambridge University Press, 2006.

Coles, Harry L. *The War of 1812.* Edited by Daniel J. Boorstin. Chicago History of American Civilization. Chicago: University of Chicago Press, 1966.

Conrad, Susan Phinney. *Perish the Thought: Intellectual Women in Romantic America, 1830–1860.* New York: Oxford University Press, 1976.

Cott, Nancy F. *The Bonds of Womanhood.* New Haven: Yale University Press, 1977.

Cutter, William Richard, and William Frederick Adams, eds. *Genealogical and Personal Memoirs Relating to the Families of the State of Massachusetts.* Vol. 4. New York: Lewis Historical Publishing, 1910.

Davidson, Cathy N. *Revolution and the Word: The Rise of the Novel in America.* New York: Oxford University Press, 1986.

Dorsey, Bruce. *Reforming Men and Women: Gender in the Antebellum City.* Ithaca NY: Cornell University Press, 2002.

Dull, Jonathan R. *The Age of the Ship of the Line: The British and French Navies, 1650–1850.* Lincoln: University of Nebraska Press, 2009.

Eysenck, Hans J. *The Biological Basis of Personality.* 1967. New Brunswick NJ: Rutgers University Press, 2006.

Ferguson, Moira. *First Feminists: British Women Writers, 1578–1799.* Bloomington: Indiana University Press, 1985.

Ferguson, Robert A. *The American Enlightenment, 1750–1820.* Cambridge: Harvard University Press, 1997.

Grunes, Rodney A. "James Madison and Religious Freedom." In *James Madison: Philosopher, Founder, and Statesman*, edited by John R. Vile, William D. Pederson, and Frank J. Williams. Athens: Ohio University Press, 2008.

James, Janet Wilson. *Changing Ideas about Women in the United States, 1776–1825*. New York: Garland, 1981.

Karlsen, Carol F. *The Devil in the Shape of a Woman: Witchcraft in Colonial New England*. New York: Norton, 1987.

Kelley, Mary. *Learning to Stand and Speak: Women, Education, and Public Life in America's Republic*. Chapel Hill: University of North Carolina Press, 2006.

Kerber, Linda K. *Toward an Intellectual History of Women*. Chapel Hill: University of North Carolina Press, 1997.

Kilcup, Karen, ed. *Nineteenth-Century American Women Writers: A Critical Reader*. Malden MA: Blackwell, 1998.

Koengeter, L. W. "Crocker, Hannah Mather." In *American Women Writers: A Critical Reference Guide*. Vol. 1, *From Colonial Times to the Present*, edited by Lina Mainero. New York: Ungar, 1979.

Laffrado, Laura. *Uncommon Women: Gender and Representation in Nineteenth-Century U.S. Women's Writing*. Columbus: Ohio State University Press, 2009.

Levy, Leonard W. *The Establishment Clause: Religion and the First Amendment*. Chapel Hill: University of North Carolina Press, 1994.

Loane, Nancy K. *Following the Drum: Women at the Valley Forge Encampment*. Washington DC: Potomac Books, 2009.

Macdonald, D. L., and Kathleen Scherf. *The Vindications: The Rights of Men and The Rights of Women*. Peterborough, Canada: Broadview Press, 1997.

Mayer, Holly A. *Belonging to the Army: Camp Followers and Community during the American Revolution*. Columbia: University of South Carolina Press, 1996.

Melden, Keith E. *Beginnings of Sisterhood: The American Woman's Rights Movement, 1800–1850*. New York: Schocken Books, 1977.

Middlekauff, Robert. *The Glorious Cause: The American Revolution, 1763–1789*. New York: Oxford University Press, 1982.

Moers, Ellen. "Performing Heroinism: The Myth of Corrine." In *Literary Women*. New York: Doubleday, 1977.

New England Historical and Genealogical Register, for the Year 1862. New England Historic-Genealogical Society. 2nd ed. Vol. 16. Boston: Charles E. Goodspeed, 1906.

Norton, Mary Beth. *Liberty's Daughters: The Revolutionary Experience of American Women, 1750–1800.* Boston: Little, Brown, 1980.

Post, Constance J. "Hannah Mather Crocker." In *The Dictionary of Literary Biography: American Women Prose Writers to 1820*, edited by Carla Mulford with Angela Vietto and Amy E. Winans. Detroit: Bruccoli-Clark-Layman, 1998.

———. "Making the A-List: Reformation and Revolution in Crocker's *Observations on the Real Rights of Women*." *Resources for American Literary Study* 29 (2005): 67–88.

———. "Old World Order in the New: John Eliot and 'Praying Indians' in Cotton Mather's *Magnalia Christi Americana*." *New England Quarterly* 66 (September 1993): 416–33.

———. *Signs of the Times in Cotton Mather's Paterna: A Study of Puritan Autobiography.* New York: ASM Press, 2000.

Richards, Jeffrey. *Theatre Enough: American Culture and the Metaphor of the World Stage, 1607–1789.* Durham: Duke University Press, 1991.

Riegel, Robert. *American Feminism.* Lawrence: University of Kansas Press, 1963.

Shawcross, John T. *The Self and the World.* Lexington: University of Kentucky Press, 1993.

Shields, David S. *Civil Tongues and Polite Letters in British America.* Chapel Hill: University of North Carolina Press, 1997.

Silverman, Kenneth. *A Cultural History of the American Revolution.* New York: Thomas Y. Crowell, 1976.

Simpson, Henry. *The Lives of Eminent Philadelphians, Now Deceased.* Philadelphia, 1959.

Stark, James H. *The Loyalists of Massachusetts and the Other Side of the American Revolution.* Boston: James H. Stark, 1910.

Stone, Lawrence. *The Family, Sex, and Marriage in England, 1500–1800.* New York: Harper and Row, 1977.

Wells, Amos. *A Treasury of Hymns*. Boston: United Society of Christian Endeavor, 1914.

Welter, Barbara. "The Cult of True Womanhood: 1820–1860." *American Quarterly* 18 (1966): 151–74.

Wills, Gary. *James Madison*. New York: Times Books, 2002.

Wood, Gordon S. *The Creation of the American Republic*. Chapel Hill: University of North Carolina Press, 1969.

———. *Empire of Liberty: A History of the Early Republic, 1789–1815*. New York: Oxford University Press, 2009.

———. *The Radicalism of the American Revolution*. New York: Knopf, 1992.

Woolf, D. R. *Reading History in Early Modern England*. New York: Cambridge University Press, 2000.

Zagarri, Rosemarie. *Revolutionary Backlash: Women and Politics in the Early Republic*. Philadelphia: University of Pennsylvania Press, 2007.

Zinn, Howard. *A People's History of the United States: 1492–Present*. New York: HarperCollins, 2003.

Index

son, and Wisdom of the American
Nation," xxiv–xxv; "An humble
imitation of Dwight's 'Columbia,'"
xxvi, 35–36; humor of, xxx; letter
to, from parents, 175–76; "[Lines
to be Read at Opening School],"
181; and Mather chair, 188; *The
Midnight Beau*, xxvii, xliii–xlv, xlvii, 197n30, 245n16; "North Square
Creed, 30 Years ago," xxi–xxii,
xlvii; *Observations on the Real
Rights of Women*, xviii, xxxiii–xliii,
xlvii, 198n35; "[On Launching the
Frigate *Independence*]," 179–80;
"[On Physicians Who Require
Double Fees]," 178–79; "[On
Reading the Federal Nomination],"
185–86; "On seeing the solemnities," 58–59; "[On the Choice
of Governor in 1823]," 185; "[A
Petition for Pen and Ink]," xv–
xvi, 182–83; as political theorist,
xxxvi, 199n37; "Reminiscences
and Traditions of Boston," xviii–
xix, xlv–xlvii, xlviii, 246; and
respect for differing opinions,
xx; *The School of Reform*, xxvii,
xxxi–xxxiii, xlvii, 214; *A Series
of Letters on Free Masonry*, xviii,
xxvii–xxx, xlviii; and sermons,
xviii; "A Short Address," xxi,
55–57, 214n28; "A Song," 57–58,
214n30; and Stamp Act riot, xiii–
xiv, 167; "Thanksgiving Sermon,"
xxiii–xxiv, 204; "[To a Friend for
Sending a Loaf of Bread]," 180–81;
on tolerance, 8; "[To the Overseer
of Ward No. 2 in Boston]," 183–84;
as writer, xix–xxii, xlvii–xlix; writings of, xv–xvi, xviii–xix
Crocker, Joseph, xv
"cult of true womanhood," xl, 200n46

Dalton, John, 172
Daniel, 131
David, 20–21, 30, 171
Deborah, 94–96
Demosthenes, 99, 222n74
Dexter, Samuel, 139, 239n232
Dio Cassius, 132, 233n196
Dryden, John, 137, 236n223
Dummer, William, 163, 247n14
Dwight, Timothy: "Columbia,"
xxvi

Edes, Thomas, 167, 249n31
education, 16, 27–28, 86, 139–40. *See
also* women's education
election of 1821, 185–86
election of 1823, 185
Elements of Useful Knowledge (Kett),
xxxv
Elijah, 17, 35
Eliot, John, 138, 161, 237n229
Elizabeth I (queen of England), 101,
224n93
Elkanah, 97
Embargo Act, 147, 244n8
Enlightenment values, xviii, xxi–xxii,
xxxiii, 195n11, 212n18
Epistles on Women (Aikin), 107–8,
217n10, 217n12
equality, 95, 124, 128, 130. *See also*
women's equality
The Equality of the Sexes (Poullain de
La Barre), 100
Erskine, Thomas, 137, 139, 235n220,
236n223, 240n233
*Essay on the Character, Manners, and
Genius of Women in Different Ages*
(A. L. Thomas), xxxv, 123, 221n66
Euclid, 124, 231n176
Euroclydon, 63, 215n2
Eustis, William, 185, 252nn59–60,
253n64

In the Legacies of Nineteenth-Century American
Women Writers series

The Hermaphrodite
By Julia Ward Howe
Edited and with an introduction
by Gary Williams

*In the "Stranger People's"
Country*
By Mary Noailles Murfree
Edited and with an introduction
by Marjorie Pryse

Two Men
By Elizabeth Stoddard
Edited and with an introduction
by Jennifer Putzi

Emily Hamilton *and Other
Writings*
By Sukey Vickery
Edited and with an introduction
by Scott Slawinski

*Nature's Aristocracy: A Plea for
the Oppressed*
By Jennie Collins
Edited and with an introduction
by Judith A. Ranta

*Selected Writings of Victoria
Woodhull: Suffrage, Free Love,
and Eugenics*
By Victoria C. Woodhull
Edited and with an introduction
by Cari Carpenter

*Christine: Or Woman's Trials
and Triumphs*
By Laura Curtis Bullard
Edited and with an introduction
by Denise M. Kohn

Observations on the Real
Rights of Women *and Other
Writings*
By Hannah Mather Crocker
Edited and with an introduction
by Constance J. Post

To order or obtain more information
on these or other University of
Nebraska Press titles, visit
www.nebraskapress.unl.edu.